SHELLEY'S "THE TRIUMPH OF LIFE": A CRITICAL STUDY

SHELLEY'S "THE TRIUMPH OF LIFE": A CRITICAL STUDY

Based on a Text Newly Edited from the Bodleian Manuscript

DONALD H. REIMAN

ILLINOIS STUDIES IN LANGUAGE AND LITERATURE

55

UNIVERSITY OF ILLINOIS PRESS, URBANA, 1965

Second Printing, 1966

Board of Editors: BURTON A. MILLIGAN, JOHN R. FREY, AND PHILIP KOLB

For Royal A. Gettmann

PREFACE

When "The Triumph of Life" first appeared in Shelley's *Post-humous Poems* (1824), Hazlitt found it an emblem and type of Shelley's genius—a genius that he believed to be as perverse and misguided as it was brilliant. Reviewing *Posthumous Poems* in the *Edinburgh Review,* Hazlitt declared of the closing lines of "The Triumph": "Any thing more filmy, enigmatical, discontinuous, unsubstantial than this, we have not seen; nor yet more full of morbid genius and vivifying soul." Later commentators were not so willing to see "The Triumph of Life" as the epitome of Shelley's poetic achievement. The Victorians, who as a group admired Shelley for all the wrong reasons, wished to keep their beautiful lyric angel unspotted by the darkness of his fragmentary final major effort. Mary Shelley, who like Leigh Hunt admired *The Cenci* and the lyrics, deprecated "The Triumph of Life" in both the Preface and the notes to her collected editions of Shelley's works. To George Gilfillan, an enthusiastic early Victorian admirer of Shelley, "The Triumph" was "a piece of misty melancholious confusion," in no way characteristic of the poet. In our century, after a revolution in taste, T. S. Eliot sees "The Triumph of Life" as a glorious exception to the repeated failures of Shelley's poems. In his oft-quoted essay on "The Metaphysical Poets" Eliot finds in "one or two passages of Shelley's *Triumph of Life*" and in Keats's *Fall of Hyperion* "traces of a struggle toward unification of sensibility," dissociated since the mid-seventeenth century. From his general condemnation of Shelley's ideas and art in *The Use of Poetry and the Use of Criticism,* Eliot once again excepts "The Triumph of Life": "His views remained pretty fixed, though his poetic gift matured. It is open to us to guess whether his mind would have matured too; certainly, in his last, and to my mind greatest though unfinished poem, *The Triumph of Life,* there is evidence not only of better writing than in any previous long poem, but of greater wisdom. . . ." From the time of this pronouncement by Eliot until the present day, the words of a teacher of mine have been a reasonable estimate of the place of "The Triumph of Life" in the state of Shelley's reputation: "Anyone wishing to defend Shelley's poetry must begin with 'The Triumph of Life.' "

I did not begin my study of "The Triumph," let me add, with the object of defending or promoting either Shelley or this poem; I simply wished to understand Shelley's enigmatic swan-song and to learn how this poem related to what he had thought and done and written before 1822. As my study progressed and carried me from the printed poem to Shelley's other writings, to Shelley criticism, to the Bodleian manuscript of "The Triumph of Life," and to some of the works that Shelley read and admired during the final years of his life, I found that the problems surrounding "The Triumph of Life" and leaving a majority of critics admittedly baffled upon encountering this fragmentary effort were, in fact, the same barriers that have kept readers and critics from seeing Shelley plain from the time his first poems were published to the present and that the difficulty of "The Triumph" *was* intimately related to the course of Shelley's reputation. The barriers that tend to obscure the achievement of every artist and every thinker who rises above mediocrity were, I found, unusually prominent in the history of the attempt to ascertain Shelley's place in the English poetic tradition; these obstacles are: first, unnatural piety; second, literary fundamentalism; third, critical ignorance; and fourth, the fallible editor and typesetter.

The "unnatural piety" of Mary Shelley, her daughter-in-law, Lady Jane Shelley, and their coadjutors toward the dead poet is a matter of record (though that record is not by any means complete). Those like Trelawny who had known Shelley were disgusted by the sanctimonious atmosphere of the shrine at Boscombe Manor and repelled by efforts to sentimentalize Shelley's mental vigor into languid white marble memorials such as that which now avenges Shelley for his expulsion from University College. This sentimentalizing produced three evils: first and most serious, Shelley, that urbane and willful aristocrat who had been brought up with a horse and a gun as well as books and who never lost his eye for a pretty girl even after he learned to say "no" to his eyes, was mythologized into a disembodied angel for whom the adjective "ineffectual" was the natural one from a partially reformed Philistine. Second, the unnatural piety provoked unusual reactions by debunkers who in attacking the "Shelley legend" seemed determined to prove that, in the case of Shelley's reputation for benevolence, where there is smoke, there is *no* fire. Finally, "The Triumph of Life" and many of Shelley's other poems suffered because in collecting the MSS of Shelley's poetry in Boscombe Manor and then showing them only to confirmed worshipers, Lady Shelley minimized the opportunity for solid scholarly work on the texts of Shelley's poems, especially correction of the texts that Mary Shelley had published for the first time.

The second barrier, literary fundamentalism, is near kin to religious fundamentalism and its stock in trade is the attempt to transubstantiate mythical truth into fact—historical, scientific, or biographical. It ignores the *personae* to whom the poet gives individual speeches in dramas or dramatic dialogues: if Shelley portrayed the chorus of a play saying, "The world's great age begins anew," no mere warning by Shelley himself in a footnote suffices to prevent this class of readers from seizing on this line as a literal statement of Shelley's view of the historical future. If the words of Shelley's prose preface seem at all at variance with those of the *persona* who eulogizes the dead Poet at the end of *Alastor*, Shelley must have been confused and uncertain of his intention. Of the fundamentalists, the worst were the biographical critics who, ignoring both the literary tradition out of which Shelley's art grew and the intellectual, ethical, social, and aesthetic preoccupations of his prose and even his personal letters, tried to read Shelley's poetry as lightly disguised autobiography. Shelley wrote purely personal poems (like the "Stanzas Written in Dejection, Near Naples") but he was not responsible for publishing most of his purely personal lyrics, which Mary Shelley published after his death. There are, of course, personal elements in many of the poems he did publish or (like "Julian and Maddalo") desired to have published, but, as in the works of Dante and Milton, the two great guiding spirits of his mature art, Shelley's published works always go beyond the personal dilemma to the problems of mankind, the *persona* of the poet becoming merely the type of the imaginative human soul. The biographical critics, especially those who fed either on the unnatural piety of the "Shelley legend" or on its muckraking opposite, have built immeasurable barriers between Shelley's poetry and its readers.

A third great barrier to understanding Shelley's poetry has been critical myopia. Two Oxford Professors of Poetry, Matthew Arnold and A. C. Bradley, regretted the ignorance of the English Romantic poets, who either did not read enough or else did not understand what they read. The intellectual vitality of the Romantics as a group is no longer, I think, seriously questioned by informed people, but only recently have specialized studies on various aspects of Shelley's reading begun to dispel our ignorance of his particular intellectual heritage. In the past many passages in Shelley's works were like hieroglyphics to the layman, but scholars have recently been discovering keys to greater understanding of his ideas and his artistry. The recovery of Shelley's intellectual milieu is by no means complete, but the results of the studies produced during the past twenty-five years indicate that it has been Shelley's critics rather than their subject who did not know enough. The critics' condescension has, however, enabled many a superficial reader of Shelley's poems to condemn as confusion or incoherence on Shelley's part what he failed to understand. For example, many annotators of "mistakes" in Shelley's use of the word "Celtic" in "Lines Written Among the Euganean Hills" or "mother-in-law" in the Preface to *The Cenci* would have been spared embarrassment had they respected Shelley's intelligence enough to check in the *Oxford English Dictionary* the meanings of these terms in Shelley's time.

A fourth barrier that shields Shelley from his readers has been thrown up by fallible editors and typesetters. Shelley was acutely conscious of the errors that occurred in the printed texts of his poems; after almost every volume appeared, he offered to send to the publisher a list of errata for the second edition. Unfortunately, only *The Cenci* went into an authorized second edition during his lifetime, and thus, unlike Pope, Wordsworth, Yeats, or other long-lived poets, not only was Shelley unable to rewrite inferior passages in his poems, but he was unable to correct even the typographical errors. Moreover, many of Shelley's poems, "The Triumph of Life" among them, were first published by Mary Shelley from uncorrected and incomplete rough drafts. Charles H. Taylor, Jr., has traced in *The Early Collected Editions of Shelley's Poems* other vicissitudes of the Shelley canon during its early years, and the story of human error could be extended and broadened down to the present time. In the case of "The Triumph of Life" (and other works drawn from Shelley's drafts and notebooks), the difficulty of correcting

such errors has until recently been compounded by the nonavail-
ability of the only authoritative source of the text. With the
exception of the few poems that Shelley himself saw through the
press or that, like *Hellas,* he acknowledged to have been relatively
well printed, his intention has been obscured by texts that are not
good even by the standards of nineteenth-century printing and
very deficient by the standards of modern textual criticism. One
has to reconstruct as nearly as possible each poem as Shelley wrote
it before he can presume to explicate it, much less evaluate its
worth or place in the English poetic tradition.

During the past twenty-five years the barriers between Shelley's
poems and their readers have begun to go down. Shelley's halo and
horns have been removed and his life and literary career put into
historical perspective chiefly by three American scholars and one
versatile Englishman: Newman Ivey White, Frederick L. Jones,[1]
Kenneth Neill Cameron, and Edmund Blunden. Literary fundamentalism and dangerous biographical criticism have been answered
by a number of scholar-critics whose readings of Shelley's poems
derived from a study of his literary heritage and of the symbolic
patterns recurring from poem to poem; writers of recent books
that emphasize Shelley as artist (rather than as thinker or man)
include Carlos Baker, R. H. Fogle, Peter Butter, Harold Bloom,
Milton Wilson, and Earl R. Wasserman. Other scholars who
centered their attention on the sources of characteristic ideas in
Shelley's prose and poetry have, likewise, helped to disperse the
critics' ignorance of Shelley's attitudes and purpose: these include,
notably, Carl Grabo, James A. Notopoulos, David Lee Clark, and
C. E. Pulos. Still others have begun to attack the problem of inac-
curacy and incompleteness of the Shelley canon. Seminal for such
recent studies was Neville Rogers' *Shelley at Work.* K. N. Cameron,
G. M. Matthews, Irving Massey, Lawrence John Zillman, and
others have contributed to our understanding of Shelley texts.

In the present study, I have profited from the scholarship and
criticism of those just named, the footnotes recording my substantive borrowings from their writings but not the larger debt of

---

[1] Professor Jones's edition of *The Letters of Percy Bysshe Shelley* appeared
after this monograph had left my hands and was being put through the press;
therefore, although I have collated all my quotations from Shelley's letters with
Professor Jones's text, I have altered those quotations (and added references to
the Jones edition) only where there are substantive differences between the two
texts.

attitude and approach to Shelley and his art. Here I wish to acknowledge my special obligation to the work of two of them: Neville Rogers' *Shelley at Work* first called to my attention the Bodleian MS of "The Triumph of Life," and his prompt and helpful response to my inquiry enabled me to procure a microfilm of the MS and thus to coordinate the early stages of my critical study of "The Triumph" with a reexamination of its text. Shortly before I ordered this microfilm, G. M. Matthews studied the MS itself at Oxford and laid the foundation for his studies of "The Triumph of Life." Thus by the time I went to Oxford to check my text and transcription of the MS against the original, I was fortunate enough to have also Mr. Matthews' independent text; his careful editing has, of course, saved me from numerous errors.

In the present study I have endeavored to pursue scholarly methods that have already contributed much to our understanding of Shelley's poetry and that will, I believe, contribute even more during the years immediately ahead. I began by reediting the text of "The Triumph" from Shelley's holograph draft—in this instance, the sole authority. Because a new interpretation of the poem was my goal and remains, I believe, the chief contribution of this study, I have placed the Textual Study after the Critical Study as a reference source for those who wish to examine the details of the particular text upon which I base my reading and the relation of this text to other texts. Having established a critical text, I explicated the poem in the light of certain basic principles that scholars have recently shown to be characteristic of Shelley's thought and artistic method. While explicating "The Triumph of Life," I studied Shelley's other poems and many of the works that he is known to have read and admired, noting parallels and differences as they illuminated the meaning of "The Triumph"; in these studies I was, naturally, guided by the work of other scholars. (I have made a genuine effort to read every original comment on "The Triumph of Life.") My notes record, however, only those suggestions that I find convincing in the light of both the revised text and the poem's structure and symbolic development. Having in another place set down my ideas concerning the relation of "The Triumph of Life" to Shelley the man and taken issue with Mr. Matthews' biographical interpretation of the poem,[2] I here abjure biographical speculation and polemics.

2 "Shelley's 'The Triumph of Life': The Biographical Problem," *PMLA*, LXXVIII (December 1963), 536–550.

As I suggested near the beginning of this Preface, I began to study "The Triumph of Life" not as a partisan of Shelley but as a student of nineteenth-century English literature who found work to be done with this particular poem. Having committed my time and efforts to Shelley's works, I became, in the existential way, more and more deeply involved with my subject until I am now, perhaps, too close to Shelley to render an objective judgment of him, his ideas, or his art. Such commitment to the subject of one's study has, however, virtues to compensate for its obvious drawbacks: I have been willing to assume that Shelley knew what he was doing and that my task was to study and search until I learned what it was. If in a few instances I have been disappointed (at *my* lack of knowledge rather than at Shelley's), this attitude has, nevertheless, taught me more than would a supercilious condescension. This approach is, I believe, the right one to establish the initial comprehension of a subject; once the English poets have been thoroughly explicated by specialists, critics with a broader perspective can estimate their relative worth in our cultural history. My aim has been to illuminate the total intellectual, emotional, and aesthetic significance of "The Triumph of Life" through a detailed study of its text, structure, echoes and allusions, imagery, symbols, prosody, and—from these—theme. If I have succeeded, this study should provide students not only with a text and a reading of one of Shelley's best poems, but also with a method that can be applied to the study of other difficult works.

For support of the research leading to this study I wish to thank the Research Board of the University of Illinois for a Special Postdoctoral Summer Fellowship (1960) that enabled me to begin revision and extension of my doctoral dissertation on "The Triumph of Life"; the American Council of Learned Societies for a Grant-in-Aid of Research that enabled me to spend the summer of 1961 working with the Shelley MSS in the Bodleian Library, Oxford; the Duke University Library Council for purchasing microfilms of the Bodleian Shelley MSS; the Duke Research Council for funds with which to purchase supplies and materials and to aid in the preparation of the typescript.

I wish to thank several members of the Department of English at the University of Illinois, not merely for contributing to research specifically on "The Triumph of Life," but for strengthening my grasp of scholarly methods and literary values: Professors T. W. Baldwin, Gwynne Blakemore Evans, Harris F. Fletcher, Burton A.

Milligan, Robert W. Rogers, and Roland M. Smith; Rosario Paul Armato and James L. Scoggins (now of the University of Minnesota); and, especially, Professor Jack Stillinger, who read an earlier version of the Textual Study and suggested several significant improvements. Among my former colleagues at Duke University I am indebted for help and encouragement of my research to Professors Merle M. Bevington, Benjamin Boyce, Oliver W. Ferguson, Clarence Gohdes, S. K. Heninger, Jr., Lewis Patton, Joseph N. Riddel, Charles Richard Sanders, Lionel Stevenson, Marcel Tetel (Romance Languages), Arlin Turner, Paul Welsh (Philosophy), and George Walton Williams, and especially to Grover Smith, who read a late typescript of the entire book, caught several errors, and made other valuable suggestions. Allan H. Gilbert, Emeritus Professor of English, Duke University, gave me invaluable aid and encouragement.

The staffs of a number of libraries have contributed greatly to my research: among the unfailingly helpful and courteous staff of the University of Illinois Library, I recall with gratitude especially the help of Miss Eva Faye Benton, Miss Isabel Grant, and Miss Alma De Jordy; at the Duke University Library, that of Dr. Benjamin Powell, the Librarian, and of Miss Florence Blakely, Miss Gertrude Merritt, Mrs. Amanda Morris, Miss Mary Plowden, and Mr. Pietro Tavernise; at the Bodleian Library, Oxford, that of Dr. R. W. Hunt, Keeper of Western Manuscripts, and his fine staff, especially Mr. D. H. Merry. To the Delegates of the Clarendon Press, through their Secretary, Mr. D. M. Davin, I am grateful for permission to publish materials from the Bodleian Shelley MSS. For other help I am indebted to the Library of Wesleyan University, the Pierpont Morgan Library, the Keats-Shelley Memorial, Rome, and its able and gracious curator, Signora Vera Cacciatore. I wish also to thank Professor Terence Martin, Indiana University, and Professor Ernest J. Lovell, University of Texas, for their help with specific problems, and Mrs. Jacob Kaplan, who typed the monograph with extraordinary diligence and care.

I am grateful to Professors John R. Frey, Philip Kolb, and Burton Milligan, the board of editors of Illinois Studies in Language and Literature, who offered a number of helpful suggestions, and to Donald Jackson and the staff of the University of Illinois Press, particularly Mrs. Elizabeth G. Dulany, assistant editor, and Mrs. Bruce McDaniel and Miss Carolyn Holmstrand, the editorial assistants for the volume.

Finally, I cannot end without remarking that this book, like all first works, owes debts to the many individuals, organizations, and institutions that helped to shape its author. Most important are one's family and very close personal friends and one's teachers at all levels. An autobiographical accounting beginning in the manner of Marcus Aurelius might do some justice to this indebtedness, but this preface cannot. Two individuals, however, epitomize those to whom I am debtor for the pervasive influences that go far beyond scholarship: my wife, Mary Warner Reiman, and the teacher and friend under whose guidance this study was begun, Professor Royal A. Gettmann, to whom this book is dedicated for reasons that will be self-evident to scores of his students and colleagues at the University of Nebraska and the University of Illinois during the past quarter-century.

CONTENTS

PART ONE

"THE TRIUMPH OF LIFE": A CRITICAL STUDY

KEY TO BRIEF CITATIONS IN PART ONE

Bloom   Harold Bloom. *Shelley's Mythmaking*. New Haven, 1959.

Bradley   A. C. Bradley. "Notes on Shelley's 'Triumph of Life,'" *Modern Language Review*, IX (October 1914), 441–456.

Julian   *The Complete Works of Percy Bysshe Shelley*, eds. Roger Ingpen and Walter E. Peck. Julian ed. 10 vols. London and New York, 1926–30.

Julie   Jean-Jacques Rousseau. *Julie, ou La Nouvelle Héloïse*. Quotations are from *Œuvres complètes de J. J. Rousseau*. 2nd ed. 25 vols. Paris, 1826.

"New Text"   G. M. Matthews. " 'The Triumph of Life': A New Text," *Studia Neophilologica*, XXXII (1960), 271–309.

"On Shelley's *TL*" G. M. Matthews. "On Shelley's 'The Triumph of Life,'" *Studia Neophilologica*, XXXIV (1962), 104–134.

PL   John Milton. *Paradise Lost*. Quotations from Milton's works are from *The Student's Milton*, ed. Frank Allen Patterson. Rev. ed. New York, 1933.

P.W.   *The Complete Poetical Works of Percy Bysshe Shelley*, ed. Thomas Hutchinson. London, 1934.

Prose   *Shelley's Prose; or the Trumpet of a Prophecy*, ed. David Lee Clark. Albuquerque, 1954.

"S and JW"   G. M. Matthews. "Shelley and Jane Williams," *Review of English Studies*, N.S., XII (February 1961), 40–48.

Stawell   F. Melian Stawell. "Shelley's 'Triumph of Life,'" *Essays and Studies by Members of the English Association*, V (Oxford, 1914), 104–131.

TL   "The Triumph of Life."

Commedia (Inferno, Purgatorio, Paradiso)
                 Dante Aligheri. Italian text from *La Divina Commedia*, ed. C. H. Grandgent. Rev. ed. Boston, 1933. English translations from the Temple Classics editions of the *Inferno, Purgatorio*, and *Paradiso*, ed. H. Oelsner. London, 1956–58.

Trionfi (Trionfo d'Amore, Trionfo della Castità, Trionfo della Morte, Trionfo della Fama, Trionfo del Tempo, Trionfo della Divinità)
                 Francis Petrarch. Italian from *Rime di Francesco Petrarca*, ed. Giacomo Leopardi. Firenze, 1896. English translations from *The Triumphs of Petrarch*, trans. by Ernest Hatch Wilkins. Chicago, 1962.

CHAPTER ONE

THE PURPOSE AND METHOD OF SHELLEY'S POETRY: A MORAL IMPERATIVE AND A SYMBOLIC UNIVERSE

Fundamental and central to all of Shelley's writings—poetry and prose—was the moral law that Shelley found within himself. It is, perhaps, profitless to speculate about what aspects of his childhood training and experience formed the young Shelley's conscience or how his later readings in the eighteenth-century humanitarian authors like Godwin molded his concepts of virtue and justice. Shelley recorded in the Dedication to *The Revolt of Islam* (iii-v) a boyhood experience in which he imagined that the sound of voices "from the near schoolroom . . ./ Were but one echo from a world of woes," but he whose ear could thus catch the still sad music of humanity had listened attentively long before that "fresh May-dawn" dispersed "the clouds which wrap this world from youth." Shelley's early formative influences, like those of most men, are shrouded in obscurity; only the results of those lost experiences remained in the cast of his adult mind.

The moral law that governed Shelley's mature thought and action insisted upon both the right and the duty of each individual to rule his own destiny: Each human being was entitled to the liberty to seek his own happiness, but, at the same time, he was obligated to do all in his power to secure this freedom for the less fortunate. From these axioms Shelley dedicated his efforts to the destruction of tyranny in all its forms—the tyranny of marital, parental, pedagogical, political, and religious authoritarianism, the tyranny of poverty and ignorance. He believed that the individual

3

human spirit was the measure of all values within the limitations of mortal experience and that institutions were good only insofar as they promoted the welfare of the individual. Societies and institutions were abstractions, whereas men were real, and a family, a church, or a nation derived its only value from the benefit it conferred on the men and women who constituted it.[1] Like the ethical philosophy of Kant, Shelley's ideas depend ultimately upon the single, categorical imperative that human beings must be treated always as ends, never as means.

Besides the doctrines of benevolence and sympathy, derived from philosophers of the eighteenth century, which gave shape to Shelley's humanitarian ideals,[2] Shelley (again like Kant) inherited the epistemological dilemma of the British empirical philosophers. After reading Locke, Berkeley, Hume, and Sir William Drummond, he concluded that there are no innate ideas, that sense impressions initiate the learning process, and that, since one cannot be certain that the impressions of the senses correspond to an external reality, one must remain ultimately sceptical on all ontological questions.[3] Such a sceptical epistemology thwarted Shelley's desire to discover a firm metaphysical foundation for the moral values that he found so strong within himself. At the same time, however, the limitations of human knowledge made it impossible for experience or reason to destroy his hope that the ultimate character of the universe was good rather than evil, for even if all empirical evidence and all rational arguments indicated that human moral values were an anomaly in an amoral universe, that evidence and those reasonings, the products of fallible cognitive powers, might yet be mistaken. Shelley's severe intellectual honesty forced him to write an

[1] "Government can have no rights: it is a delegation for the purpose of securing them to others. . . . The strength of government is the happiness of the governed. All government existing for the happiness of others is just only so far as it exists by their consent, and useful only so far as it operates to their well-being." *Proposals for an Association of Philanthropists . . ., Prose*, p. 64. See also *A Declaration of Rights, Prose*, p. 70.

[2] See Roy R. Male, Jr., "Shelley and the Doctrine of Sympathy," *University of Texas Studies in English*, XXIX (1950), 183–203.

[3] The antecedents and nature of Shelley's scepticism have been admirably outlined by Pulos in *The Deep Truth: A Study of Shelley's Scepticism*. Professor Pulos' claims for the influence on Shelley of Sir William Drummond's *Academical Questions* (London, 1805) are conservative; the sceptical ideas and attitudes expressed by Drummond seem to permeate every area of Shelley's philosophy, though Shelley found it impossible to accept fideistic theism, Drummond's implicit solution to the sceptical dilemma.

"Essay on a Future State," in which he concluded that there was absolutely no evidence of immortality and that something akin to the physical law of inertia, a "desire to be for ever as we are, the reluctance to a violent and unexperienced change which is common to all the animated and inanimate combinations of the universe," was the sole origin of the hope for "a future state" *(Prose,* p. 178); but with his sceptical distrust of human reasoning, he could continue to hope that beyond the ken of mortal understanding the "Everlasting No" of ordinary human experience would give place to the "Everlasting Yea" of a realm in which the Good, the True, and the Beautiful would triumph.

Shelley sought support for his ethical ideals in the inner caverns of the human mind. An acute observer of the events of nature and society (as his letters from abroad, for example, prove), he could portray in concrete terms the interactions of people and things about him, and sometimes, when it furthers his purpose, he does so; but as a student of the natural sciences who saw behind the appearances of these events to their underlying psychological or physical causes, he often describes the operations of these hidden forces, and as a follower of the "intellectual philosophy" [4] that denied the authority of the senses and even postulated the ultimate unreality of the physical universe, he often turned to an examination of the processes of the mind, from which, he believed, one could learn more about the relationship between the impressions apprehended by the mind and the nature of reality. Through examination of the instrument that responds to sensory impressions and molds them into organic relationships, Shelley attempted to gather knowledge that external impressions themselves could not give. His best poems fuse three levels of experience into images that at the "phenomenal" level describe in detail an event or scene (often one that Shelley has actually witnessed), at the "scientific" level suggest the underlying physical or psychological causes of the

[4] Shelley speaks repeatedly of the "intellectual system" and "Intellectual Philosophy" in his "Essay on Life," where he says, "Perhaps the most clear and vigorous statement of the intellectual system is to be found in Sir William Drummond's *Academical Questions"* *(Prose,* p. 173). C. E. Pulos has demonstrated that the term "intellectual philosophy" was used to designate the thought of Berkeley and Hume as contrasted to the "common sense" philosophy that reacted against them. Drummond and Shelley, as classicists, connected Hume's scepticism with the Greek sceptics of the New Academy, with Cicero, and with Bacon and Montaigne and the Renaissance revival of scepticism. See Pulos, *The Deep Truth,* Chapters 2. 3.

phenomenon, and at the "philosophical" level infer its hidden moral implications.[5]

One cannot understand Shelley's philosophical position—ethical, epistemological, or ontological—without a thorough knowledge of his prose. Once the main outlines of his thought are clear, the corpus of Shelley's poetry, together with the prefaces and notes he himself supplied, is usually sufficient to clarify the theme of any single poem, but when one wishes to plumb its subtleties, not only Shelley's essays, letters, and recorded conversations, but even the books he read illuminate modulations of meaning.[6] No English poet is more allusive than Shelley, and certainly few read more widely or brought to their poetry a more varied range of symbolic reference: He knew the literature, history, and science of Western civilization from Homer and the Pentateuch to Goethe and Coleridge. He read ceaselessly and omnivorously, devouring books on agricultural chemistry, the histories of Gibbon and Sismondi, the myths of Plato and the scepticism of Hume, the dramas of Athens and England, Calderón and Alfieri, the theological and philosophical works of Aristotle and Augustine, Lucretius and Spinoza—all in their original languages, which he mastered so that he might not lose the harmonious sounds and subtleties of diction.[7] Shelley, far from becoming merely eclectic, however, integrated with his personal philosophical perspective the knowledge and wisdom he garnered from his studies.

[5] Elsewhere I have attempted to show how these three levels are integrated in one of Shelley's earlier poems: "Structure, Symbol, and Theme in 'Lines Written Among the Euganean Hills,'" *PMLA*, LXXVII (September 1962), 404–413.

[6] Though it may be, in our day, superfluous to justify poetic obscurity, the writings of most poets contain many references that are meaningless to the casual reader. Obscurities resulting from recondite biographical, historical, or literary allusions or from the author's individual symbolic vocabulary can usually be explained after intensive study of the author's life, works, and reading. The sole difference between legitimate obscurity and the other kind is that the former results from complexity rather than from indistinctness or confusion of poetic attitude and conception. Shelley's allusions, almost without exception, enrich and modify the surface statements of his poetry, usually in such a manner that one cannot imagine the same subtlety and complexity being achieved by more direct means.

[7] ". . . the language of poets has ever affected a certain uniform and harmonious recurrence of sound, without which it were not poetry, and which is scarcely less indispensable to the communication of its influence than the words themselves, without reference to that peculiar order. Hence the vanity of translation" (*A Defence of Poetry, Prose,* p. 280). See also Shelley's letter "To a Lady," Spring, 1821 (Julian, X, 267–268), where he inveighs at length against studying a literary work in any but its original language.

Throughout his maturity Shelley never changed his basic attitudes and ideals; he persisted in his desire to extend liberty of thought under the guidance of benevolent love to every human being, and he continued also to hold the sceptical epistemology that prevented him from declaring categorically that the ideal to which he aspired was in fact congruent with an objective reality. He attempted, therefore, to portray through his poetry the ideals that he found both within himself and in the records of the greatest human spirits. The conceptions of man, nature, history, and immortality in Shelley's poems are not declared to be objectively true, but are, like the myths of Plato, poetic "guesses at truth"; of the problem of evil and the immortality of the soul Shelley wrote: "Let it not be supposed that I mean to dogmatise upon a subject, concerning which all men are equally ignorant. . . . [but] as it is the province of the poet to attach himself to those ideas which exalt and ennoble humanity, let him be permitted to have conjectured the condition of that futurity towards which we are all impelled by an inextinguishable thirst for immortality." [8] To "exalt and ennoble humanity," to embody the highest human ideas in such attractive forms that men will desire the good, and to image evil in such repulsive forms that they will abhor it, in short, to familiarize men "with beautiful idealisms of moral excellence" [9]—this was the purpose of Shelley's poetry. He could honestly declare that didactic poetry was his abhorrence because he never pretended to "teach" in an intellectual sense; despite the vast range of knowledge he brought to his poetry, his purpose was never to discuss the nature of things, scientifically or philosophically. He attempted, rather, to purify and stretch the imaginations of his readers through self-acknowledged myths that tell not what exists, or even what within the limitations of the mortal world *can* exist, but what according to the profoundest moral insights of Western civilization *should* exist; Shelley, unlike most poets, never confused the realm of "is" with that of "ought." Those critics who have concluded that Shelley's picture of human history in a poem like *Prometheus Unbound* is

[8] Note to *Hellas, P.W.,* p. 478.

[9] Preface to *Prometheus Unbound, P.W.,* p. 207. Cf. Sir William Drummond: "If you wish to make men virtuous, endeavour to inspire into them the love of virtue. Show them the beauty of order, and the fitness of things. . . . Represent vice, as indignant virtue will always represent it, as hideous, loathsome, and deformed. . . . will cannot be changed, while sentiment remains unaltered. There is no power, by which men can create, or destroy their feelings. Sensation alone overcomes sensation." *Academical Questions,* pp. 20–21.

"unrealistic" had only to turn to Shelley's Preface to find him admitting as much.[10] In *The Cenci* Shelley exhibits the "sad reality" of the world that "is," a world starkly contrasting with the moral world of "ought" that appears in *Prometheus*. This sharp division between "is" and "ought," between the hard limitations of the human situation and man's apprehension of ideal perfection, remained for Shelley the basic ethical dilemma, and the poet's problem was to find a language through which the two worlds, irreconcilably disparate in "phenomenal" human experience, might be harmonized—or at least related—in the artistic universe of the poem.

Since 1900 when William Butler Yeats wrote his significant essays on "The Philosophy of Shelley's Poetry," [11] critics have recognized with more or less perception that Shelley transmits his meaning partly through a system of symbols that remain relatively consistent from poem to poem. The useful criticism of Carl Grabo, Carlos Baker, Peter Butter, Neville Rogers, Harold Bloom, Milton Wilson, and Earl R. Wasserman begins with the assumption that Shelley's language is functional to his ideas—that for him, as for other poets, subtleties of diction were the heart and soul of poetry.[12]

Anyone who has worked with the manuscripts of Shelley's poetry —or who has read the criticism of those who have—ought to be aware that Shelley corrected and revised in a never ending search for the exact words to convey his meaning, though in his struggle to communicate his apprehensions exactly as they came to him, he became cognizant of the limitations of language and the difficulty

---

10 ". . . it is a mistake to suppose that I dedicate my poetical compositions solely to the direct enforcement of reform, or that I consider them in any degree as containing a reasoned system on the theory of human life. Didactic poetry is my abhorrence; nothing can be equally well expressed in prose that is not tedious and supererogatory in verse. My purpose has hitherto been simply to familiarise the highly refined imagination of the more select classes of poetical readers with beautiful idealisms of moral excellence; aware that until the mind can love, and admire, and trust, and hope, and endure, reasoned principles of moral conduct are seeds cast upon the highway of life which the unconscious passenger tramples into dust, although they would bear the harvest of his happiness" (Preface to *Prometheus Unbound*, *P.W.*, p. 207).

11 First published in *The Dome* (July 1900); reprinted in *Ideas of Good and Evil* and, more recently, in *Essays and Introductions* (New York, 1961).

12 A contrary opinion has recently been expressed—though in no respect documented—by David Perkins in *The Quest for Permanence* (Cambridge, Mass., 1959), p. 109. Shelley's own statements on the value of language are unequivocal: see *A Defence of Poetry*, *Prose*, pp. 279–280; Letter "To a Lady," Julian, X, 267–268.

of communication: "These words are ineffectual and metaphorical. Most words are so—No help!" [13] Although in *A Defence of Poetry* Shelley first designates as "poetry" any product of human imagination, he soon narrows his definition, first to "those arrangements of language and especially metrical language which are created by that imperial faculty. . . ." [14] As a sceptic who denied that there was a necessary correspondence between the mind's impressions and any external causes, Shelley believed that the "nature itself of language" could provide "a more direct representation of the actions and passions of our internal being and is susceptible of more various and delicate combinations than color, form, or motion . . ." because language, the medium of thought itself, "is more plastic and obedient to the control of that faculty of which it is the creation. For language is arbitrarily produced by the imagination and has relation to thoughts alone; but all other materials, instruments, and conditions of art" have physical relations and properties "which limit and interpose between conception and expression." [15] Moreover, the sounds of language, he believed, constitute a sensory medium apart from the intellectual content of words and have relations both with one another and with the ideas they represent; the poetic mind must, therefore, perceive "the order of those relations" at the same time that it perceives "the order of those relations of thoughts." [16] Since, therefore, the imagination will harmonize not only the ideas of words but their sounds as well into meaningful relationships, "the authors of revolutions in opinion are not only necessarily poets as they are inventors, nor even as their words unveil the permanent analogy of things by images which participate in the life of truth but as their periods are harmonious and rhythmical . . ." (*Prose,* p. 281).

The poetic imagination for Shelley thus perfectly integrated three aspects of language: first, the relations of words to "ideas," their complex denotative and connotative significance; second, the

---

[13] Note to "Essay on Love," *Prose,* p. 170. But although Shelley recognized the metaphorical—we would say "symbolic"—nature of language, he did not impugn its value within his sceptical epistemology; though it is "vain . . . to think that words can penetrate the mystery of our being . . . rightly used they may make evident our ignorance to ourselves, and this is much" ("Essay on Life," *Prose,* p. 172).

[14] *Prose,* p. 279.

[15] *Prose,* pp. 279–280.

[16] *Prose,* p. 280. See note 7 above. In Shelley's discussions of the nature of poetry, he discusses only the aural characteristics of language, never the visual appearance or arrangement of words on the printed page.

relations through analogies or metaphors of these verbal concepts to the "impressions" that a nonsceptic would term "objective reality"; and third, the relations of both the "ideas" and the "impressions" of words to their sounds. For Shelley, then, the best poetry first exhibits unity of conception as an organic creation according to the laws of an integrated imagination; it expresses this truth in images that have coherent analogical relations to the "things of nature" or the world of sensory apprehension; and, finally, it orders the sounds of the words in a way that not only commends its meaning through the delight of pleasant harmonies but supports that meaning wherever possible by onomatopoeic effects.

The relation of two of these three aspects requires some elaboration and explanation. That Shelley sought coherent analogical relations between the terms in his poems and the natural objects or beings commonly designated by those words does not mean that he used words "naturalistically" or "realistically." On the contrary, Shelley did not believe in the truth of relations between words and the so-called "physical" entities they designated (their referents) but only between words and the concepts of the mind that the words expressed; that is, because the reality of external nature must remain ever doubtful to the limited human mind, words take their significance not from an external world but from the ordered laws of the mind itself. Man's understanding of the phenomenal world is continually in flux, as science describes and postulates more and more about the behavior of animals, the causes of meteorological phenomena, and the like, but the individual human mind retains conceptions and attitudes that give to each word connotations quite distinct from the "objective" nature of its referent. In most instances, however, the connotative "idea" designated by the word bears some relation to the qualities of the "external object" also designated by the word. The lion, for example, may not in fact be the King of Beasts: it may actually fear the rhinoceros or the elephant. But its regal appearance and its carnivorous habits lend to it associations that justify the "idea" of the lion as King of Beasts. Shelley, therefore, never restricted his use of referential words to the empirical nature or behavior of their referents, though he did utilize such scientific "facts" as would contribute to the "idea" of the word. He drew his poetic symbol of the eagle, for example, more from Pliny's *Natural History* and from Biblical and bestiary tradition than from nineteenth-century knowledge of the eagle's nature and habits, because the ancient traditions gave moral and symbolic dimensions to the bird that Shelley—like the American republic [17]—found useful in symbolizing his ideas. Inasmuch as he did not assign symbolic values to his words and images on empirical grounds, his mind could chart a consistent significance for each word.[18] From his reading and his own experience Shelley came to associate various words with particular phases of man's moral life. Heat and cold, light and darkness, owls and eagles, violets and roses, sun and moon, all came to symbolize certain moral and epistemological concepts. To communicate his ideas to the reader, he drew these symbolic significances from earlier poetic tradition, modifying the usages of earlier poets only as he had to in order to express his individualized conceptions of man and the universe.

Shelley's symbolic universe will be fully elucidated only after scholars have examined dozens of key words in various contexts in his poetry (and prose) and have then studied the associations of these same words in the philosophical, religious, and literary writings that are known to have impressed Shelley. Because such study of his symbolism is still in its infancy, readers of his poetry have often been unable to grasp the significance of a recurring word or phrase that seems to symbolize something beyond itself. Some critics have assumed that many of Shelley's symbols were original and arbitrary, having little relation to those of other writers, while others have attempted to trace all of his symbols to a single tradition, usually Platonism. Recent studies of Shelley's use of Lucretius and of Bacon,[19] however, joined with previous recognition of his

[17] Benjamin Franklin, an eighteenth-century rationalist, attempted to overthrow this traditional symbolism and to prevent the United States from adopting the bald eagle as its national bird, preferring the turkey, whose characteristic habits he found more in accord with the ideals of the American republic.

[18] Since Shelley was not especially concerned with the referents of words, but with language itself, which "is arbitrarily produced by the imagination and has relation to thoughts alone" (*Prose*, p. 279), he often gives synonyms quite different symbolic connotations in his poetry. For example, as I shall try to show in my explication of "The Triumph of Life," the word "Sun" has good associations, whereas the word "day" has bad connotations. Or, to turn to the eagle again, in *Prometheus Unbound*, where Jupiter is evil, Jupiter's sacred bird cannot be called an "eagle" (which, in spite of continued misreading, always carries good connotations in Shelley's poetry); instead, the bird is referred to as "Heaven's wingèd hound" (I.34). Hounds, like wolves, are always symbols of evil in Shelley's poetry.

[19] William O. Scott, "Shelley's Admiration for Bacon," *PMLA*, LXXII (June 1958), 228–236; Paul Turner, "Shelley and Lucretius," *RES*, N.S., X (August 1959), 269–282.

debts to the Bible, Plato, Æschylus, Spenser, Milton, Dante, Calderón, Goethe, and others, demonstrate the variety of Shelley's sources, and Earl R. Wasserman's brilliant reading of *Adonais* shows the complexity with which Shelley syncretized symbolic overtones from many sources into his highly original poetry.[20]

In the "Essay on Life" (perhaps the most important single document of Shelley's intellectual development), Shelley divides natural phenomena into two major categories: First he speaks of "the system of the sun, and the stars, and planets . . . the spectacle now afforded by the nightly cope of heaven," and then of "the scenery of this earth. . . ."[21] This distinction between celestial and terrestrial phenomena—between the "cope of heaven" and the "scenery of this earth"—plays an important role in Shelley's symbolism. Shelley adopted for poetic purposes a pre-Copernican cosmology that considered all created things beneath the moon subject to mutability, whereas the sun, planets, and stars beyond the moon existed in a realm of permanence. The moon, "to whom alone it has been given/ To change and be adored forever," [22] was mutable but eternal and regular in its mutations; it governed the sublunar world and was the abiding symbol of its limitations. Whereas the celestial bodies consisted of but the single element of fire, terrestrial creation contained the four elements—fire, air, water, and earth. Earth—often referred to as dust—represented inert matter; water symbolized purely mortal or terrestrial generation; fire, the element of the sun and stars, symbolized spiritual energy; and the air, which existed between the earth and waters of the mutable and the fires of the eternal, was the realm of those ideas and abstractions that raise men above the merely mortal perspective but which are limited and distorted by the imperfections of human condition.

Besides distinguishing between the pure fires of Heaven and the sublunar creation, Shelley recognized two subdivisions within terrestrial nature. The quotation from the "Essay on Life" continues: "the scenery of this earth, the mountains, the seas, and the rivers; the grass, and the flowers, and the variety of the forms and masses

[20] *"Adonais:* Progressive Revelation as a Poetic Mode," *ELH,* XXI (December 1954), 274–326. Slightly revised and reprinted in *The Subtler Language.*

[21] *Prose,* p. 172. Clark, in a headnote to the "Essay on Life," dates it 1812–14, an error that his first footnote refutes. (He shows that in 1818 Shelley probably first saw the quotation from Tasso that he uses in the essay.) The holograph of "Essay on Life" (now in the Pierpont Morgan Library) was originally part of the same notebook (now in the Carl H. Pforzheimer Library) that contained the holograph of *A Philosophical View of Reform* (1819–20) (see Kenneth Neill Cameron, *Shelley and His Circle: 1773–1822,* II, 897).

[22] "Lines Written in the Bay of Lerici," 2–3 (see "S and JW," p. 41).

of the leaves of the woods, and the colors which attend the setting and the rising sun, and the hues of the atmosphere, turbid or serene . . ." (*Prose*, p. 172). As the punctuation of this passage indicates,[23] Shelley distinguished those elemental natural forms such as mountain, sea, and river (that consist of a single one of the three terrestrial elements of earth, water, and air) from those slighter phenomena such as cloud, wave, leaf, dew, mist, rainbow, moth, and flower.

A terrestrial feature like an ocean, a continent, or even a river or a mountain, exhibits the qualities of its element (water or earth) in a general or abstract way. The sea or ocean in Shelley's poetry, for example, often symbolizes the realm of temporal existence upon which man pursues his voyage of life.[24] Sometimes a small stream symbolizes the course of life of some particular individual, whereas a river may signify the history of some particular community.[25] The smaller, ephemeral terrestrial creatures frequently image a particular aspect of man, or man in a specific condition or situation. The cloud, for example, is a recurring symbol of the human mind or soul, a product of the moisture of mortal generation but existing above the merely mortal and vivified by the light of the celestial bodies. Or, a mimosa, the "sensitive plant," becomes the symbol of man, with his unfulfilled longings for the Good, the True, and the Beautiful, as contrasted with the other transitory creatures, whose natures seem fulfilled and satisfied within the realm of temporal experience.[26]

Occupying a unique position in Shelley's symbolic universe was the wind, which in its wilder manifestations as "storm," "tempest," or "whirlwind" was Shelley's symbol of Necessity. As a follower of Hume and Drummond, Shelley rejected the Aristotelian-Thomistic theory of causation and believed that the mere conjunction of two sensory impressions (even when they conjoined repeatedly) demonstrated no necessary causation of the second by the first. Because

---

[23] I have examined a photostat of the Pierpont Morgan MS of "On Life," which does not have the same punctuation as Clark's edition, but in this instance there is clearly a division between the two types of terrestrial phenomena such as that indicated by Clark's punctuation. Shelley scholars require a new critical edition of the prose based where possible on Shelley's MSS, but this undertaking will not be feasible on a full scale until the Pforzheimer papers have been published.

[24] "Lines Written Among the Euganean Hills," 1–26 (*P.W.*, p. 554) and "Time" (*P.W.*, p. 637).

[25] "Euganean Hills," 184 (*P.W.*, p. 556) and "Evening: Ponte al Mare, Pisa," 13–16 (*P.W.*, p. 654).

[26] Wasserman, *The Subtler Language*, p. 257.

Shelley held that the causes for both sensory "impressions" and psychic "ideas" were unknown and unknowable, he used the wind, which "blows where it wills" though nobody knows "whence it comes or whither it goes," to symbolize the concept that philosophers had postulated to explain the relations between series of physical, historical, or psychological events. Because air is the element symbolizing human concepts and ideas, the wind, a connected movement of this element, proves an effective sceptical symbol of the concept of Necessity that had played so large a part in eighteenth-century thought. Among the celestial symbols the moon, which "as Mother of the Months" [27] is associated with time and mutability, is also "the planet of frost, so cold and bright" that makes things "wan with her borrowed light" [28] and is usually identifiable with reason, the analytic faculty, which in *A Defence of Poetry* Shelley distinguishes from imagination, the vital, synthetic faculty. In a proposed letter to Ollier answering Peacock's *Four Ages of Poetry*, Shelley wrote: "He would extinguish Imagination which is the Sun of life, and grope his way by the cold and uncertain and borrowed light of that moon which he calls Reason, stumbling over the interlunar chasm of time where she deserts us, and an owl, rather than an eagle, stare with dazzled eyes on the watery orb which is the Queen of his pale Heaven." [29] In *Epipsychidion* he speaks of

> The cold chaste Moon, the Queen of Heaven's bright isles,
> Who makes all beautiful on which she smiles,
> That wandering shrine of soft yet icy flame
> Which ever is transformed, yet still the same,
> And warms not but illumines.
>
> 281–285; *P.W.,* pp. 417–418

In a fragment "To the Moon" Shelley asked,

> Art thou pale for weariness
> Of climbing heaven and gazing on the earth,
> Wandering companionless
> Among the stars that have a different birth,—
> And ever changing, like a joyless eye
> That finds no object worth its constancy?
>
> *P.W.,* p. 621

The moon in Shelley's poetry is beautiful but cold, pale, and inconstant, of a different order from the stars, giving one only the

[27] "The Witch of Atlas," 73 (*P.W.,* p. 373).
[28] "To Constantia," 5–6 (*P.W.,* p. 541).
[29] ?March 1821. Julian, X, 246.

borrowed, secondary light of rational analysis, which is eternal but not immutable and shines only upon certain aspects of our experience.

The Sun, on the other hand, is associated with the vivifying creative imagination, a burning fountain of warmth and light out of which flow the spiritual natures of created things. At the universal level the Sun signifies the Deity; in the world of human experience it represents Imagination, the divine in man. Shelley always distinguishes, however, between the light of the celestial Sun and the same light as filtered through the earth's atmosphere. In the first note to *Queen Mab* he wrote: "Beyond our atmosphere the sun would appear a rayless orb of fire in the midst of a black concave. The equal diffusion of its light on earth is owing to the refraction of the rays by the atmosphere, and their reflection from other bodies." [30] Thus, the earth is surrounded by a "veil of light," and the white radiance of pure sunlight is broken into the colors of the visible spectrum. The rainbow, product solely of the distortion of the white light of the One Reality into the multiple colors of this earth, symbolizes the unreal appearances of earthly life, a "painted veil" that hides from human vision the nature of things-in-themselves, and, with the epistemological dilemma clearly in his thoughts, Shelley speaks of the human mind as diffusing truth and casting "rainbow hues" over the external world.[31] The cosmic Sun thus plays what seems to be an ambiguous role in Shelley's symbolism. In itself it vivifies and illuminates in the highest sense, but because of the double distortion by the earth's atmosphere (the conditions of limited, terrestrial existence) and by the cloudy human mind, the light of the sun cannot be trusted; in "Letter to Maria Gisborne" Shelley recalls

> . . . how we spun
> A shroud of talk to hide us from the sun
> Of this familiar life, which seems to be
> But is not:—or is but quaint mockery
> Of all we would believe, and sadly blame
> The jarring and inexplicable frame
> Of this wrong world. . . .
>   154–160; *P.W.*, pp. 366–367

---

[30] *P.W.*, p. 800.

[31] See "Fragment: To the Mind of Man" (*P.W.*, pp. 634–635). Because water droplets act as light-refracting prisms, such phenomena as dew, mist, and cloud assume symbolic overtones that relate them both to the human mind (*Hellas*, 215–217; "The Sunset," 1–4, *P.W.*, p. 528) and to the mind's distortion of reality.

The sun as seen by men is deceptive, and in such later poems as "The Sensitive Plant" and "To Night," Shelley praises the night and its dreams as fountains of higher knowledge.

The "fixed stars" symbolize the immutable realm of Being that enjoys all the conditions for which men long but which are impossible in this life under the rule of "Fate, Time, Occasion, Chance, and Change." In the terrestrial realm of cyclical necessity, not only do individuals prosper and suffer, live and die, without regard for moral differences, but there is no discernible permanent progress in history: If "the world's great age begins anew," it too shall pass away to be succeeded by a return of "hate and death." [32] The stars, shining with an unchanging light that does not obscure them in their own bright veil (as does the Sun, deity itself), offer the hope to mortals that they, too, can rise above the mutability of this existence into an unchanging fulfillment of the highest human aspirations. In *Adonais* the stars symbolize the souls of great and good men of the past, "the splendours of the firmament of time" who "may be eclipsed, but are extinguished not." [33] Since the true Sun is obscured by its veil of light, man depends upon the inner sun of his own imagination (which partakes of the nature of the Divine but is subject to the limitations of the terrestrial world) and upon the example of those noble dead who, like stars, beacon "from the abode where the Eternal are" (*Adonais*, 495).

Finally, the planet Venus receives considerable attention throughout Shelley's poetry. Shelley believed strongly in two of the "theological virtues," Hope and Love, though "Faith" was always a term of opprobrium in his vocabulary because of what he regarded as the black moral record of all fideisms, Pagan, Christian, or Moslem.[34] For him full use of human reason was a moral responsibility, even though reason's ultimate success lay in defining the narrow limits of its own competence. In the "Essay on Life" he says of the "intellectual philosophy" (Humean scepticism): "It establishes no new truth, it gives us no additional insight into our hidden nature, neither in its actions nor itself. Philosophy, impatient as it may be to build, has much work yet remaining as pioneer for the overgrowth of ages. It makes one step towards this object: it destroys

[32] Final Chorus of *Hellas* (*P.W.*, pp. 477–478).
[33] *Adonais*, 388–389 (*P.W.*, p. 441). Allan H. Gilbert has pointed out to me that Shelley probably derived his use of "splendours" from Dante's *Paradiso*, e.g., Canto XXI, 32.
[34] See Shelley's note (8) to *Hellas*, 1090–91 (*P.W.*, p. 480).

error and the roots of error. It leaves, what is too often the duty of the reformer in political and ethical questions to leave, a vacancy" (*Prose*, p. 173). But whereas "Faith" was, in Shelley's eyes, a moral liability, "Love" and "Hope" were the cornerstones of his ethical philosophy, Love its motivating force, and Hope for the ultimate triumph of Good over Evil the sustainer of its energy. Venus, as the morning star Lucifer (the light-bearer), was the sign of man's regeneration within his earthly life—his awakening to spiritual Love; as Hesperus or Vesper, the evening star, it promised fulfillment of man's aspirations beyond the grave and thus symbolized Hope; as Dante's "third sphere" [35] it also symbolized Love in its highest manifestations.

The celestial symbols remain relatively consistent in their associations throughout Shelley's poetry, as do many of the terrestrial symbols. Each individual poem, however, develops its particular symbolic universe, drawing nuances and associations from specific traditions (the pastoral elegiac tradition in *Adonais*), from literary models (the *Persae* of Æschylus in *Hellas*), or from relevant historical events (the Peterloo Massacre in *The Mask of Anarchy*), and (since the symbolic force is primarily "philosophical") also from the "scientific" and the "phenomenal" levels of meaning. In explicating Shelley's individual poems, then, one cannot impose his "symbolic universe" in a Procrustean fashion; one must read each work on its own terms, keeping in mind the approximate values of these symbols and observing how they interrelate within the poem. The symbolism is consistent, but it evolves in forms as individual as Shelley's poetry is different from the literary sources he used.

In the chapter that follows I attempt to explicate "The Triumph of Life," putting to the best use I can all that I have learned from other students of Shelley as well as from my own study of the corpus of Shelley's poetry, prose, and letters, but I base every statement on the text of "The Triumph" itself, a text newly edited from the Bodleian manuscript. The temptation for the critic of Shelley, friendly or hostile, is immediately to give him or his individual poems a rank or niche in the English poetic tradition. Unfortunately, the present state of Shelley studies does not permit this, for until one knows what the poet actually wrote and what it means, one can

---

[35] *Paradiso*, VIII–IX; cf. also Shelley's translation of the First Canzone of the *Convito*: "Ye who intelligent the Third Heaven move . . ." (*P.W.*, p. 726).

hardly determine whether his poetry is better or worse than that of other poets (whose work may or may not be better understood). Until all of Shelley's works are scrutinized anew, beginning with a reconsideration of the authority of their texts and concluding with a line-by-line, word-by-word explication of literal, "scientific," and symbolic-philosophical implications, every effort to determine Shelley's place in the Romantic movement or to evaluate his poetic achievement must remain perilously tentative and approximate. I have attempted, therefore, chiefly to explore what, in fact, Shelley wrote and what this means. Some criticisms of Shelley's poetic theory and practice and of his philosophical ideas have been based upon misunderstanding of his works, but to point out that a group of critics may have been mistaken about this or that aspect of his work does not, obviously, prove that Shelley was a great poet or a profound thinker; it means only that those who value the qualities that actually characterize Shelley's poetry be able to appreciate it more when they recognize these qualities in it. If, as I believe, Shelley belongs to the great tradition of Western writers that includes Dante, Shakespeare, and Milton, the proper explication of his works ought to go far toward reestablishing his literary reputation; if not, then his writings deserve, perhaps, to remain less read than abused.

CHAPTER TWO

A READING OF
"THE TRIUMPH OF LIFE"

DUST AND FOAM

"The Triumph of Life" is a mythopoeic work that explores the human situation in its various actual manifestations, while contrasting with this "sad reality" the inherent possibilities open to the man who exercises his will to liberate himself from bondage both to external necessity and to his own blind passions. Shelley, who in his "Sonnet: Political Greatness" wrote that "Man who man would be,/ Must rule the empire of himself," knew that man's free self-rule is constantly endangered by the power of amoral Necessity, by the tyranny of custom and the arbitrary power of human institutions, and by the unruly desires of his own heart: "All spirits are enslaved which serve things evil." [1]

Shelley adopted not only the rhyme-scheme of his poem but also many substantive details from Dante and Petrarch; he also, as in his earlier works, borrowed freely from Milton, from Lucretius, from Bacon, from Plato, from Sismondi, and from Rousseau's *Julie, ou la Nouvelle Héloïse*.[2] In *Julie* Rousseau tells how a consuming passion for a worthy but unattainable object (Julie) nearly destroyed an intelligent, well-meaning, and sensitive but too impulsive young man (Saint-Preux) and how this excess of love, which thus threatened to consume both Saint-Preux and his beloved, was

---

[1] *Prometheus Unbound* II.iv.110.

[2] Shelley apparently reread *Julie* early in 1822, for in his letter to John Gisborne, 10 April 1822, he wrote: "Do you remember the 54th letter of the 1st part of the Nouvelle Héloïse? Göthe, in a subsequent scene evidently has that letter in his mind . . ." (Julian, X, 372).

transformed by Julie's strength of will and virtue into a chaste devotion that ennobled both lovers. Elsewhere I have attempted to suggest how Shelley's situation in 1822 may have resembled that of Rousseau when he wrote *Julie*.[3] But biography plays little part in "The Triumph of Life" and must be considered at most a factor in the execution rather than the conception of the poem. "The Triumph" is a philosophical poem that explores the possibilities for human values in a seemingly amoral universe, and most of the key concepts in the poem parallel those from such earlier works as *Alastor, The Revolt of Islam, A Philosophical View of Reform,* and *Epipsychidion.* In the Preface to *Alastor* Shelley had divided men into three classes: first, "the luminaries of the world" who are destroyed by an uncontrollable passion for a vision of an unattainable ideal; second, the "selfish, blind, and torpid" multitude "who constitute . . . the lasting misery and loneliness of the world"; and third, those who do *not* "attempt to exist without human sympathy" but who dedicate themselves according to their talents to the love and service of their fellow men as "friends," "lovers," "fathers," "citizens of the world," or "benefactors of their country." This third class of men was the subject of *The Revolt of Islam.* In Canto I, stanzas xxxv-xlvi, the beautiful, sad Woman tells the story of her dream encounter with the vision of Intellectual Beauty, an account that parallels very closely the vision of the Youth in *Alastor*.[4] But this woman, instead of being blinded by the vision (as was the Youth), used it as the inspiration for her life of service to her fellow men; immediately after her ideal antitype says, "A Spirit loves thee, mortal maiden,/ How wilt thou prove thy worth?" she, like the Youth in *Alastor,* suddenly awakes to find herself left desolate:

[3] "Shelley's 'The Triumph of Life': The Biographical Problem," *PMLA,* LXXVIII (December 1963), 536–550.

[4] There is some suggestion in *The Revolt of Islam* that this poem was intended as a sequel to *Alastor,* with its outcome reversing that inflicted upon the Youth by the avenging "Spirit of Solitude." The beautiful, sad Woman in Canto I of *The Revolt* tells the Poet,

> A dying poet gave me books, and blessed
> With wild but holy talk the sweet unrest
> In which I watched him as he died away—
> A youth with hoary hair—a fleeting guest
> Of our lone mountains: and this lore did sway
> My spirit like a storm, contending there alway.
> *Revolt,* 454–459

"And to the shore I went to muse and weep;
But as I moved, over my heart did creep
A joy less soft, but more profound and strong
Than my sweet dream; and it forbade to keep
The path of the sea-shore: that Spirit's tongue
Seemed whispering in my heart, and bore my steps along.

xliv
"How, to that vast and peopled city led,
    Which was a field of holy warfare then,
I walked among the dying and the dead,
    And shared in fearless deeds with evil men,
    Calm as an angel in the dragon's den—
How I braved death for liberty and truth,
    And spurned at peace, and power, and fame—and when
Those hopes had lost the glory of their youth,
How sadly I returned—might move the hearer's ruth."

Revolt, 508–522

These same three groups of human beings—the "unforeseeing multitudes," the enraptured dreamers, and the dedicated humanitarians [5]—appear in "The Triumph of Life" and are judged much as they were in Shelley's earlier works, but his last major poem exhibits greater complexity and explores subtler variations within these three categories.

Shelley has given his reader in the first two lines of "The Triumph" an objective correlative that, when recognized, becomes a key to the theme. The initial simile contains both an echo from and an allusion to the Attendant Spirit of Milton's *Comus*. In the opening speech of Milton's masque the Spirit, after describing the perils faced by travelers in "the perplex't paths of this drear Wood," announced his mission:

Therefore when any favour'd of high *Jove*,
Chances to passe through this adventrous glade,
Swift as the Sparkle of a glancing Star,
I shoot from Heav'n to give him safe convoy.

ll. 78–81

[5] These three groups are also mentioned in Keats's "The Fall of Hyperion: A Dream" (107–215), but though Keats praises those "who love their fellows even to the death" (156), he never really shows much interest in them in this or other poems. If *Endymion* is (as some have seen it) an answer to *Alastor* and if *The Revolt of Islam* is (as I believe) a sequel to *Alastor*, Keats's solution to the dilemma of the idealistic dreamer is evidently a far more individualistic and "romantic" one than Shelley's: Shelley's solution takes the form of humanitarian service to others, while Keats's answer centers on self-fulfillment through romantic love. Of course, Keats's poem was written at an earlier stage of his development than Shelley's, and as a poem *Endymion* is not inferior to *The Revolt*.

Shelley's first line both echoes line 80 of *Comus* and alludes to the Spirit who hastens to the good and glorious task of giving safe convoy through the world's wilderness to chosen men. In this echo and allusion Shelley tells his reader for the first of many times that, although "The Triumph of Life" presents a dark picture of human existence, it is not a hopeless one. In fact, though in *Comus* Milton seems to be optimistic about the unvanquishable power of virtue, the opening speech of that masque presents as dark a picture of the mortal world as Shelley ever drew:

> Before the starry threshold of *Joves* Court
> My mansion is, where those immortal shapes
> Of bright and aëreal Spirits live insphear'd
> In Regions milde of calm and serene Ayr,
> Above the smoak and stirr of this dim spot,
> Which men call Earth, and with low-thoughted care
> Confin'd, and pester'd in this pin-fold here,
> Strive to keep up a frail and Feaverish being
> Unmindfull of the crown that Vertue gives
> After this mortal change, to her true Servants
> Amongst the enthron'd gods on Sainted seats.
> Yet som there be that by due steps aspire
> To lay their just hands on that Golden Key
> That ope's the Palace of Eternity:
> To such my errand is, and but for such,
> I would not soil these pure Ambrosial weeds,
> With the rank vapours of this Sin-worn mould.
>
> ll. 1–17

Shelley announces his purpose in the opening simile: to give safe convoy to those few who aspire to the Palace of Eternity, though in doing so it will be necessary for him to encounter also "the rank vapours of this Sin-worn mould." Likewise, the Sun, which sprang forth like the Attendant Spirit, inevitably soils his pure beams in the earthly vapors, and this refraction of the white radiance of the sun into the rainbow hues of the terrestrial world is a key image of the poem. In the third line Shelley includes a verbal reminiscence of Psalm 19, where the sun is said to be "as a bridegroom coming out of his chamber, and rejoiceth as a strong man to run a race," the verbal echo reinforcing the favorable associations of the Attendant Spirit.[6] Finally, the "mask of darkness" falls from

---

[6] Cf. *PL* IV.13, where Milton contrasts Satan's progress to that of the sun in Psalm 19. Another echo in *TL*, line 2, is more ambiguous: Byron's "Michael flew forth in glory and in good," *The Vision of Judgment*, 233.

the earth, an event that any student of Shelley will recognize as joyous. The Sun is, *in itself,* a symbol of the Good.

The following lines (5–20) record the natural worship of the Sun by terrestrial creation, worship that expresses itself through four of the five senses. The mountains become flaming altars of both heat and light, the Ocean raises an orison while a choir of birds sings matins, and the flowers swing odorous censers; [7] as the Sun's rays reach across the Apennines toward the west, first the mainland, then an island, the Mediterranean, and all the slighter forms that inhabit them—all things that

> . . . in them wear
> The form & character of mortal mould
> Rise as the Sun their father rose, to bear
>
> Their portion of the toil which he of old
> Took as his own & then imposed on them. . . .[8]

Bradley has compared these lines to "The Boat on the Serchio" (30ff.), where Shelley wrote:

> All rose to do the task He set to each,
> Who shaped us to His ends and not our own;
> The million rose to learn, and one to teach,

and it is claimed that, since the Sun is a symbol of the Good, perhaps of God, Shelley was approaching orthodoxy. Harold Bloom is certainly correct, however, in pointing to the succeeding lines of "The Boat on the Serchio" to refute this speculation:

> What none yet ever knew or can be known.
> And many rose
> Whose woe was such that fear became desire;—
> Melchior and Lionel were not among those;
> They from the throng of men had stepped aside. . . .
> *P.W.,* p. 655

At dawn all merely mortal creatures respond in harmony to the Sun and its creative power, obeying the Necessity of their respective natures, but the Poet is "not among those"; while all other created things are rising in automatic response to the power of the Sun, the Poet, who has remained awake all night, stretches himself under a tree and prepares to sleep. Bloom has rightly suggested that the contrast emphasizes Man's more-than-natural destiny, a destiny

---

[7] This analysis is based on Harold Bloom, *Shelley's Mythmaking,* pp. 224–225.

[8] Stawell and Bradley note a resemblance between *TL,* 18, and *Paradiso* XXII. 116: "Quegli ch'è padre d'ogni mortal vita. . . ."

which, however (as the lines from "The Boat on the Serchio" imply), "the throng of men" do not fulfill. In *Queen Mab* Shelley had described the same problem at somewhat greater length (italics mine):

> . . . the fruits, the flowers, the trees,
> *Arise in due succession;* all things speak
> Peace, harmony, and love. The universe,
> In Nature's silent eloquence, declares
> That all fulfil the works of love and joy,—
> All but the outcast, Man.
>
> III.194–199

Man is an outcast because he is greater than other created things, but an outcast nonetheless. Once the "magnificence and beauty of the external world" cease "to suffice," and his mind, "at length awakened," "thirsts for intercourse with an intelligence similar to itself": when, in short, "Power" and "First Cause" become inadequate names for God and the human spirit seeks for its ideal antitype in the nature of things, man becomes a dissatisfied alien in the natural world.[9] Though man is superior to other terrestrial creatures, the very aspiration and self-awareness that lift him also doom him to stand forever outside the merely natural fulfillment that he observes around him. The Furies had mocked Prometheus about man's plight:

> . . . We laugh thee to scorn.
> Dost thou boast the clear knowledge thou waken'dst for man?
> Then was kindled within him a thirst which outran
> Those perishing waters; a thirst of fierce fever,
> Hope, love, doubt, desire, which consume him for ever.
>
> I.541–545

Identifying himself not with the sunlight of dawn, which is the atmosphere-distorted "light of common day" that manifests the Power of natural creation, but rather with the eternal and immutable stars, celestial symbols of human ideals, the Poet prepares to sleep once these stars have been obscured by the veil of sunlight.[10]

---

[9] Preface to *Alastor* (*P.W.*, p. 14). *TL*, 5–20, echoes Milton's description of the worship of God by the natural creatures of Paradise (*PL* IX.192–199). Shelley contrasts man's outcast state with the perfect harmony between man and nature in Milton's lines, where Adam and Eve "joynd their vocal Worship to the Quire/ Of Creatures wanting voice," but he parallels Milton's account of Adam and Eve's night after their fall (*PL* XI.171–175), where "the Morn,/ All unconcern'd with our unrest, begins/ Her rosie progress smiling. . . ."

Cf. with *TL*, 15–18, *Inferno* II.1–3.

[10] As a number of critics have observed, the "cone of night" to which Shelley refers (23) is the cone-shaped shadow that the Earth casts into space away from

F. Melian Stawell has sketched the physical setting of the Poet's vision: "The slope is on a spur of the Apennines near the coast (such as those that surround Spezia itself), and from it there is a view westward to the sea. The poet's back is, at first, turned to the east. The car that passes him I understand to have come up behind him over the spur, from the east, up from 'the oblivious valley' of Rousseau's birth, on the further side of which (the eastern side) rises 'the great mountain' of l. 452. This assumes, as I think we should, that the vision described by the poet and all that is seen by Rousseau before their meeting are meant to form one picture, on the whole coherent." [11] Behind the description of the physical setting is that of the Poet's moral situation: "the Deep/ Was at my feet, & Heaven above my head" (27–28). The Poet stands on the brink of the abyss with Heaven, the ideal life, apparently out of reach above him. Man always finds himself struggling between perdition and the ideal, and the phrasing here seems to indicate that the Poet stands, "as it were, upon a precipice," [12] staring down into the jaws of chaos.

Once the Poet is settled under the chestnut tree, his consciousness is slowly overcome by a waking trance. Shelley carefully distinguishes this state from ordinary dream (it "was not slumber") and from mystical experience; in these states the Poet's consciousness would be a passive instrument, such as is the Youth's mind during his dream vision in *Alastor* or Shelley's in the experiences he relates in "Hymn to Intellectual Beauty" and the Dedication to *The Revolt of Islam*.[13] The phenomenon described in lines 29–33

---

the sun. Locock compares *Prometheus* IV.444, *Epipsychidion*, 228, *Hellas*, 943; Bradley compares *Adonais*, 352, *PL* IV.776, *Paradiso* IX.118–119; Turner compares *De Rerum Natura* V.762–764.

[11] "Shelley's *Triumph of Life*," *Essays and Studies*, V (Oxford, 1914), 112[n].

[12] Letter to John Gisborne, 18 June 1822 (Julian, X, 404). Note that these lines of "The Triumph" were probably written before the letter; often biographical critics forget that not only is art not a mere transliteration of biographical experience, but art can sometimes provide the conceptual categories under which the author, as well as his reader, can organize and interpret his experiences. Shelley's letters provide numerous examples of life experiences being given significance through reference to Shelley's earlier writings or those of other authors.

[13] In *A Defence of Poetry* Shelley writes of "the best and happiest moments of the happiest and best minds": "We are aware of evanescent visitations of thought and feeling . . . arising unforeseen and departing unbidden, but elevating and delightful beyond all expression. . . . It is as it were the interpenetration of a diviner nature through our own; but its footsteps are like those of a wind over the sea, which the coming calm erases, and whose traces remain only as on the wrinkled sand which paves it" (*Prose*, p. 294). This experience is

of "The Triumph" is best explained by Shelley's note to *Hellas:*
"I have preferred to represent the Jew as disclaiming all preten-
sion, or even belief, in supernatural agency, and as tempting
Mahmud to that state of mind in which ideas may be supposed to
assume the force of sensations through the confusion of thought
with the objects of thought, and the excess of passion animating
the creations of imagination." [14] The "trance of wondrous thought"
(41) is, then, like Mahmud's, the child of the Poet's own active
imagination, thus bearing a direct relation to those "thoughts which
must remain untold" (21); those unstated hopes and untold thoughts
and fears project themselves in the vision that is cast like "a veil
of light" over the consciousness of the Poet.

Miss Stawell has rightly suggested that the physical setting remains
unaltered throughout the poem; in describing the onset of the
Poet's imaginative vision, Shelley shows carefully that the operation of time, however, is suspended and that the experience is a
universal one, perhaps one that the Poet and certainly one that
other imaginative men have experienced before. G. M. Matthews
has shown parallels between the description of the Poet's sur-
roundings and a passage in Rousseau's *Confessions,* [15] and both "The
Triumph" itself and close resemblances between Rousseau's story in
"The Triumph" and Shelley's idealized autobiography in *Epipsychidion* clearly indicate that Rousseau is one forerunner who had
experienced the same kind of imaginative vision in a similar
setting. [16]

Superimposed upon the Poet's continuing awareness of the natural setting is his imaginative apprehension of "a public way/
Thick strewn with summer dust," which is not part of the physical

---

not that which the Poet undergoes during the introduction of "The Triumph,"
though it is probably the nature of Rousseau's vision of the "shape all light";
while these visitations last, "self appears as what it is, an atom to a universe"
(*Prose,* p. 294), whereas the Poet in "The Triumph" enjoys a certain degree of
separation and distance from the vision he witnesses.

[14] *P.W.,* p. 479. Cf. Shelley's "Essay on Life": "By the word *things* is to be
understood any object of thought—that is, any thought upon which any other
thought is employed with an apprehension of distinction" (*Prose,* p. 174).

[15] "On Shelley's 'The Triumph of Life,'" *Studia Neophilologica,* XXXIV (1962),
109. Barnard, in *Shelley: Selected Poems, Essays, and Letters* (New York, 1944),
has glossed lines 31–33 with *Prometheus* IV.211–212.

[16] Shelley could also have been thinking of such a return to place and a
renewal of vision as Wordsworth describes in "Tintern Abbey," which contains
a slight verbal parallel: "The day is come when I again repose/ Here, under
this dark sycamore . . ." (9–10).

scene but rather the Poet's metaphorical vision of the course of human life willfully followed by the mass of mankind.[17] The people who hurry to and fro "numerous as gnats" [18] lead ephemeral and meaningless lives; ignorant of their course, they follow blindly in a turbulent procession which, once they enter its train, sweeps them along like leaves in the wind.[19] Men of all ages, from infancy to old age, are "mixed in one mighty torrent," some, the oppressed, "flying from the thing they feared" and some, the oppressors, "seeking the object of another's fear." Others, seeing only the sordid side of life and the horrors of death, "pored on the trodden worms that crawled beneath," while still others, blinded by their own self-centered gloominess, mistook their private disappointments for the real death of spirit into which they blindly trod. Some, fleeing from their shadows, tried to escape from all their morbid thoughts but only wasted their breath in vain attempts to escape themselves (52–61). A greater number of men, less introspective, governed their actions by "shadows the clouds threw" (those unreal shades of transient and ephemeral human ideas, fashions, and modes) or oriented themselves by the shadows that "birds within the noonday ether lost,/ Upon that path where flowers never grew," following only the *shadows* of eagle spirits who (as we shall see) aspired to the noonday sun, and thus worshiping the eclipse instead of the Sun itself.

Lines 43–73 of "The Triumph" gain in power if one recalls the third canto of Dante's *Inferno*, in which Dante and Virgil pass through the great door of Hell and first encounter those who are odious both to God and to His enemies, since they were neither good nor evil in life. These remain naked, stung by hornets and wasps that "made their faces stream with blood, which mixed with tears, was gathered at their feet by loathsome worms." [20] After

17 Stawell and Bradley compare Shelley's "public way" (43) to Petrarch's "pubblico viaggio" (*Trionfo della Morte* II.14). The phrase occurs frequently in Wordsworth's poetry (e.g., "Michael," 1).
18 On "gnats" cf. Shelley to Mary, 20 August 1818: "the only thing that incommodes me are the gnats at night, who roar like so many humming tops in one's ear . . ." (Julian, IX, 324). Cf. *Inferno* XXVI.25–30.
19 Cf. *Paradise Lost* I.301–302: "His Legions, Angel Forms, who lay intrans't/ Thick as Autumnal Leaves that strow the Brooks. . . ."
20 Elle rigavan lor di sangue il volto,
   Che, mischiato di lagrime, ai lor piedi,
   Da fastidiosi vermi era ricolto.
                   III.67–69

Dante and his guide reach the "joyless strand of Acheron," they behold Charon driving the souls of the damned into his boat

> Come d' autunno si levan le foglie
> L' una appresso de l' altra, fin che 'l ramo
> Vide a la terra tutte le sue spoglie. . . .
> > III.112–114

> as the leaves of autumn fall off one
> after the other, till the branch sees
> all its spoils upon the ground. . . .

The opening scene of the Poet's vision in "The Triumph," read in the light of Canto III of the *Inferno*, becomes the Poet's entrance into the borders of Hell and his encounter with "the dreary souls of those who lived without blame, and without praise." [21]

The aimless wandering of these lost souls is tragic because the Poet knows that their condition is not the inevitable heritage of men, but the result of their own blindness. Near the dusty road are rest for the weary and living waters for those who thirst. The fountains, breeze, and grassy paths represent the same earthly environment that the weary multitude find oppressive but that becomes beautiful and peaceful when seen from another perspective and put to a different use. Banks of violets, Shelley's symbol-flower of regeneration, bring "sweet dreams," intimations, perhaps, of man's exalted destiny. The unforeseeing multitude, however, pursue "their serious folly as of old . . ." (73).

The first part of the Poet's vision contrasted the "serious folly" of the masses with the beauty and bountiful provision of nature; this earth, which could and should be a garden, has become a dusty highway upon which men seek their lives only to lose them. The remainder of the poem's first movement (74–175) restates and expands in three parts the motif of human impotence before the power of Necessity from without and rebellious passions from within. As in 43–73 the Poet stood on the threshold of the Inferno and witnessed the sad plight of those who blew neither hot nor cold, so in the one hundred lines that follow he enters into Hell itself. This second part of the vision begins with a reiteration of the wind-leaf simile, but whereas the earlier figure (50–51) had

---

[21] III.35–36. Stawell (p. 115) compared this phase of "The Triumph" to similar groups in the *Commedia*. T. S. Eliot uses some phrases from the *Inferno* III and IV to describe a similar crowd in "The Burial of the Dead," *The Waste Land*, 63–64; line 65 ("And each man fixed his eyes before his feet") resembles *TL*, 57.

utilized the seasonal cycle of necessity, the simile that introduces
the intensified restatement of the theme is, appropriately, limited
to the daily cycle: "The throng grew wilder, as the woods of June/
When the South wind shakes the extinguished day.—" (75–76).
This transitional figure marks the approach of the wilder throng
who surround the cold, bright Car; the advent of the chariot itself
is preceded by a "cold glare, intenser than the noon" that obscures
"the Sun as he the stars." The light of common day that was the
element of the first aimless wanderers gives place to a more pernicious influence, destructive even of mediocrity.

The Poet compares the curved chariot and its gloomy passenger
to the new moon bearing the ghost of the old moon in its arms,
a harbinger of approaching storm, according to the ballad of "Sir
Patrick Spens" and Coleridge's "Dejection: An Ode." That is,
within the chariot, bent over in the crouching position that the old
moon assumes within the new moon's slim outline, sits a dark
Shape.[22] As I. A. Richards pointed out many years ago, Shelley
here alludes once more to Milton, this time to the memorable
description of Death in *Paradise Lost:*

> . . . The other shape,
> If shape it might be call'd that shape had none
> Distinguishable in member, joynt, or limb,
> Or substance might be call'd that shadow seem'd,
> For each seem'd either; black it stood as Night,
> Fierce as ten Furies, terrible as Hell,
> And shook a dreadful Dart; what seem'd his head
> The likeness of a Kingly Crown had on.
>
> II.666–673

The crouching, formless Shape in "The Triumph" not only resembles Death, but Shelley includes a verbal echo of *Paradise Lost*
II.672: "And o'er what seemed the head . . ." (91).[23] The Shape
is thus portrayed in terms of Death, the guardian of the gate of
Hell. The Shape represents, then, not merely the everyday stulti-
fying, mundane existence of those wandering masses whom the

[22] The description of the chariot in "The Triumph" parallels at almost every
point Ione's description of the "chariot like that thinnest boat,/ In which the
Mother of the Months is borne" in the fourth act of *Prometheus Unbound* (IV.
206–235). One should remember that the final act of *Prometheus* describes the
universe as seen by man's regenerated soul, not, as in "The Triumph," by fallen
man. Therefore, in *Prometheus* IV the moon and time itself have taken on more
favorable associations.

[23] Richards, *Principles of Literary Criticism* (London, 1955), p. 217.

Poet witnessed as they aimlessly pursued the public way; it is a positive evil, a destructive force into whose power men are delivered by Sin, a deadly threat within that dusty road.

"The Triumph of Life," like all Shelley's best poems, is not allegorical but symbolic in Coleridge's distinction and not only symbolic but mythopoeic.[24] Shelley's symbols are many faceted; although within a specific context they may be more or less equated with a particular entity, they never lose their vitality or sink into lifeless, cardboard counters for abstractions. The Shape, like Death in *Paradise Lost,* is a mythic creation that overflows the boundaries of any equation with a multiplicity of suggestions. Besides the obvious parallels with the chariots of the *Trionfi,* Shelley's Car of Life (lines 79–106) contains reminiscences of Milton's "Chariot of Paternal Deitie," Dante's Car of the Church, and Ezekiel's vision of God's manifest glory.[25] Bloom rightly suggests that Shelley consciously contrasts his symbol with these three antecedents, but one must still clarify the implications of this opposition. The chief attribute of the symbolic chariots of Ezekiel, Dante, and Milton was *power*—the irresistible might of God, or of His Church, to force obedience to an arbitrary will; again and again in the journey of Dante and his guide through the Inferno, Virgil silences the overseers of various circles of Hell by invoking the untrammeled power of the Divine will: "Thus it is willed there where what is willed can be done." [26] But to Shelley there could be no truly divine power that did not conform to some law of justice, and no exhibition of

24 In *The Statesman's Manual* Coleridge wrote: "an allegory is but a translation of abstract notions into a picture-language. . . . On the other hand a symbol . . . is characterized by a translucence of the special in the individual, or of the general in the special, or of the universal in the general. . . . It always partakes of the reality which it renders intelligible; and while it enunciates the whole, abides itself as a living part in that unity of which it is the representative" (*Complete Works,* ed. W. G. T. Shedd [New York, 1884], I, 437–438). "The Triumph," like "The Rime of the Ancient Mariner," contains the additional dimension of mythopoeic creation; Rousseau, Napoleon, Alexander, etc., are obvious "symbols" in Coleridge's sense, just as Abraham was, but a mythic chariot or Sun or "shape all light" must be given associations within the mythical world of the poem before one can decide what unity or unities it represents. The moon-like chariot has movement, cold light, power, thus participating in certain universal aspects of the phenomenal world. But it "abides itself as a living part" of the larger categories.

25 *Paradise Lost* VI.710–718, 749–766, 832–852, XI.126–133; *Purgatorio* XXIX. 16–21, 52–120; Ezekiel x:4–22. Bloom discusses these parallels in *Shelley's Mythmaking,* pp. 231–236.

26 *Inferno* V.23–24 ("Vuolsi così colà dove si puote/ Ciò che si vuole . . .").

omnipotence could make right an arbitrary decision; the will of man or God, to be righteous, must be obedient to the law of love.[27] Thus the power that to Ezekiel, Dante, and Milton bespoke the majesty of God, to Shelley simply epitomized the rule within phenomenal experience of amoral Necessity, and the human being who bowed down to worship such power in any of its numerous manifestations became enslaved by a demonic force. Coercion by its very nature participated in evil, because free choice was the corner-stone of the moral life. To be forced into actions either by external, physical necessity or by one's own unruly passions was a sign of the collapse of the autonomy requisite for ethical decisions.

Shelley's Car of Life, which symbolizes arbitrary power, exhibits other attributes that enrich the conception: The cold, fascinating light of the moon-like car suggests mere reason, "mind contemplat-ing the relations borne by one thought to another." [28] The concept of Time is also implicit in the description; in *Prometheus Unbound* Shelley's depiction of the chariots of the immortal Hours closely parallels that of the Car of Life, the cycle that brings the new moon is a universal measure of time, and the course of the chariot as it is later described by Rousseau is temporal. Finally, the move-ment of the car fuses the attributes of power and time into a representation of the forces of the cause and effect that work through Time.[29] The Janus-visaged charioteer is clearly analogous to Destiny as he appears in *Hellas*: "The world's eyeless charioteer,/ Destiny, is hurrying by!" (711–712). Such a charioteer is an amoral, untrustworthy driver.[30] In the Prologue to *Hellas* Satan calls Destiny

[27] Cf. Peacock's anecdote about Shelley's interpretation of *Faerie Queen* V.iii: "Shelley once pointed out this passage to me, observing, 'Artegall argues with the Giant; the Giant has the best of the argument; Artegall's iron man knocks him over into the sea and drowns him. This is the usual way in which power deals with opinion.' I said, 'That was not the lesson Spenser intended to convey.' 'Perhaps not,' he said; 'it is the lesson which he conveys to me. I am of the Giant's faction.' In the same feeling with respect to Thomson's *Castle of Indo-lence*, he held that the Enchanter in the first canto was a true philanthropist, and the Knight of Arts and Industry in the second an oligarchical impostor overthrowing truth by power" (Julian, X, 21[n]).

[28] *A Defence of Poetry, Prose*, p. 276.

[29] "The Shapes which drew it" were lost "in thick lightnings" because unlike Dante's Car of the Church, which was drawn by a griffon symbolic of Christ, Shelley's car of reason-time-necessity has no obvious external motive force. To Shelley, a follower of Hume and Drummond, both the prime mover and the connections among events were unknown and unknowable.

[30] The four faces of the charioteer derive from Ezekiel, Dante, and Milton (*PL* XI.128ff.), but the numerous eyes of Shelley's cherubic figure are blinded,

"Vicegerent of my will, no less/ Than of the Father's" (142–143), and Mont Blanc's glaciers and the River Arve, emblems of natural Necessity, signify the alternatingly destructive and revivifying operations of a Power, "remote, serene, and inaccessible" (*P.W.*, p. 534). Neither the cold, rational beams "that quench the Sun" of imagination nor Destiny's potential ability to read the shadow of the future on the past (cf. *Hellas*, 805)—to "pierce the sphere/ Of all that is, has been, or will be done"—can compensate, from the human perspective, for the charioteer's moral blindness. That the chariot is described as moving "with solemn speed majestically on" is not ironic but simply one more evidence that pomp and majesty were to Shelley signs of the degenerate use of power: In two early Gothic revenge poems Shelley used the word "majestic" to describe the advance of avenging spirits,[31] in *Prometheus* the phantasm of Jupiter looked cruel "but calm and strong,/ Like one who does, not suffers wrong" (I.238–239), and in *The Mask of Anarchy*, the chariot of Anarchy advanced "with a pace stately and fast" (38).

The Poet, who has hitherto remained relatively detached and aloof from the scene before him, now becomes emotionally involved and when he rises—or does so in imagination—to scrutinize the pageant more closely, he sees "the million" swept "like clouds upon the thunder blast." In "Ode to the West Wind" the power of the wind of Necessity to control leaf, cloud, and wave was a relative

---

not "more wakeful" than Argus. Here again Shelley first recalls antecedents and then inverts the significance of the picture. The four faces are appropriate to Shelley's purpose, four being the number traditionally associated with mundane, terrestrial creation, as in the four elements (earth, water, air, and fire), four corners of the world, four winds, four seasons, and four moral virtues (prudence, temperance, fortitude, justice), The four faces of the cherubim in Ezekiel and the theological-poetic tradition need not conflict with these mundane associations: the four-faced creatures, though they are manifestations of the unseen Divinity, are commensurate with mortal understanding and, thus, undeserving of the perfect numbers one (Deity), three (Trinity, theological virtues), seven (four plus three, the number of all things, mortal and divine), or twelve (four times three). Locock (II, 480) and Baker (*Shelley's Major Poetry*, p. 261ⁿ) compare *TL*, 105–106, with Spenser's *Faerie Queen:*

> Scarse could he once uphold his heavie hedd,
> To looken whether it were night or day.
> May seeme the wayne was very evill ledd,
> When such an one had guiding of the way,
> That knew not whether right he went, or else astray.
>   I.iv.19

[31] "Revenge," 58 (*P.W.*, p. 853); "Ghasta; or, the Avenging Demon," 31 (*P.W.*, p. 854). Cf. Kurtz, *The Pursuit of Death*, p. 330.

good,[32] but in "The Triumph," where any compromise with the power of natural necessity is seen to be corrupting, the leaf, cloud, and wave, impelled by external power, symbolize the conquest and destruction of human moral freedom. The scene before the Poet reminds him of a triumph in which the Roman citizenry welcomed the conquering leader who would soon seize absolute power in Rome.[33] Shelley's use of the word "jubilee" in line 111 is, I think, deliberately ironic, for the Year of Jubilee should be marked by giving freedom to the slaves instead of enslaving others.[34] The irony of the single word prepares one for the proliferating ironies of the lines that follow: "imperial Rome," the ruler of the world, is itself enslaved as the result of its own false values; men in the "living sea" ("deaf as is the sea which wrath makes hoary" [477]) are, like clouds and leaves, swept along by external powers; their homes are senate house, prison, and theater—they are rulers, slaves, and actors who feign what they do not believe; in forcing others to stoop under the symbolic yoke, the oppressors themselves become beasts of burden. Every image, every phrase, almost every word carries the paradoxical relationship of power and virtue—that one cannot extend his power over the wills of other men and still remain free himself.

Chained to the chariot are a captive multitude that include the more noteworthy among those whom the Shape has conquered.

---

[32] In "Ode to the West Wind" and several other poems written in the same period, Shelley, seeing no sign that "love and reason" were able to legislate away the old order and thereby break the chains of Necessity, resolved to ally himself with historical Necessity as exhibited in the revolutionary forces alive in Europe, forces that he believed were about to destroy the old tyrannies. "Ode to the West Wind" thus marks Shelley's temporary compromise with the limitations of terrestrial existence and his decision to write such poems as *The Mask of Anarchy*, "Ode to Naples," and "Men of England." But, perhaps influenced by his failure to find publishers for his revolutionary poems and by the inability of his limited audience to comprehend the significance of his published poetry, Shelley later renounced his pragmatic compromise with amoral Necessity and turned once again to the elucidation of the Ideal.

[33] See J. C. L. Simonde de Sismondi, *A History of the Italian Republics, Being a View of the Origin, Progress, and Fall of Italian Freedom* (Everyman Edition; London, n.d.): "Rome held sway over the greatest part of the known world; but, under the necessity of employing despotic authority, in order to secure the obedience of the army, and the distant provinces, she finally became herself the property of the master whom she had imposed on others" (p. 6). Shelley alludes to Sismondi's book in the first note to *Hellas*.

[34] This "jubilee" is an ironic echo of *PL* VI.882–886. See also "Lines Written Among the Euganean Hills," 122–123.

If the punctuation of Shelley's rough draft is a guide to the syntax of the passage, this multitude seems to consist of two kinds of captives: first, those "who had grown old in power" and then those who had grown old in "misery." Shelley elaborates these identifications: The groups consist of those who had startled their respective eras (for so I read "age") [35] in either exceptional action (the oppressors) or remarkable suffering (the oppressed) and whose "hour" (the brief time of a human life as contrasted to the world's great "age") endured the full measure of their roles as doers or sufferers, so that the vigor of youth and maturity gave place to the decadence of age. ("So that the trunk survived both fruit & flower.") All are included, then, of those "whose fame or infamy must grow" in human history until the extinction of the sun turns the earth into "a mass of frost" [36] except "the sacred few."

Most critics of "The Triumph" have been unduly pessimistic, I think, about the number of those who escape the bondage of Life, some interpreting the phrase "sacred few" as sacred two, Jesus and Socrates. (Some critics have been trying to prove that "The Triumph" is a grimly pessimistic poem because such a view is necessary to their own biographical or philosophical theses about Shelley.) Obviously the "few" are few compared to the multitude of captives, and even men whom Shelley admired as highly as Homer, Plato, and Rousseau are or have been captives in Life's train. But even so I find the poem little more pessimistic than Shelley's earlier works. As G. M. Matthews has pointed out, "Shelley's fullest picture of the immediate future is in *The Revolt of Islam* (1818), where massacre, famine, and disease reach their climax in the burning alive of the popular leaders. *The Mask of Anarchy* (written 1819) anticipated a far greater slaughter of unarmed civilians than at Peterloo. *Hellas* (1821) ended in the betrayal and massacre of the resurgent Greeks. 'The Triumph of Life,' therefore, does not differ from its 'optimistic' predecessors except in its concentration on the past and present. . . ." [37]

"The Triumph of Life" contains a grimly realistic picture of the

---

[35] See Textual Note to lines 120–124 (p. 153).

[36] Shelley to Peacock, 24 July 1816: "It is agreed by all that the snows on the summit of Mont Blanc and the neighbouring mountains perpetually augment. . . . The glaciers must augment and will subsist at least until they have overflowed this vale. I will not pursue Buffon's sublime but gloomy theory, that this earth which we inhabit will at some future period be changed into a mass of frost" (Julian, IX, 186).

[37] "On Shelley's *TL*," p. 104.

human situation and of the mass of mankind, but below that panorama of this modern Dance of Death is a caption to warn those who
"by due steps aspire" to reach eternity: "forbear/ To join the
dance" (188–189). Those critics, sympathetic to Shelley or otherwise,
who have naively accepted Mrs. Shelley's opinion, "Shelley believed
that mankind had only to will that there should be no evil, and
there would be none,"[38] have been, no doubt, shocked by the
apparently small percentage of "the Wise,/ The great, the unforgotten" (208–209) who resisted evil in their own lives, and such
critics have been panicked into calling "The Triumph" a palinode
to Shelley's earlier works. But Shelley himself, who never closed
his eyes to the magnitude of the problems facing those who worked
for human amelioration, did not find it necessary in "The Triumph" to darken his picture of the human predicament. The
imaginative humanitarian who would be the benefactor of his
fellow men must still attempt, through the power of his free will,

> To suffer woes which Hope thinks infinite;
> To forgive wrongs darker than death or night;
> To defy Power, which seems omnipotent;
> To love, and bear; to hope till Hope creates
> From its own wreck the thing it contemplates;
> Neither to change, nor falter, nor repent. . . .
> *Prometheus* IV.570–575

Shelley's belief in the capacity of man's moral will to resist, as
Prometheus does, the otherwise omnipotent forces of "Fate, Time,
Occasion, Chance, and Change" was not a wild, foolish hope based
on his own private desire; he believed that he had seen the efficacy
of this human hope admitted even by the sharpest critics of liberal
perfectibilitarianism; in a note to the Preface to *The Revolt of
Islam* (1818) he wrote: "It is remarkable, as a symptom of the
revival of public hope, that Mr. Malthus has assigned, in the later
editions of his work, an indefinite dominion to moral restraint
over the principle of population. This concession answers all the
inferences from his doctrine unfavourable to human improvement,
and reduces the *Essay on Population* to a commentary illustrative
of the unanswerableness of *Political Justice*" (*P.W.*, p. 34). The
"sacred few," then, offer the hope of human salvation even as they
warn of the difficulty of obtaining "that Golden Key/ That ope's
the Palace of Eternity."[39]

---

[38] Note on *Prometheus Unbound, P.W.*, p. 271.
[39] *Comus*, 13–14. Cf. *Trionfo della Morte* i.13–16.

The "sacred few," like the captives, include men of two classes; first are those who "as soon/ As they had touched the world with living flame/ Fled back like eagles to their native noon" (129–131). These men died relatively young at the height of their idealistic powers; they, whose pure spirits have flowed back to the burning fountain whence they came, from the contagion of the world's slow stain are now secure (*Adonais*, 338–339, 356–357). Nothing indicates that these would not include "the inheritors of unfulfilled renown" who were among "the splendours of the firmament of time" in *Adonais*: Keats, Chatterton, Sidney, and even Lucan, "by his death approved" (388–404). From Shelley's remarks on Jesus in "Essay on Christianity" and from the tradition that Jesus was thirty-three at the time of the Crucifixion, it seems probable that he should be included in this group.

The second class of those great names who were *not* captive to Life consists of "those who put aside the diadem/ Of earthly thrones or gems," those who, though they did not die young, had power to resist the corrupting force of the mundane. This group, I should think, would include Milton, that "Sire of an immortal strain" who "went, unterrified,/ Into the gulf of death," but whose "clear Sprite/ Yet reigns o'er earth; the third among the sons of light" (*Adonais*, 30–36). It would probably include Dante, to whom Shelley pays a compliment later in "The Triumph" that would be inappropriate for a captive in Life's train; it might well include Petrarch, whose urn in the Euganean Hills yet burns with love, "a quenchless lamp by which the heart/ Sees things unearthly" ("Euganean Hills," 200–203). Socrates would, presumably, find his place among this second group of eagle spirits. I suggest these names not in the way of a complete catalogue; certainly "The Triumph" gains in power by its very vagueness as to which men belong among the sacred few, "they of Athens & Jerusalem" who represented the best in the Hellenic and Hebraic traditions and who preserved the purity of their ideals and lives from conformity to the mundane.[40] But they are probably not fewer than the spirits of those Great who, in *The Revolt of Islam*, "sate on many a sapphire throne . . ./ A mighty Senate . . ." (604–606).

All others, however, "till the last one" were either amid these mighty captives or else among "the ribald crowd that followed

---

40 See Rousseau's footnote to *Julie* VI.xi (*Œuvres*, X, 343[n]), quoted in note 78 of this chapter.

them/ Or fled before" (136–137). Ahead of the Conqueror dance the Maenadic [41] devotees of sensuality who, like the carnal sinners of the Second Circle of the *Inferno* (V), are tortured, convulsed, and spun on "the rapid whirlwinds" of their own uncontrolled lust. They are first compared to moths whose own desires destroy them [42] and then to a pair of clouds which, crowded together in a valley, neutralize one another through the exchange of their opposite electrical charges, "and die in rain." [43] In this scientific simile, with its implications of a physical necessity, Shelley (who had in several of his later poems regretted the psychological reaction that followed the release of passions through sexual consummation) [44] admirably expressed the slavery of the lustful. As a cloud is dispersed in rain or as a wind-driven wave is spent in foam, the devotees are juggernauted by the chariot of Life; [45] the desolation is not "single" (160) because, again as in *Inferno* V, lust destroys people in pairs and also because its destructive power not only corrupts the soul itself but also saps the energy that could effectively operate in the great world at large.

Behind the chariot follow aged men and women for whom, because they are impotent, the winds of passion are "insulting." Though these people struggle to keep up with the values of the mundane, they, no less impotent of will than the lustful young, "wheel" (as the others were "spun") in a sexual dance around each other and the "ghastly shadows" that interpose. These shadows, as later lines of "The Triumph" suggest, may be the masks or false

[41] Bradley compares Shelley's description of sculptured Maenads on an altar to Bacchus (*Prose*, p. 349). Both "fierce spirit" (145) and "her who dims the Sun" (148) refer to the shape in the moon-like chariot, which had already been said to obscure the Sun (77–79).

[42] *Adonais*, 473–474: "what still is dear/ Attracts to crush, repels to make thee wither." See also *Julie* III.xx (*Œuvres*, IX, 111–112): "Il n'y a point de passion qui nous fasse une si forte illusion que l'amour . . . c'est son ardeur même qui le consume; il s'use avec la jeunesse, il s'efface avec la beauté, il s'éteint sous les glaces de l'âge; et depuis que le monde existe on n'a jamais vu deux amants en cheveux blancs soupirer l'un pour l'autre."

[43] See *Prometheus Unbound* II.ii.48–63 and *Julie* I.xxxix (*Œuvres*, VIII, 201): "quelques heures agréables s'éclipsent comme un éclair et ne sont plus. . . ."

[44] See, for example, the lyric beginning "When passion's trance is overpast" (*P.W.*, pp. 645–646). Bradley cites: "Her touch was as electric poison" (*Epipsychidion*, 259).

[45] One should note how leaf, wave, and cloud, with which the Poet wished to identify himself in "Ode to the West Wind," in "The Triumph" assume completely negative connotations. Amiyakumar Sen (*Studies in Shelley*, pp. 264–267) compares with *TL*, 138–164, Southey's *The Curse of Kehama*, xiv.

images of themselves which those create who are enslaved to the forms and mores of society. Although the elder forms attempt to sustain the same mundane passions as their youthful counterparts, not only is impotence of body joined to impotence of will, but they cannot even know the true selves of their partners. When Life inevitably leaves them behind, they sink, not like the youthful into the waters symbolic of animal vitality, but into the dust symbolic of inert matter, a death befitting their aridity of soul. Lightning-like fires of passion consume the lustful, but the calculating, the avaricious, and the gluttonous—inhabitants of Dante's Third and Fourth Circles of Hell (Cantos VI, VII)—are destroyed by "frost." [46]

In the opening movement of the poem (which ends with line 175) the Poet first described his relation to the universe about him and the beginnings of his trance-vision (1–40); second, the vision of the thoughtless multitude who wander aimlessly on the dusty road of Life while nearby a new Eden awaits them if they would only see and choose it (41–73); and, third, both mundane existence and the three classes of men who become its slaves—the mighty captives who are chained to the Car of Life, the passionate who are overcome by their undisciplined lusts, and the selfishly calculating who end their lives not with a bang but a whimper. "The Triumph of Life," like other major poems by Shelley, develops around a central image, a single motif (correlating other, related images) that recurs again and again, each time slightly modified, until like a musical theme it is at last resolved in fulfillment of the expectations that earlier statements of it have aroused in the reader. The first 175 lines introduce all the elements basic to "The Triumph of Life" (as it exists in its fragmentary state); later descriptions of the pageant merely elaborate or modify this picture, and each later discussion of an individual captive merely particularizes one of its alternatives. The poem, as it stands, moves from the portrayal of one individual (the Poet) through a general vision of human life (with brief sketches of particular historical figures) to an idealized life story of an individual (Rousseau) whose experience more or less parallels that of the Poet.

[46] Though the variety of punishments in Dante's *Inferno* stands as the basic analogue, a likelier verbal antecedent for *TL*, 175, is *Paradise Lost* II.594–595: "the parching Air/ Burns frore, and cold performs th' effect of Fire." See also Byron's *Don Juan* IV.65–72.

POWER AND WILL

The second movement of "The Triumph of Life" begins when the Poet, "struck to the heart by this sad pageantry" (176), asks the meaning of his vision. He receives a response from the depths of his own soul, projected in a self-induced vision of a decayed derelict from the procession. The tattered form seems to rise in place of an old root in the natural scene, the dried grass around it being transformed into "thin discoloured hair"; the Poet imagines that holes, partially covered by the grass hair, "were or had been eyes" (188),[47] a significant detail because of the importance that Shelley always attached to eyes and vision. In a juvenile fragment he had written:

> How eloquent are eyes!
> Not the rapt poet's frenzied lay
> When the soul's wildest feelings stray
> Can speak so well as they.
>   *P.W.*, p. 842

Throughout Shelley's poetry keenness of vision or brightness of eye symbolizes the spiritual condition of men. The eagle was a favorite symbol of spiritual vision and aspiration in part because traditionally it was able to renew its keen vision by flying into the sun (symbolic of the Ideal), which burned the scales from its eyes, and then to rejuvenate itself by plunging back into the fountain (symbol of the mortal life). In "The Triumph" the eagle spirits fled back into the Sun without redescending to the mundane element: They achieved perfect vision, but in solving the great mystery they cut themselves off completely from their fellow men. Rousseau, on the other hand, damaged his vision when he went to the opposite extreme by immersing himself completely in mortality. Rousseau's spirit (not blind, as Bloom asserts [48]) possesses natural knowledge and experiential wisdom—enough, certainly, to guide the Poet of

---

[47] Cf. *Julie* I.xxvi (*Œuvres*, VIII, 154): "Dans les violents transports qui m'agitent, je ne saurois demeurer en place; je cours, je monte avec ardeur, je m'élance sur les rochers, je parcours à grands pas tous les environs, et trouve partout dans les objets la même horreur qui règne au dedans de moi. On n'aperçoit plus de verdure, l'herbe est jaune et flétrie, les arbres sont dépouillés, le séchard et la froide bise entassent la neige et les glaces; et toute la nature est morte à mes yeux, comme l'espérance au fond de mon cœur."

[48] *Shelley's Mythmaking*, p. 255. Bloom's reading seems plausible until one recalls the instances later in the poem where Rousseau can and does see; at least he can see the pageant, which is the concern of the fragment: *TL*, 234–238, 252–253, 260–261, 274, 281–282, and, especially, 544–546.

"The Triumph" through Hell and perhaps part of Purgatory, as Virgil guided Dante—but if we remember Rousseau's limitations we must suppose that, had "The Triumph" been extended into a vision of the Ideal to balance the vision of sublunary experience in the existing fragment, Rousseau would certainly have given place to another guide, as Beatrice replaced Virgil in Canto XXX of *Purgatorio*.[49]

One should notice also the point at which Rousseau breaks in upon the Poet's questions: The Poet has asked, half to himself, *"what* is this?" (the pageant), *"whose* shape is that within the car?," and is just beginning to ask *"why* is all here amiss?" when the unidentified creature replies, "Life." [50] Which question is Rousseau answering, the first (What is this pageant?) or the second (Whose shape is in the car?)? Critics have assumed that "Life" answers the second question, or perhaps both. But inasmuch as the shape in the car is, as we shall see later in the poem, equated with another shape that cannot be called "Life" (certainly not life in the mundane sense), one ought, perhaps, to reserve judgment on the exact extent of Rousseau's answer until one explores these further implications. Meanwhile, note that the Poet has not yet actually asked his third and most important question, "Why?"

The decayed form of Rousseau in his first speech delivers a conditional promise:

> . . ."If thou canst forbear
> To join the dance which I had well forborne,"
> Said the grim Feature, of my thought aware,
>
> "I will now tell that which to this deep scorn
> Led me & my companions, and relate
> The progress of the pageant since the morn."
>   188–193

The phrase "grim Feature," originally used by Milton to describe

---

[49] Bloom has, once again, noted the detail of Rousseau's relation to Virgil (p. 252), but ignored its implications, which conflict with his theory of Shelley's developmental cycle. Because according to his formula "The Triumph" must show the failure of myth, he ignores the unfinished state of the poem and the structural patterns both of Shelley's earlier poems and of the literary analogues to "The Triumph."

[50] Italics mine. *Trionfo d'Amore* i.42–81 roughly parallels the questions and answers of *TL,* 176ff., though the conquering power in Petrarch's poem is identified by the disguised spirit as "Love" rather than "Life."

Shelley's use of "crew" in *TL,* 184 (and 445), parallels Milton's use of the word in *PL* (I.51, V.879, XII.38) to denote a group committed to a course of evil.

Death in *Paradise Lost*,[51] again suggests the limited nature of Rousseau's guidance. Rousseau knows the Poet's thoughts before they are expressed because he is only a projection of the Poet's internal questionings. Rousseau goes on to say that, if his story does not satisfy the Poet's "thirst of knowledge," the Poet should follow the dance "even to the night." The thirst for further knowledge is an unwholesome desire that would drive the Poet to enter upon a course that the decayed Rousseau knows, through bitter experience, *he* should have resisted. Rousseau sardonically implies that he expects the Poet to disregard his warning, but the gravity—even horror—of what lies ahead for the Poet if he does so, staggers the decayed spirit.

To the Poet's question "who art thou?" the grim Feature answers in a truly masterful example of Dantesque compression:

. . ."Before thy memory

"I feared, loved, hated, suffered, did, & died,
And if the spark with which Heaven lit my spirit
Earth had with purer nutriment supplied

"Corruption would not now thus much inherit
Of what was once Rousseau. . . ."

199–204

Although Rousseau seems to imply that his environment was responsible for the corruption of his soul, he adds immediately, "nor this disguise/ [have] Stained that within which still disdains to wear it.—" (204–205). This qualification implies that, in spite of the unfavorable "nutriment" supplied to his Heaven-born soul by his earthly environment, something within his soul "disdains," perhaps resists, that corruption of the world's slow stain. In the uncanceled alternative reading of line 205, this implication gains in force: "Stained that which ought to have disdained to wear it.—"[52] The textual problem seems clear: In the line as given by *PP* and *SN*, Rousseau says that, though he had an obligation to resist the force of his environment, he did not do so (perhaps even accepting his corruption and conforming himself to this world); the line as given in my text says that Rousseau's soul still despises the corrupting forces but fails to indicate that Rousseau had the capacity to resist

---

[51] *PL* X.279. Forman first pointed this out in a note to his text (III, 337ⁿ–338ⁿ). Cf. Scott's *The Heart of Midlothian* (1818), Chapter XVIII, where the phrase describes Meg Murdockson.
[52] See Textual Note, p. 163.

them successfully. Shelley's indecisiveness in completing this line, I believe, stemmed from his desire to include both the idea that Rousseau was morally responsible and able to overcome his environment *and* the idea that even though he has been subdued by life, his inner soul is yet restive in its bondage. (Another possibility is that although the first ending [*PP* and *SN*] was closer to Shelley's own opinion, the second [*T*] better fitted the dramatic character of Rousseau as Shelley conceived him.)

Certainly in Shelley's view a man's spiritual condition usually resulted from an interaction of his Heaven-sent soul and his environmental opportunities. Of the historical (or legendary) Beatrice Cenci he wrote: "The young maiden . . . was evidently a most gentle and amiable being . . . and thus violently thwarted from her nature by the necessity of circumstance and opinion. . . . Beatrice Cenci appears to have been one of those rare persons in whom energy and gentleness dwell together without destroying one another. . . . The crimes and miseries in which she was an actor and a sufferer are as the mask and the mantle in which circumstances clothed her for her impersonation on the scene of the world" (*P.W.*, pp. 275, 278). And in the Preface to *The Revolt of Islam* he admitted that the development of genius demanded favorable external circumstances: "There is an education peculiarly fitted for a Poet, without which genius and sensibility can hardly fill the circle of their capacities" (*P.W.*, p. 34). On the other hand, Shelley, unlike the naturalists of a later generation, never regarded man as simply a hopeless victim of circumstances, a moral puppet. The human will—like Prometheus, its titanic emblem—is both able and morally obligated to resist all the forces of natural Necessity. From the viewpoint of the Ideal, at least, Beatrice's revenge was a "pernicious mistake," and from the perspective of the Absolute, Rousseau, in spite of his appearance on the stage of history at an unpropitious time and his career in a degenerate country, "ought to have disdained" the unhealthy nutriment and should "still disdain" to wear his horrible disguise.

Rousseau assures the Poet, however, that although he himself did not emerge unscathed from his encounter with the mundane world, his life was not in vain: " 'If I have been extinguished, yet there rise/ A thousand beacons from the spark I bore.'—"(206–207).[53]

[53] Shelley's lines echo a speech in which Statius speaks of his master, Virgil, in Dante's *Purgatorio* XXI.94–97:

This declaration is another sign of hope in the grim vision, for if "a thousand beacons" are aflame in the Europe of Shelley's time, lit from the single Heaven-given fire of Rousseau's Promethean spirit, there were surely many surviving flames from such earlier great ages of the world as fifth-century Athens and Renaissance England.

The Poet, temporarily satisfied with Rousseau's account of himself, turns back to the pageant before them, asking, "And who are those chained to the car?" to which Rousseau replies: " 'The Wise,/ The great, the unforgotten . . .' " (208–209). The principle on which these captives are bound together to the car of time [54] is their common possession of worldly power—ecclesiastical ("mitres"), military ("helms"), political ("crowns"), or intellectual ("wreathes of light,/ Signs of thought's empire over thought"). Whereas those who voluntarily rushed before the chariot, or limped after it in a vain attempt to stay within its light, had in common "impotence of will," these Men of Power, "the top and head of those who have a proper self," [55] were vanquished not by the external pressures of Necessity but their own recalcitrant souls: "their lore/ Taught them not this—to know themselves; their might/ Could not repress the mutiny within" (211–213). The captivity of these Men of Power reiterates the paradox of worldly might and wisdom, almost Pauline in its severity, that had occupied Shelley's mind at least since his journey to Italy: In "Lines Written Among the Euganean Hills" the Austria that ruled Venice was "the slave of slaves," [56] and in *Prometheus Unbound* Jupiter's omnipotence in the external world does not give him true mastery of himself, for "all spirits are enslaved which serve things evil." [57] Shelley's "Sonnet: Political Great-

---

Al mio ardor fuor seme le faville
(Che mi scaldar) de la divina fiamma
Onde sono allumati più di mille—

De l' *Eneïda* dico. . . .

The sparks which warmed me, from the divine
flame whence more than a thousand have been
kindled, were the seeds of my poetic fire:
of the Æneid I speak. . . .

[54] Cf. *Adonais*, 234: "But I am chained to Time, and cannot thence depart!"

[55] Keats to Benjamin Bailey, 22 November 1817 (*Letters*, ed. Hyder Rollins, I, 184).

[56] "Euganean Hills," 123.

[57] II.iv.110.

ness" contains, perhaps, the most complete declaration of this principle:

> . . . Man who man would be,
> Must rule the empire of himself; in it
> Must be supreme, establishing his throne
> On vanquished will, quelling the anarchy
> Of hopes and fears, being himself alone.[58]

Even a man's own will must be vanquished for him to be himself. But what *is* to rule, if not his own will? Shelley, as Milton Wilson has shown,[59] attempted throughout his life to get free of the burr of self, to project his values outside himself in benevolent identification with others; he upheld his ideal in spite of personal defeats and disappointments, and that he, like other mortals, failed to achieve complete selflessness should not blind one to either the nobility of the attempt or the considerable measure of his success. In Shelley's writings "Love is celebrated everywhere as the sole law which should govern the moral world." [60] This Love, the self-giving *agape* of the New Testament, must rule in a man's heart if he is to achieve his true humanity:

> His will, with all mean passions, bad delights,
> And selfish cares, its trembling satellites,
> A spirit ill to guide, but mighty to obey,
> Is as a tempest-wingèd ship, whose helm
> Love rules, through waves which dare not overwhelm,
> Forcing life's wildest shores to own its sovereign sway.
> *Prometheus* IV.406–411

Because "the Wise, the great, the unforgotten" subjected their wills, not to benevolent love but to unworthy, selfish passions, and because they feigned a "morn of truth" that no mortal can possess, "deep night/ Caught them ere evening." [61]

The Poet next centers his attention on a single Man of Power who sulks with "chin/ Upon his breast." Rousseau replies that this "child of a fierce hour," [62] product of the new tide of time that was the age of the French Revolution, sought to win the world, but lost both that world and his own soul—"more/ Of fame & peace"

---

[58] *P.W.*, p. 642.

[59] *Shelley's Later Poetry*, pp. 148–170.

[60] Preface to *The Revolt of Islam, P.W.*, p. 37.

[61] Stawell (p. 122n) and Bradley (p. 442n) compare *TL*, 214–215, to Petrarch's *Trionfo della Morte* i.39: "Gente a cui si fa notte innanzi sera."

[62] As elsewhere in the poem "hour" refers to the lifespan of an individual, whereas "age," meaning era, encompasses a larger period of time.

than even Virtue can give if it lacks such opportunity. Napoleon, a mere climber, was borne to the pinnacle by the necessity of histori-cal forces beyond individual control, but like another "thousand climbers" before him, he grew giddy on the heights, plunging to worldly ruin and to moral enslavement. Once again Rousseau stresses the need for moral responsibility. In his own life he had allowed his Heaven-given flame to be extinguished by an unfavor-able environment, whereas Napoleon, granted every opportunity by external circumstance, fell prey to his own mutinous self-will.[63] Yet Rousseau left a "thousand beacons" (207) flaming on the night, whereas Napoleon joined "a thousand climbers" fallen.

It is little wonder that the Poet, contrasting the ineffectual rela-tive virtue of Rousseau's soul with the meteoric rise of an amoral self-seeker like Napoleon, should question the reconcilability of "Power" and the "Will for Good." In *Queen Mab* Shelley had articulated the core of his moral philosophy in these words: "when the power of imparting joy/ Is equal to the will, the human soul/ Requires no other Heaven" (III.11–13). The cornerstone of the good life was the hope, if not the certainty, that virtue would ulti-mately triumph over evil, but Shelley's experience continually reiterated the unpleasant lesson that, in this world at least, the power of imparting joy is never equal to the will. Nevertheless, the Poet's despair in "The Triumph" goes beyond the facts of his experience in this vision:

> . . . much I grieved to think how power & will
> In opposition rule our mortal day—
>
> And why God made irreconcilable
> Good and the means of good. . . .
>
> 228–231

His despair is so deep that he even wishes to turn away from the

[63] Shelley's early attitude toward Napoleon can be seen in his irregular sonnet "Feelings of a Republican on the Fall of Bonaparte" (*P.W.*, pp. 526–527), in which Shelley, who admits that though, "I hated thee, fallen tyrant! . . ./ I know/ Too late . . ./ That Virtue owns a more eternal foe/ Than Force or Fraud: old Custom, legal Crime,/ And bloody Faith the foulest birth of Time." The view that Napoleon's worst crime was a disrupting "anarchy" that merely prepared the way for renewed tyranny reappears in "Ode to Liberty," 174–180 (*P.W.*, p. 607). "Lines Written on Hearing the News of the Death of Napoleon" (*P.W.*, pp. 641–642) uses Napoleon as the symbol of human energy in its relations with elemental Earth. The deaths of the greatest men have no harmful effect on the natural world, which feeds on those it fed (33). But after Napoleon's destructive career "the millions who follow" can "mould/ The metal before it be cold," reshaping society into "hopes" as well as "his shame."

pageant of recent history, "the spent vision of the times that were/ And scarce have ceased to be" (233–234).

But this despair, seen in its dramatic context, is not the message of the poem any more than were, in *Prometheus Unbound*, Prometheus' visions of the evils which had sprung from the perversions of Jesus' life and teachings and from the French Revolution. Some critics, who find in lines 224–234 Shelley's final analysis of the human predicament, have compared these lines with *Prometheus* I.625–628:

> The good want power, but to weep barren tears.
> The powerful goodness want: worse need for them.
> The wise want love; and those who love want wisdom;
> And all best things are thus confused to ill.

These lines, however, are spoken, not by Prometheus, but by one of the Furies who attempt to drive him to despair.[64] Just as these seducing words and visions are beginning to have their effect, just as Prometheus succumbs and yearns for death, the Spirit of the Earth sends to him "those subtle and fair spirits/ Whose homes are the dim caves of human thought" (I.658–659). After the Poet, or Shelley himself, or any other idealistic humanitarian, has scanned in vain external creation and the course of human history for any sign of the ultimate victory of good over evil, the inner spirits of

[64] A partial analogue to the Poet's outcry of despair at *TL*, 224–234, can be found in *Inferno* XXXI.46–57, where in the lowest depth of Hell Dante and Virgil see among the tortured giants Nimrod, the author of tyranny. The poet considers that Nature was wise in ceasing to join such huge and powerful bodies to men who can serve Mars: "Chè dove l' argomento de la mente/ S' aggiunge al mal volere ed a la possa,/ Nessun riparo vi può far la gente" (XXXI.55–57). But though "men can make no defence" against the combination of mind, evil will, and potency, Shelley's outcry in "The Triumph" significantly alters the situation: the men of evil will and power who rule after Napoleon are not, like Nimrod, giants but rather pygmies (227), and thus God wisely (as Dante says) does not join human tyranny to giant's strength. In Hesiod's *Theogony* Zeus avenges himself upon man for receiving the stolen fire from Prometheus by sending Pandora (with her jar of troubles) to become the bride of Epimetheus; after the evils, troubles, and diseases escape into the world, only Hope remains as a comfort. Shelley, like Spenser and Bunyan, believed the Giant Despair to be the most dangerous of all foes. See his letter to Maria Gisborne, 13 or 14 October 1819: "Let us believe in a kind of optimism in which we are our own gods. . . . it is best that we should think all this for the best even though it be not, because Hope, as Coleridge says is a solemn duty which we owe alike to ourselves & to the world—a worship to the spirit of good within, which requires before it sends that inspiration forth, which impresses its likeness upon all that it creates, devoted & disinterested homage" (Julian, X, 93; corrected from Jones, II, 125).

man's own soul generate the hope he needs to see beyond the distorted vision of the outward eye. In "The Triumph" Rousseau, a creature of the Poet's own imagination, forces the Poet to study the pageant in spite of himself.

The problem of evil that was certainly to be the central concern of the entire poem is epitomized in the ten lines in which the Poet reflects on Napoleon's fate. Shelley's use of the word "God" in line 230 is significant. Critics who wish to bring Shelley into the fold of orthodox Christianity have seized upon this reference to "God" as one indication that Shelley accepted the concept in a conventional way. But, of course, in its context the use of the term is anything but favorable, for "God" remains a being of power, not of virtue. At an earlier point in "The Triumph," where the Poet cried out for the Divinity to have mercy on the wretchedness of Rousseau's decayed spirit (181), *MS* shows that Shelley replaced "God" with "Heaven" (even though the line was metrically stronger with "God"). Shelley there clearly meant to avoid suggesting by his diction that he accepted the conventional Deity. As C. E. Pulos has demonstrated [65] Shelley's continued and unshaken opposition to Christian orthodoxy was based on historical and moral grounds rather than theological ones. The "Essay on Christianity" could place Shelley theologically with many liberal or existential Protestants of our own day. Shelley, however, influenced by Gibbon and the *philosophes* (and hardened by the reactionary churches of his day, both in England and on the Continent), remained convinced that the influence of the Christian church, like that of other vested institutions, was morally pernicious, persecuting the very men who tried most diligently to follow in the steps of Jesus; he would probably have accepted Dostoevski's "Legend of the Grand Inquisitor" as a just critique of established Christianity.

In summary, the dramatic context of the Poet's despairing declaration of the incompatibility of "power" and "will" does not permit one either to accept it as the poem's final message or to garner from it a pious optimism. Rousseau, the Poet's guide through this ambulatory Inferno, does not permit him to mourn over the evil influence of Napoleon, but turns him back to the pageant of history that passes before them: "Dost thou behold" (imperative, not interrogative) "those spoilers spoiled" (234–235). The Poet, instructed to

[65] *The Deep Truth*, pp. 89–104.

watch conquest dragged captive,[66] sees other figures of the years that "scarce have ceased to be": Voltaire and Kant, sages who possessed intellectual power, walk with anarchs [67] and demagogues such as the "enlightened Despots" were—each one seeming "already old" to the "fresh world." [68] The presence of these sophists and tyrants of much greater ability than the pygmies of the restored monarchies who succeeded Napoleon, assures the Poet that those pygmy-tyrants will, in their turn, fall to the power of historical Necessity. The message of history is not completely black; Necessity, which raises and destroys the just and the unjust indiscriminately, is not evil but amoral, and amoral forces can be shaped and utilized by the good and wise to promote human improvement, just as they can be manipulated by self-seeking climbers for their own aggrandizement.[69]

Rousseau contrasts his own defeat with Life's conquest of the Enlightened Despots and their flatterers:

> ". . . I was overcome
> By my own heart alone, which neither age
>
> "Nor tears nor infamy nor now the tomb
> Could temper to its object."
>
> 240–243

Rousseau, unlike those who sacrificed the Ideal by tempering their hearts to the influence of external circumstances, seeking their salvation in "things" and "machinery," was an idealist who, like the Youth in *Alastor,* found the sublunar world incommensurate

---

[66] *Prometheus Unbound* IV.556.

[67] Shelley's use of "anarch" has its most notable literary antecedents in *Paradise Lost* (II.988) and *The Dunciad* (IV.655). Milton's use of the term for Chaos was probably Shelley's source, since it occurs in the same passage from which Shelley had earlier drawn the name of Demogorgon.

[68] Cf. Shelley's first letter to William Godwin, 3 January 1812: "The name of Godwin has been used, to excite in me feelings of reverence and admiration. . . . Considering, then, these feelings, you will not be surprised at the inconceivable emotions with which I learned your existence and your dwelling. I had enrolled your name in the list of the honourable dead" (Julian, VIII, 232–233). See Textual Note to line 238, p. 167.

[69] Cf. Shelley on Malthusian necessity: "war, vice, and misery are undeniably bad—they embrace all that we can conceive of temporal and eternal evil. Are we to be told that these are remediless, because the earth would, in case of their remedy, be overstocked? . . . What opinion should we form of that man who, when he walked in the freshness of the spring . . . should find fault with this beautiful order, and murmur his contemptible discontents because winter must come, and the landscape be robbed of its beauty for a while again? Yet this man is Mr. Malthus" (*Proposals for an Association of Philanthropists, Prose*, p. 68).

with his heart's thirst for perfection. He was lost, as his story later in the poem shows, because he insisted on seeking in the real world the embodiment of what must, ultimately, remain eternal.[70] In the terms of twentieth-century theology, he tried to absolutize the relative.

The Poet, however, fails to recognize the implications of Rousseau's commentary for his own situation and tries once more to turn his back on the procession. The world, he says contemptuously, has not improved so greatly that he has any reason to worship those older generations who made it what it is today, those who "drew/ New figures" on the world, creating new values as the old order passed away (243–248). Rousseau retorts sharply that values of one kind or another will "rise on the bubble" of this phenomenal world no matter who paints them or what they may be; one implication is that if the virtuous cease to devote their energies to the molding of philosophical attitudes and political actions, the state of the world can become even worse than it is.[71] The best we can do, says Rousseau, is to cast "our shadows" on the ever changing phenomenal world and expect no more in the way

[70] My reading agrees with the first of the four alternative readings proposed by Bradley (pp. 450–452) and the one that Bradley himself thought "the most probable": "its" (243) refers to "age," "tears," "infamy," or "tomb" (241–242), and "object" refers to the purpose or aim of each of these external pressures. But the steadfastness of Rousseau's commitment to the Ideal amid the grim realities of life served only to betray him more deeply, first into the vain pursuit of phantoms and later into attempts to find an incarnation of the Ideal: cf. *Julie* III.vi (*Œuvres*, IX, 20), where Saint-Preux writes: "Les tristes remords ont chassé l'amour. Tout est changé pour moi; mon cœur seul est toujours le même, et mon sort en est plus affreux."

Shelley's uses of the verb "temper" indicate that he saw the need for a golden mean of accommodation between the individual's ideals and the recalcitrant facts of experience. One must avoid, on the one hand, excessive conformity and, on the other, the pursuit of unrealistic desires. Of this latter danger he warned Claire Clairmont (italics mine): "If you would take my advice you would give up this idle pursuit after shadows, & *temper* yourself to the season . . ." (Julian, X, 365; corrected from Jones, II, 400). And of the danger of conforming too much to this world, he wrote to Horace Smith: "all, more or less, subdue themselves to the element that surrounds them, and contribute to the evils they lament by the hypocrisy that springs from them" (Julian, X, 410).

[71] Cf. *A Defence of Poetry*: "it exceeds all imagination to conceive what would have been the moral condition of the world if neither Dante, Petrarch, Boccaccio, Chaucer, Shakespeare, Calderon, Lord Bacon, nor Milton had ever existed; if Raphael and Michael Angelo had never been born; if the Hebrew poetry had never been translated; if a revival of the study of Greek literature had never taken place; if no monuments of ancient sculpture had been handed down to us; and if the poetry of the religion of the ancient world had been extinguished together with its belief" (*Prose*, pp. 292–293).

of permanent amelioration than was accomplished by the great minds of the past. "But," he continues, "mark . . . the mighty phantoms of an elder day."

As I suggested earlier, the pageant is divided historically, the mighty captives whom Rousseau and the Poet discuss being grouped by the same chronological epochs into which Shelley divided European history in *A Philosophical View of Reform:* first, there appear the leaders of the Enlightenment and Napoleon, representatives of the new age, the groundwork of which was first laid by the poets and philosophers of the Renaissance and which achieved its first practical success in the establishment of the American republic.[72] Next Shelley returns to the "world's great age" of the Hellenic period, introducing Plato, Aristotle, Alexander, and the "great bards of old" (cf. *MS:* "Homer & his brethren"). Finally, he shows how the seeds of tyranny sown by "the tutor & his pupil" emerged in the Roman emperors to Constantine ("the heirs/ of Cæsar's crime"); later, when Christianity had become the established religion in the Roman Empire, the tyranny divided into two branches, a secular one comprising the "Anarchs" who founded the dynasties of Medieval Europe that, in their continuation through the age of exploration and conquest, had "spread the plague of blood & gold abroad," and, on the ecclesiastical side, "Gregory" (the pontifical name taken by Hildebrand [Gregory VII], who established the power of the papacy), and "John" (the name most frequently used by popes), representing the establishment that in Shelley's view exercised an unbroken tyranny over thought throughout the Middle Ages.[73] The poem thus discusses the captives neither randomly nor arbitrarily; each appears because his fate relates directly to the Poet's central problem, the apparent impossibility of reconciling "good & the means of good." That this question—the problem of evil itself—emerges as the dominant, pervading, and ultimate question posed by "The Triumph of Life" as a whole, justifies one, I think, in assuming that this problem underlay those "thoughts which must remain untold" troubling the Poet through his sleepless night at the outset of the poem (21–23).

Rousseau commands the Poet to look upon "all that is mortal of great Plato" (254). Commentators, focusing their attention on the

---

[72] *Prose,* pp. 231–234.

[73] Notice that the "Anarchs old" (285) and the sun-eclipsing hierarchy parallel Milton's and Pope's "Chaos and old Night" (of whom Chaos is called "Anarch"), who represent the antithesis to the culture and moral order that remained the ideals of all three poets.

subsequent lines, have explained that the "star that ruled his doom" was the youth Aster, of whom, according to tradition, Plato became enamored late in life.[74] Because Plato failed to control his passions, he, unlike his master Socrates, had to suffer for his sins in chains behind the victorious chariot. Critics commonly slight, however, the qualifications "all that is mortal" and "expiates": the first phrase seems to indicate that not all of Plato's spirit is in bondage to Life, and the verb implies that Plato's suffering is not eternal but purgatorial.

Most twentieth-century critics have read Shelley not so much in the light of his own writings as in reaction against nineteenth-century admirers. Both groups tended to equate Shelley's life and writings, assuming that the rapt bard versified every tingle of his sensitive soul. To his sentimental admirers, this myth somehow gave his poetry sincerity and genuineness of emotion; his tough-minded critics found that this made his poetry sentimental and in bad taste. As recent studies have demonstrated, however, Shelley was a self-conscious artist who successfully transmuted his personal experiences into impersonal, universal symbols.[75] What has not yet been sufficiently emphasized is that Shelley in his poetic theory held a view of the separation of man and artist that accords with the best balanced and sanest modern theories of impersonality. There is not space here to demonstrate all the ramifications of his theory, but one can find its cornerstone in the oft-quoted sentence from the *Defence*: "Poetry is the record of the best and happiest moments of the happiest and best minds." [76] A poet is at all times more sensitive than other men, but only in certain moments in which his imaginative powers seem to raise him above his ordinary nature does he write immortal works. What Shelley says, amid the rhetorical flourishes of *A Defence of Poetry*, is that the author puts his "best self" into his writings. Wayne C. Booth, in his valuable study *The Rhetoric of Fiction* (Chicago, 1961), has shown that one can solve the epistemological dilemma of the critic who accepts and takes literally the "intentional fallacy" and the "affective fallacy" if one remembers that there is, on the one hand, a difference be-

---

[74] A. C. Bradley (pp. 449–450) first explained these allusions.

[75] Among recent studies of Shelley as an artist, rather than as man and thinker, are Earl R. Wasserman's *The Subtler Language* and Milton Wilson's *Shelley's Later Poetry*. Another statement of my view, together with substantiating evidence, appears in "Structure, Symbol, and Theme in 'Lines Written Among the Euganean Hills.' "

[76] *Prose*, p. 294.

tween the actual, historical author and the "implied author," or the set of values and attitudes that the author has embodied in his work (in other words, the author's "best self") and, on the other hand, a vast gap between the reader's ordinary nature and the "best self" that emerges as he gives himself up to the imaginative universe of a great work. Much discussion of the writings of the Romantic poets has nothing to do with their poetry—the chief, if not the only, reason they are intrinsically worthy of attention—but actually consists of *argumentum ad hominem* that would be discredited at once in a more rigorously intellectual discipline. Shelley (who could distinguish between Byron, the dilatory, parsimonious profligate he knew at Venice, and Byron, the moral satirist who was composing in *Don Juan* an immortal poem) never lost sight of the distinction between the ideal man who emerged only at inspired intervals and the natural man, in bondage to sin, who reigned throughout most of a human being's life in this phenomenal world.[77] Thus he could eulogize the noble dead without forgetting or denying their feet of clay: "Let us assume that Homer was a drunkard, that Virgil was a flatterer, that Horace was a coward, that Tasso was a madman, that Lord Bacon was a peculator, that Raphael was a libertine, that Spenser was a poet laureate. . . . Their errors have been weighed and found to have been dust in the balance; if their sins were as scarlet, they are now white as snow" (*Prose*, p. 295).

Such passages as this indicate that Shelley's attitude toward Plato could not be as severe as some critics of "The Triumph" have assumed it to be, and two features of the relevant lines of the poem itself confirm this. Just as lines 256-258 allude to Plato's epigram on the youth Aster, "Thou wert the morning star among the living," line 254 alludes to another Greek epigram that Shelley translated:

> Eagle! why soarest thou above that tomb?
> To what sublime and star-ypaven home
>   Floatest thou?—
> I am the image of swift Plato's spirit,
> Ascending heaven; Athens doth inherit
>   His corpse below.
>
> *P.W.*, p. 721

[77] Cf. *Essay on Christianity:* "According to Jesus Christ, and according to the indisputable facts of the case, some evil Spirit has dominion in this imperfect world" (*Prose*, p. 204). Cf. also *A Defence of Poetry:* "In the intervals of inspiration . . . a poet becomes a man and is abandoned to the sudden reflux of the influences under which others habitually live" (*Prose*, p. 296).

"All that is mortal of great Plato," then, would except, perhaps, not only his immortal writings, but the best side of his soul. If not, at least the verb "expiates" implies that Plato's soul, though it must submit to the pain of purification, is not irredeemably damned.[78] Certainly Rousseau was once one of the mighty captives chained to the car, and yet he has "fallen by the way side" (541), somehow freed from the painful procession. Furthermore, love was the cause of Plato's defeat, and Rousseau affirms later, in his allusion to Dante (472–480), that Dante told "how all things are transfigured, except Love." [79]

The "tutor & his pupil," Aristotle and Alexander, were both Men of Power, even Dominion,[80] in the intellectual and military-political senses respectively. The arbitrary authority they exerted transformed their spirits into vultures instead of eagles—Alexander as a thunderbearing favorite of fame, one of the "Worthies" whose self-seeking ambition was held up as an example for emulation by generations of misguided teachers,[81] and Aristotle, an authority whose prescriptions prevented men from examining the data of experience until Bacon's treatises signaled the Renaissance renewal of scientific inquiry. Once again Shelley enriches his poem through meaningful allusion, for as William O. Scott has shown, the lines on "the tutor & his pupil" echo "Bacon's comment on Aristotle . . . 'I will think of him that he learned that humour of his scholar, with whom it seemeth he did emulate, the one to conquer all opinions, as

[78] Cf. Rousseau's footnote to *Julie* VI.xi (*Œuvres*, X, 343n): "Platon dit qu'à la mort les âmes des justes qui n'ont point contracté de souillure sur la terre se dégagent seules de la matière dans toute leur pureté. Quant à ceux qui se sont ici-bas asservis à leurs passions, il ajoute que leurs âmes ne reprennent point si tôt leur pureté primitive, mais qu'elles entraînent avec elles des parties terrestres qui les tiennent comme enchaînées autour des débris de leurs corps."

[79] Cf. *Julie* V.xiii (*Œuvres*, X, 185): "L'amour en lui-même est-il un crime? N'est-il pas le plus pur ainsi que le plus doux penchant de la nature? n'a-t-il pas une fin bonne et louable? ne dédaigne-t-il pas les âmes basses et rampantes? n'anime-t-il pas les âmes grandes et fortes? n'ennoblit-il pas tous leurs sentiments? ne double-t-il pas leur être? ne les élève-t-il pas au-dessus d'elles-mêmes? Ah! si pour être honnête et sage il faut être inaccessible à ses traits, dis, que reste-il pour la vertu sur la terre? Le rebut de la nature et les plus vils des mortels."

[80] The relative clause in lines 261–262 modifies both "the tutor & his pupil."

[81] Very pertinent is the discussion of Alexander the Great by Falkland and Caleb in Godwin's *Caleb Williams*. Caleb, representing a more natural and liberal viewpoint than Falkland, cites Dr. Prideaux and Fielding's *Jonathan Wild* in an attack on the Macedonian's right to the appellation "Great"; to Falkland, whose mind has been poisoned by the illusions of chivalry, this constitutes "accursed blasphemy!" (*Caleb Williams*, ed. George Sherburn [New York, 1960], pp. 127–130).

the other to conquer all nations.' " [82] The compliment to Bacon has
its ironic side, however, in other symbols and allusions. Bacon's spirit
(*not* an "eagle" spirit, as Mrs. Shelley made it; see Textual Note,
p. 173) leaped "like lightning out of darkness"; this, like the lightning simile at lines 155–158, is a symbol of necessity—in this case,
historical necessity. As in the literary rebirth of his own age, Shelley
believed that he saw "the cloud of mind . . . discharging its collected
lightning" to restore "the equilibrium between institutions and
opinions," [83] so Bacon's genius expressed the judgment of intellectual history, the need at his time for an updating of the corpus of
scientific thought to conform with the advances of the earlier
Renaissance. Moreover, the metaphor in which a Proteus nature un-
bars "the caves that held/ The treasure of the secrets of its reign,"
echoes Spenser's Cave of Mammon [84] and reminds one that for
Shelley advances in material wealth or technology of any kind,
though not evil, were amoral and subject to misuse ("poetry and the
principle of self, of which money is the visible incarnation, are the
God and Mammon of the world" [85]); it also recalls Bacon's chief
human weakness. In pointing to the shades of Plato and Bacon,
Rousseau reiterates the moral ambiguities of the sublunary world,
where "all best things are thus confused to ill" (*Prometheus* I.628).

The "great bards of old" (274), identified in a canceled fragment as "Homer & his brethren," are the great classical poets. *A
Defence of Poetry* clarifies the judgments that they "inly quelled/
The passions which they sung" and that "their living melody/
Tempers its own contagion to the vein/ Of those who are infected
with it" (274–278). Referring to the decline of the arts during the
Hellenistic period, Shelley declared that not the presence of sensual
elements but the absence of synthesizing and transmuting imaginative power rendered this literature erotic and decadent:

> An equal sensibility to the influence of the senses and the affections is
> to be found in the writings of Homer and Sophocles; the former, espe-
> cially, has clothed sensual and pathetic images with irresistible attrac-

[82] "Shelley's Admiration for Bacon," *PMLA*, LXXIII (June 1958), 229. Scott
also notes that *TL*, 271, where Shelley speaks of "the Proteus shape of Nature's
[spirit]," echoes Section XIII of *The Wisdom of the Ancients*, in which Bacon
discusses the myth of Proteus as an allegorical fable of Matter and its changes.
[83] Preface to *Prometheus Unbound*, *P.W.*, p. 206.
[84] *The Faerie Queene* Book II. Canto vii. Scott cites Bacon's quotation from
Democritus: "the truth of nature lieth hid in certain deep mines and caves"
(p. 229).
[85] *A Defence of Poetry, Prose*, p. 293.

tions. Their superiority over these succeeding writers consists in the presence of those thoughts which belong to the inner faculties of our nature, not in the absence of those which are connected with the external; their incomparable perfection consists in a harmony of the union of all.[86]

The Hellenic writers from Homer through the Golden Age of fifth-century Athens "inly quelled" their passions by harmonizing them with their higher or "inner" natures. In other words, through the power of imagination, they transmuted their private, personal feelings, even erotic emotions, into universal art, which is always moral because, by enlarging and ennobling the imagination of the reader, it "defeats the curse which binds us to be subjected to the accident of surrounding impressions." [87] Why, then, should the classic writers be captive to the Car of Life? Remembering the qualifying phrases that describe Plato's captivity, one might assume that the slavery of even these unnamed writers is not irrevocable, although inasmuch as they are certainly slaves in the pageant, they, like Plato, must have in their private lives fallen under the dominion of the passions that in their art they purified. Rousseau says of himself, on the other hand, that his sufferings and writings were too nearly an equation: "I have suffered what I wrote, or viler pain!" Rousseau, like Hellenistic and Roman writers—and like the young Shelley himself—lacked in his writings "that tranquillity which is the attribute and accompaniment of power." [88]

In "The Triumph of Life: A New Text" G. M. Matthews revised the text of lines 281-282 in a way that made meaningful for the first time this difficult passage, where Mary Shelley herself believed there to be a "chasm" in the text. Though I diverge somewhat from Matthews' reading (see Textual Notes), his reassignment of speeches is extremely valuable. In the dramatic interplay between the Poet and his guide, Rousseau declared that his "words" (writings) were "seeds of misery—/ Even as the deeds of

---

[86] *Prose*, p. 286. Cf. in "Notes on Sculptures in Rome and Florence" Shelley's comment on the representation of the Dionysian revel: "This was indeed a monstrous superstition only capable of existing in Greece because there alone capable of combining ideal beauty and poetical and abstract enthusiasm with the wild errors from which it sprung. In Rome it had a more familiar, wicked, and dry appearance—it was not suited to the severe and exact apprehensions of the Romans, and their strict morals once violated by it sustained a deep injury little analogous to its effects upon the Greeks, who turned all things—superstition, prejudice, murder, madness—to Beauty" (*Prose*, p. 349).

[87] *A Defence of Poetry, Prose*, p. 295.

[88] Shelley to Godwin, 11 December 1817 (Julian, IX, 267).

others," and he pointed to a company in which the Poet recognized the Roman emperors, the founders of the dynasties of modern Europe, and the ecclesiastical princes of the same period. The Poet immediately objects that Rousseau's words did not have the same pernicious effect as "their" deeds. These tyrants had enslaved millions, binding the freemen of the Graeco-Roman world, using "force & murderous snares" to continue and spread the brutal rule of "blood & gold," and rising "like shadows between Man & god" [89] until men worshiped the eclipse instead of the true Sun. The charge that Rousseau makes against himself echoes Shelley's earlier judgment that "Rousseau gave license by his writings to passions that only incapacitate and contract the human heart." [90] In "The Triumph" Rousseau accepts the Poet's defense of his influence— yes, he was better than the tyrants of the old order that he fought, for "their power was given/ But to destroy . . . I/ Am one of those who have created, even/ If it be but a world of agony" (292–295).

The Poet now questions Rousseau specifically on his life story: " 'Whence camest thou & whither goest thou?/ How did thy course begin,' I said, '& why?' " (296–297), for, he declares, he is sick of the "perpetual flow/ Of people" and his "heart" is sick "of one sad

[89] Note that in Shelley's draft "Man" is capitalized whereas "god" begins with a lower-case letter. Shelley might have altered this pattern before printing the poem, but I do not think that it results from carelessness but rather from a characteristic idea (in part illustrated by the quotations in footnotes 64 and 71 above), that may be called apocalyptic humanism. Though Shelley was not an atheist in any meaningful sense of the word, the epistemological dilemma created by his adherence to Humean scepticism left as his only source of religious knowledge the hopes and desires of his own soul and his only guide to conduct the *beau idéal* created by his own imagination and the imaginations of other men; Man is, therefore, the "creator" of "god"—not the actual Supreme Being, but human conceptions of the Supreme Being. In the *Essay on Christianity* Shelley wrote: "The Universal Being can only be described or defined by negatives which deny his subjection to the laws of all inferior existences. Where indefiniteness ends idolatry and anthropomorphism begin" (*Prose*, p. 202). Earlier, in the Preface to *The Revolt of Islam*, he had written: "The erroneous and degrading idea which men have conceived of a Supreme Being . . . is spoken against, but not the Supreme Being itself" (*P.W.*, p. 37). Thus the phrase "men divine" used in conjunction with the names of Gregory and John provides an ironic contradiction in terms: men are not divine, and to assume divinity, to claim the right to guide the spiritual destinies of other men no more ignorant than oneself, was idolatry in the worst sense.

[90] *Proposals for an Association of Philanthropists, Prose*, p. 67. From a remark in Shelley's letters it seems clear that the work by Rousseau that most shocked him and that gave rise to this judgment was *The Confessions*. See Shelley to Hogg, 14 May 1811, *Shelley and His Circle*, ed. Kenneth Neill Cameron, II, 785, or Julian, VIII, 86.

thought." This untold thought that makes the Poet soul-sick must be the problem of evil that is the subject of the poem: "why God made irreconcilable/ Good & the means of good" (230–231).

The words of the Poet as he demands Rousseau's history strongly echo a passage in *Adonais:*

> Whence are we, and why are we? of what scene
> The actors or spectators? Great and mean
> Meet massed in death, who lends what life must borrow.
> As long as skies are blue, and fields are green,
> Evening must usher night, night urge the morrow,
> Month follow month with woe, and year wake year to sorrow.
>
> 184–189

In *Adonais* the Poet weeps that the natural cycle moves relentlessly onward, without regard for human life and hopes. The heart of the Poet in "The Triumph" is sick of one sad thought: that the pageant of history shows no sign of progress, gives no assurance of the survival and accumulation of humane values. As Earl R. Wasserman has shown in his explications of "The Sensitive Plant" and *Adonais,* Shelley often presents an apparently negative answer to the moral problem that has within it the seeds of a later, more optimistic interpretation of the human dilemma. Rousseau rejected the Poet's despairing judgment that it makes no difference what kind of figures one paints on the "false & fragile glass" of the phenomenal world, and the Poet himself, when confronted by Rousseau's confession that his words had become a curse, objected that there was a significant difference between the effect of Rousseau's writings and the deeds of tyrants like Constantine.[91] Thus, though the Poet finds nothing of comfort in the "perpetual flow/ Of people," he no longer ignores Rousseau's message for him. The Poet's retort to Rousseau at line 281 ("But not as theirs") thus signals a turning point in the poem.

THE UNANSWERED QUESTION

Rousseau replies to the Poet's rapid questions, Whence? Whither? How? and Why? that he can partly answer the first question—he knows "how & by what paths" he has been brought "to this dread pass" and that this much even the Poet can guess—but that he has no idea "why this should be," and still less notion "whither the con-

[91] No historical figure did Shelley despise more than Constantine. See, for example, *Prose*, pp. 125, 148, and Julian, X. 13–14. 40.

queror hurries me" (300–304). But, Rousseau continues, if you really want to know,

> ". . . follow thou, & from spectator turn
> Actor or victim in this wretchedness,[92]
>
> "And what thou wouldst be taught I then may learn
> From thee.—"
>
> 305–308

This repetition of the injunction, "If thirst of knowledge doth not thus abate,/ Follow it even to the night" (194–195), reiterates both Shelley's scepticism and the relationship between the Poet in "The Triumph" and the spirit of Rousseau. In *Hellas* the Phantom of Mahomet tells Mahmud only what he can already predict. In "With a Guitar, to Jane" Shelley writes that "the Spirit that inhabits" the guitar

> . . . talks according to the wit
> Of its companions; and no more
> Is heard than has been felt before,
> By those who tempt it to betray
> These secrets of an elder day.
>
> 81–86

Rousseau, a projection of the Poet's imagination, knows only what the Poet has learned or experienced.

Yet, paradoxically, "Rousseau" in "The Triumph" also represents the spirit of the historical Jean-Jacques Rousseau and not simply a mirror-image of the Poet (who represents, of course, the spirit of Shelley). The "Rousseau" of "The Triumph" is the Poet's (Shelley's) conception of the historical Rousseau, and thereby Shelley's sceptical admission that he could never know what the real Jean-Jacques was like; he could know only his idea of "Rousseau." Shelley presumably had reasons for choosing Rousseau, rather than some other writer, as the Poet's guide. Because critics have been relatively unsuccessful in finding convincing parallels between Rousseau's story in "The Triumph" and *The Confessions,* many have concluded that the poem merely echoes the idealized accounts of Shelley's own experience, such as that in *Epipsychidion.* Shelley's comments on Rousseau's works show, however, that whereas his only recorded judgment of the *Confessions* was that "they

---

[92] Rousseau's use of the phrase "actor or victim" may imply that Rousseau is uncertain about human responsibility for the captives' predicament, but I take these words as equivalents of oppressor and oppressed, tyrant and slave. See *TL,* 54–55.

are either a disgrace to the confessor or a string of falsehoods . . probably the latter," [93] for *Julie, ou La Nouvelle Héloïse* he had nothing but praise. He first praised the character of "Eloisa" (Julie as she appeared in the English translation [94]). Later, in his long letter to Peacock of 12 July 1816 (one of two letters of the period that Shelley believed significant enough to publish, along with "Mont Blanc," in Mary Shelley's *History of a Six Weeks' Tour* [1817]), he pays an extended tribute to "the divine beauty of Rousseau's imagination, as it exhibits itself in 'Julie,' " [95] and on 10 April 1822, about the time Shelley must have begun "The Triumph of Life," he wrote to John Gisborne of a passage in *Faust,* "Do you remember the 54th letter of the 1st part of the Nouvelle Héloïse? Göthe, in a subsequent scene evidently has that letter in his mind. . . ." [96]

In the *Confessions* (Book IX) Rousseau tells that during his stay at the Hermitage,

> ne voyant rien d'existant qui fût digne de mon délire, je le nourris dans un monde idéal, que mon imagination créatrice eut bientôt peuplé d'êtres selon mon cœur.
>
> . . . . .
>
> Je me figurai l'amour, l'amitié, les deux idoles de mon cœur, sous les plus ravissantes images. . . . J'imaginai deux amies. . . . Je donnai à l'une des deux un amant dont l'autre fut la tendre amie. . . . Épris de mes deux charmants modèles, je m'identifiois avec l'amant et l'ami le plus qu'il m'étoit possible; mais je le fis aimable et jeune, lui donnant au surplus les vertus et les défauts que je me sentois. [97]

Such a statement would have been more than enough to suggest to Shelley that the story of Saint-Preux, Julie's lover, formed an idealized picture of Rousseau's interior experience such as Shelley

[93] Shelley to Hogg, 14 May 1811, quoted from the corrected text of this letter published by Kenneth Neill Cameron, *Shelley and His Circle: 1773–1822,* II, 785.

[94] *Eloisa: Or, a Series of Original Letters,* collected and published by J. J. Rousseau, translated from the French, 3rd ed., 4 vols. (London: Printed for T. Becket and P. A. De Hondt, 1764).

[95] Julian, IX, 167.

[96] Julian, X, 372. Such an exact reference suggests either that Shelley knew *Julie* almost by heart or else that he had reread it shortly before April 1822. Shelley's remark on Goethe's use of this particular passage of Rousseau's novel suggests that conscious use of such correlatives was not foreign to his own artistic method. (Cf. Julian, X, 371: "*Cypriano* evidently furnished the germ of Faust, as Faust may furnish the germ of other poems; although it is different from it in structure and plan, as the acorn from the oak.")

[97] *Œuvres complètes de J. J. Rousseau . . .,* 2nd ed. (Paris: Baudouin Frères, 1826), XVI, 263, 268.

had himself recently depicted in *Epipsychidion*.[98] It should surprise
no one, therefore, that in "The Triumph" Shelley portrayed Rousseau's history in terms of the experience of Saint-Preux. There is, of
course, a great difference between the form in which Saint-Preux's
love for Julie develops in the lengthy epistolary novel and that in
which Rousseau relates his experience in less than 250 lines of
"The Triumph of Life" (which has, of course, its own symbols
and its larger context into which Rousseau's story must be integrated), but "The Triumph" echoes *Julie* in thought and expression
often enough and coherently enough to remove all doubt as to
Shelley's model for Rousseau's spiritual pilgrimage. Basically, Shelley simply reversed the creative process that gave birth to *La
Nouvelle Héloïse* by abstracting from the novel the seminal encounter between Rousseau and the vision of his epipsychal ideal.
In "The Triumph" Julie becomes Rousseau's vision of the "shape
all light" and Saint-Preux's love of Julie is transformed into Rousseau's pursuit of that mortal vision of the Ideal.

In "the April prime" [99] Rousseau becomes aware that he has been
sleeping "under a mountain which from unknown time/ Had
yawned into a cavern high & deep." Whether we visualize the yawn-
ing cavern as a narrow canyon cleaving the mountain (as Bradley
suggested and as I think likely) [100] or as simply a high and deep
cave, the symbolism clearly depicts the birth of man, who emerges
from the mountain (a mass of earth and thus Shelley's symbol of the

---

[98] See Shelley to John Gisborne, 18 June 1822: "The 'Epipsychidion' I cannot
look at. . . . If you are anxious, however, to hear what I have been,
it will tell you something thereof. It is an idealized history of my life and
feelings" (Julian, X, 401). Shelley apparently lent a copy of *Julie* to Emilia
Viviani (see White, *Shelley*, II, 483).

Shelley's interpretation of Rousseau's character parallels closely Byron's conception of Rousseau in Canto III of *Childe Harold's Pilgrimage*, written in 1816
at the same time that Byron and Shelley reread and discussed *Julie* (see Julian,
IX, 167–177).

[99] Matthews objected to the reading "forest tops" (309) on botanical grounds
("New Text," p. 295). But Shelley's description derives from Italy, not England,
and by April the "forest tops" would have begun to turn green. (See Shelley to
Peacock, 25 February [1819]: "The willow trees had just begun to put forth
their green and golden buds, and gleamed like points of lambent fire among
the wintry forest" [Julian, X, 29].) Cf. Shelley's other uses of "forest tops": "The
Witch of Atlas," 354; "The Woodman and the Nightingale," 46.

Rousseau's awakening to self-consciousness occurs some time after birth itself,
which would, presumably, coincide with the beginning of the year, probably
the vernal equinox (21 March) or the first of March (which was the first month
in the Roman year). Cf. Adam's awakening to life: *PL* VIII.250–256.

[100] Bradley's discussion (p. 454) concerns *TL*, 343–344; Stawell (p. 124) and
Carlos Baker (*Shelley's Major Poetry*, pp. 265–266) discuss in detail the setting
of the vision at *TL*, 311–314.

physical universe when in an inert state) from which issues the stream of mortal generation and behind which lies the "realm without a name," a world from which man finds himself cut off even at birth. All the details of Rousseau's description emphasize the impossibility of knowing what the soul's state was "before that sleep" (332). Shelley's Rousseau, unlike the child of Wordsworth's "Ode: Intimations of Immortality," enters life trailing no clouds of remembered glory: The Lethean stream of mortal generation fills the grove with a sound that causes all who hear it to forget *"all* pleasure & *all* pain, *all* hate & love," even the deepest emotions, noble and ignoble—a mother's love and a king's thwarted ambition.[101] The Poet himself, says Rousseau sardonically, would "forget thus vainly to deplore" the world's apparent wrongs over which he has no control. Rousseau does not know "whether my life had been before that sleep/ The Heaven which I imagine, or a Hell/ Like this harsh world in which I wake to weep" (327–335).[102] Lines 318–331 emphasize that Shelley's picture of awakening human self-awareness is thoroughly sceptical and directly opposed to Plato's and Wordsworth's myths in which the soul can recall an antenatal existence.

On coming to self-consciousness, Rousseau arose, and for a time the natural world seemed to glow with "a gentle trace/ Of light diviner than the common Sun/ Sheds on the common Earth" (335–339). This state of innocence is not analogous to that in Wordsworth's ode; rather, this period is that when "the magnificence and beauty of the external world sinks profoundly into the frame of [a young idealist's] conceptions, and affords to their modifications a variety not to be exhausted." [103]

Rousseau continues: "but [104] all the place/ Was filled with many sounds woven into one/ Oblivious melody, confusing sense/ Amid

101 *TL,* 314–326 (italics mine). Cf. Milton's description of Lethe (*PL* II.582–586). Another analogue—and possible (though doubtful) source—for *TL,* 321–326, is the tenth stanza of Burns's "Lament for James, Earl of Glencairn" (suggested by an anonymous critic in *Cambridge University Magazine,* I [1839], 96).

102 Bradley notes (p. 454) that "this harsh world" echoes *Hamlet* (V.ii).

103 Preface to *Alastor (P.W.,* p. 14). The stage described by Shelley has analogues in the thought of other Romantic poets: it corresponds to Wordsworth's youthful passionate love of nature alluded to in "Tintern Abbey" (ll. 72–83) and to "the Chamber of Maiden-Thought" in Keats's letter to Reynolds of 3 May 1818 (*The Letters of John Keats,* ed. Hyder Rollins, I, 280–281). The "common Sun" (338) is coeval, not with this youthful period of unreflective wonder, but with the perspective of adult experience from which both Rousseau and the Poet view the earlier period.

104 Note the change in the text from "and" to "but."

the gliding waves & shadows dun" (339–342). The mélange of sounds, moving waves, and shadows, like all manifestations of terrestrial creation (unlike the silence and calm serenity of the pure white radiance of eternity), confused the sense of the young Rousseau through its multiplicity, signaling the confusion of human cognitive faculties. The "bright omnipresence of morning" (not "a rayless orb of fire" as would be the true Sun beyond the distorting influence of the earth's atmosphere) flowed through the eastern cavern and the Sun's image was reflected "on the waters of the well that glowed/ Like gold, and threaded all the forest maze/ With winding paths of emerald fire" (346–348). The gold and green colors reflected from the water result from the refraction of white sunlight into its component colors, thus reiterating the terrestrial and phenomenal nature of the ensuing experience. Finally, amid the "Sun's image" "on the vibrating/ Floor of the fountain," there stood "a shape all light."

One can determine the nature of the "shape all light" with some precision, I think, if he remembers the basic outlines of Shelley's symbolic universe. The stream symbolizes the course of an individual mortal life,[105] whereas the well itself represents the individual human mind, at a particular point relatively static, but, of course, still consisting of a fluid, terrestrial element. The reflected image of the sun, "amid" which—and presumably out of which—the "shape all light" arises, I take to be a symbol of the human imagination—a reflection of the true Sun of cosmic energy in a mortal medium. The "shape all light" is thus equivalent to the vision seen by the Youth of *Alastor,* of whom Shelley wrote: "He images to himself the Being whom he loves. Conversant with speculations of the sublimest and most perfect natures, the vision in which he embodies his own imaginations unites all of wonderful, or wise, or beautiful, which the poet, the philosopher, or the lover could depicture." [106] The shape flings "dew on the earth, as if she were the Dawn" (that time at which the rays of the sun are most distorted

---

[105] The figure appears frequently in Wordsworth (e.g., in *The River Duddon* and in the opening simile of *The Prelude,* Book Nine). Yeats, who first pointed out Shelley's use of the symbol (*Ideas of Good and Evil*), uses it pointedly himself in "Coole and Ballylee."

[106] *P.W.,* p. 14. Shelley's Preface to *Alastor* parallels very closely *The Confessions,* where Rousseau tells how he embodied his ideals in the character of Julie, parallels it so closely, indeed, that one suspects Shelley may have had Rousseau in mind as one of the misled idealists of whom the Youth in *Alastor* was a type (though Rousseau's ultimate reaction to his vision of the Ideal was, of course, far different from the Youth's).

by the earth's atmosphere). Once I was convinced that the "shape all light" was equivalent to Iris, the rainbow, but the correction of the text at line 356 (from "still before me" to "still before her") makes clear the distinction between them. Iris, the rainbow messenger, accompanies the "shape," but they are not the same. Nevertheless, that the "shape" is accompanied by dew, rain, music, and the rainbow reemphasizes her terrestrial nature: The "shape" is composed of all that is "wonderful, or wise, or beautiful" in the young Rousseau's experience, but as the product of a limited human imagination, she is still of the earth, earthy. The moving "waters of the well" and the "flashing rays" that it disperses show the mutability and imperfection of the earthly medium's capacity to reflect the Ideal Sun.[107]

The entire passage describing the "shape all light" (343–357) has employed vivid sensory impressions, some of them synaesthetic: "emerald fire," "vibrating floor," "silver music." One recalls the opening lines of "The Triumph" in which natural creation's worship of the Sun also expressed itself in a variety of sensory impressions; the "shape all light" is, like the Witch of Atlas, a daughter of the Sun and is, therefore, worthy of worship by the terrestrial creatures. But, also like the Witch of Atlas, she is the daughter of an earthbound water spirit.[108] In Shelley's symbolic mythology, the union of the sun (or a star) and a terrestrial creature of water or earth symbolized the infusion of celestial energy into the terrestrial world (and in this sense the offspring of such a union was raised above merely mortal nature), but such a union of the Absolute and the limited, the Eternal and the temporal, inevitably resulted in the distortion of the Ideal, in an eclipse that one ought never confuse with "the true Sun it quenched" (292). Shelley fought relentlessly against all anthropomorphic conceptions of God,

[107] In *Paradise Lost* (III.372–382) Milton tells of the invisibility and inaccessibility of God "amidst the glorious brightness"; the brightest Seraphim cannot approach God even when He shades the "full blaze" of His beams in a cloud. For Milton, God's glory was visible in the "Divine Similitude," the Son (III.382–387). Though Shelley does not, of course, share Milton's theological perspective, he does share his epistemological dilemma; in lieu of a single historical incarnation of the Divinity, Shelley posits repeated, though imperfect and transitory, experiences of a more-than-human inspiration throughout the course of human history.

The phrase "burned on the waters" (346) echoes the same line in Enobarbus' description of Cleopatra's meeting with Antony (*Antony and Cleopatra* II.ii) that T. S. Eliot has used to great effect at the opening of "A Game of Chess" in *The Waste Land*.

[108] "Her mother was one of the Atlantides ("The Witch of Atlas," 57).

preferring the name of "atheist" to "the erroneous and degrading idea which men have conceived of a Supreme Being."[109] Those who identify the Witch of Atlas with the Ideal itself have been hard-pressed to explain her rather unideal pranks, but when one recognizes her as a distorted and limited (though divinely begotten) embodiment of the Ideal, one can easily understand the aberrations that her influence initiates.

Milton's *Comus* describes another offspring of the Sun:

> . . . (who knows not *Circe*
> The daughter of the Sun? Whose charmed Cup
> Whoever tasted, lost his upright shape,
> And downward fell into a groveling Swine). . . .
>   50–53

From Milton's description of Circe's son, Comus, also a seducer of virtue, Shelley borrowed several features of his "shape all light." Comus, Milton wrote:

> Excells his Mother at her mighty Art,
> Offring to every weary Travailer,
> His orient liquor in a Crystal Glasse,
> To quench the drouth of *Phoebus*. . . .
>   63–66

"Phoebus," Milton's name for God here (as in *Lycidas*, 77), is exactly equivalent in Milton's symbolism to Shelley's Sun. Thus Comus, though a descendant of the Sun, seduces men from their thirsting search for the living waters that can be found only in the Absolute. Likewise, the "shape all light" bears in her right hand "a crystal glass/ Mantling with bright Nepenthe" (358–359). Comus says to the Lady:

> And first behold this cordial Julep here
> That flames, and dances in his crystal bounds
> With spirits of balm, and fragrant Syrops mixt.
> Not that *Nepenthes* which the wife of *Thone*,
> In *Egypt* gave to *Jove*-born *Helena*
> Is of such power to stir up joy as this,
> To life so friendly, or so cool to thirst.[110]

---

[109] Preface to *The Revolt of Islam*, *P.W.*, p. 37.

[110] *Comus*, 671–677. Notice that Helen of Troy is said to be "*Jove*-born"; she whose beauty burnt the topless towers of Ilium was, like Circe, begotten by the Divinity. Throughout Greek mythology the half-divine children of gods and mortals initiated a large proportion of the destruction and chaos on earth.

Stawell (p. 126) compares *TL*, 358–359, with the "oracular vapour" of *Prometheus* II.iii.1–10.

The Nepenthe bubbling and foaming in a crystal glass borne by the "shape all light" echoes *Comus* and thus carries with it ominous overtones, as does the "fierce splendour" (359) that fell from the "shape."

The "shape," moving along the stream "with palms so tender," [111] does not break "the mirror of its billow": that is, the imaginative creature, an airy nothing, does not impinge upon the mortal world of phenomenal reality, remaining in the realm of "dream" (367), "mist" (368), "foam" (371), "airs" (372), "slant morning beams" (373), and "shadows" (374), while her feet move "to the ceaseless song/ Of leaves & winds & waves & birds & bees" (375–376)—all both literally and symbolically representative of mortal generation and the terrestrial world. Moreover, in her bending movement she assumes the shape of the rainbow, her feet and her "fair hair" both skimming along the surface of the stream (363–365). Although Shelley apparently did not wish to identify his mythic "shape all light" specifically with Iris, he associates the "shape" very closely with the rainbow, symbol of the refraction of "the white radiance of Eternity" into the colors of the visible spectrum.

The shape "moved in a measure new" as a "shape of golden dew" rising from a lake moves "where eagle never flew" (375–381); thus the movement of the "shape" is compared with a cloud of evening mist rising from the surface of a lake and receiving a golden tint from the moon rising behind it.[112] Such a figure would symbolize perfectly the infusion of the power of Reason into the embodiment of the Ideal, for the symbolic moon of Reason (which has as its attendant bird the owl) is one place where the eagle spirits of imaginative men "never flew."

As a number of critics (especially Bice Chiappelli [113]) have noted, the effect of the "shape all light" on the mind of Rousseau is not salutary. Her feet, as well as the music of terrestrial creation,

". . . seemed as they moved, to blot
The thoughts of him who gazed on them, & soon

"All that was seemed as if it had been not. . . ."
383–385

---

[111] Locock compares Shelley's use of "palms" for feet in *Prometheus* (IV.123) and *Adonais* (212). Shelley's uses in these two poems are the earliest examples of this meaning recorded in the *OED*; Browning (*The Return of the Druses*) followed him in this use, which Shelley may have derived from books on comparative anatomy or another science (see *OED*).
[112] Cf. *TL*, 378–381, with *PL* V.185–188.
[113] *Il Pensiero religioso di Shelley*, pp. 87–121.

The "gazer's mind" seemed "strewn beneath/ Her feet like embers, & she, thought by thought,/ Trampled its fires into the dust of death" (386–388). Since fire is Shelley's consistent symbol of spiritual energy, this effect must be pernicious, a conclusion confirmed by the next simile:

> "As Day upon the threshold of the east
>   Treads out the lamps of night, until the breath
>
> "Of darkness reillumines even the least
>   Of heaven's living eyes—like day she came,
> Making the night a dream. . . ."
>   389–393

Shelley could have found the simile (a traditional one) in *Julie*, where Saint-Preux writes to his beloved, "Ne te vis-je pas briller entre ces jeunes beautés comme le soleil entre les astres qu'il éclipse?" [114] But though Shelley utilizes the general effect of Saint-Preux's subjection to Julie, he changes "sun" to "Day" to preserve the consistency of his own symbolic pattern. In his published poems Shelley never used the word "sun" in a derogatory sense,[115] but he often employed "morning," "dawn," "evening," or "day" to represent the "veil of light" cast by the atmosphere's diffusion of sunlight. Finally, the conclusion of the simile ("until the breath/ Of darkness reillumines even the least/ Of heaven's [116] living eyes") foretells the same kind of renewal of vision and rebirth of celestial light for which Rousseau hopes in lines 416–423.

Rousseau, suspended "between desire and shame" (as was Saint-Preux when he wrote his first two letters to Julie), says,

> ". . . 'If, as it doth seem,
>   Thou comest from the realm without a name,
>
> " 'Into this valley of perpetual dream,
>   Shew whence I came, and where I am, and why—
> Pass not away upon the passing stream.' "
>   395–399

Rousseau's tentativeness in identifying his vision shows his (and

---

[114] Part I, Letter xxxiv (*Œuvres*, VIII, 182). See also *Julie*, Part IV, Letter ii, where Madame d'Orbe writes to Julie: "c'est de te chérir quoique tu m'éclipses. Ma Julie, tu es faite pour régner. . . . tu me subjugues, tu m'atterres, ton génie écrase le mien, et je ne suis rien devant toi" (*Œuvres*, IX, 172).

[115] Only in his verse "Letter to Maria Gisborne" (which he presumably would not have published without revision) did Shelley give the word "sun" negative associations ("Letter to Maria Gisborne," 154–160, *P.W.*, pp. 366–367).

[116] Perhaps Shelley did not capitalize "heaven's" because it refers literally to the sky and not to a symbolic value.

Shelley's) scepticism, for he carefully refrains from equating this creature of his own desires with noumenal reality. The source of Rousseau's vision was not an antenatal memory; if Shelley's account in the Preface to *Alastor* is an adequate précis of an analogous experience (as I believe it is), the attributes of the ideal entered the mind from the deep "fountains of knowledge" and from "the magnificence and beauty of the external world," avenues of knowledge acceptable to one who followed the fundamental tenets of the British empirical philosophers. At any rate, the youthful Rousseau, asking the same questions of the "shape all light" that the Poet had asked him (296–297), fears that she will pass away upon the passing stream.

" 'Arise and quench thy thirst,' was her reply," arise and "quench the drouth of *Phoebus*," quench that longing for a permanence found in no merely terrestrial creation, either of the natural world or of man's imagination. The young Rousseau, like a flower struck by the alchemist's wand of morning,[117] bent at her command and "touched with faint lips the cup she raised" (404). There need be no doubt that Rousseau drank of the cup; the events that follow imply that his condition has been changed, that he has fallen under some spell. Rousseau, in fact, comes to terrestrial knowledge of Good and Evil, as did Adam and Eve when they ate of the fruit of the tree. His brain became as a sandy beach [118] where the wave of his vision had "more than half erased" the track of deer, symbols of innocence, and where the wolf of evil "leaves his stamp visibly upon the shore" until a second wave bursts. Although that "second" never appears to wash away the wolf's track within "The Triumph," this simile, like that of lines 389–392, carries within it the seeds of an optimistic solution to the problem of evil posed by the poem, for it implies that Rousseau's vision of evil has distorted his perspective, erasing the marks of good but leaving the marks of evil until still another

[117] Oscar Kuhns (*Dante and the English Poets from Chaucer to Tennyson* [N.Y., 1904], p. 178) compared *TL*, 401–402, with *Inferno* II.127–129. The parallel is clear, but once again Shelley's echo seems to be set in ironic contrast to his source: Dante uses the figure to describe how the Poet regained his courage "as one set free" upon hearing Virgil tell how Beatrice had sent him to guide the Poet, but in "The Triumph" almost the same simile introduces the lines in which the Poet's "brain became as sand" and in which the beautiful "shape all light" waned under the influence of the second, pernicious vision.

[118] O. W. Firkins (*Power and Elusiveness in Shelley*, p. 36) compares *TL*, 405, with "The Sensitive Plant" i.102–105 and "Fragments of an Unfinished Drama," 151–154.

wave, another moment in the constant flux of human experience and knowledge, rectifies the picture.

When the "new Vision never seen before" burst on Rousseau's sight (410–411), the "fair shape" of his imaginative ideal faded in the cold, rational light of the conquering chariot, as the veils of sunlight drop one by one over the "silent splendour" (opposed to the noisy sublunary world) of Lucifer, Venus as the Morning Star.[119] Yet,

> ". . . as the presence of that fairest planet
> Although unseen is felt by one who hopes
>
> "That his day's path may end as he began it
> In that star's smile"
>
> 416–419

so Rousseau knew "in that light's severe excess/ The presence of that shape"(424–425). Intervening is a rather long simile describing Venus,

> ". . . whose light is like the scent
> Of a jonquil when evening breezes fan it,[120]
>
> "Or the soft note in which his dear lament
> The Brescian shepherd breathes, or the caress
> That turned his weary slumber to content.—"

[119] Paget Toynbee (*Dante in English Literature,* II, 230ⁿ) compares *TL,* 416, with *Purgatorio* I.19. If the entire passage *TL,* 412–423, can be considered analogous to *Purgatorio* I.13–21, then Rousseau's story might mark the beginning of Shelley's discussion of the purgatorial experience of humanity as opposed to the *Inferno* he had described in *TL,* 43–299. Certainly the break in tone when Rousseau begins to tell of his awakening in the "oblivious valley" and the approach of the "shape all light" suggests that Shelley may have intended to conclude Rousseau's story with a hope for his ultimate salvation.

[120] Earl Wasserman, discussing *Adonais,* 174–175, notes that the association of starlight and the fragrance of flowers "appears in Shelley's poetry with striking frequency" and concludes that "the flower . . . is the earthly manifestation of a star. . . . Shelley conceives of flowers and stars, fragrance and light, as related by a metaphoric transition which symbolizes the relation of earthly existence to immortal existence." In a note he compares the *Adonais* lines to *TL,* 419–420; *Revolt,* 4607; *Orpheus,* 94, 116; *Matilda,* 37; *Alastor,* 440; *Witch,* 600; *Prometheus* III.ii.47; *Question* II.2–3, IV.3; "Sensitive Plant," 35, 46, 80–81, 175–176; *Prince Athanase,* 248 (*The Subtler Language,* p. 323).

Professor Wasserman has made a good beginning in his essays on "The Sensitive Plant" and *Adonais* toward elucidating the significance of Shelley's recurring association of flowers and stars. I do not agree, however, that Shelley came upon the relationship by "thinking of the resemblance of flowers to stars, and also of the manner in which flowers feed upon light to produce their own brilliance and scent." Rather, Shelley no doubt drew upon the literary tradition for this association: he would have needed to go no farther than Milton's *Lycidas,* where the soul of Lycidas, first associated with Hyacinth (106) and other plants (1–2, 78, 133–151) at last is compared to the morning star (165–173; cf. 30–31).

In this synaesthetic imagery the light of the star is described in terms of three other senses, moving from the most abstract and indefinite, scent, through sound, and concluding with the touch of an endeared caress that soothed his troubled sleep.[121] If we remember that Rousseau called the place in which he awoke "this valley of perpetual dream" (397), the significance of the sleep image is apparent, and the image of life-as-dream makes a fitting analogue to Shelley's image of life as a painted veil. In other words, though Rousseau can no longer *see* the "fair shape," her presence becomes known through the less definite senses; though in his journey of daily life he sees nightmares, he may be only in a world of dream, and a soft caress soothes him and calms him in the knowledge that he shall wake to find his love once more. The two possibilities are carefully interwoven to convey the ambivalence and complexity of the sceptical epistemology: though Rousseau *may* be only dreaming this phenomenal experience, to his limited mortal vision he seems to "wake to weep" in a "sick day" where the vision of the ideal, "more dimly than a day appearing dream,/ The ghost of a forgotten form of sleep,/ . . . glimmers, forever sought, forever lost" (427–431). The sceptical follower of the "intellectual philosophy" always had to ask himself "Was it a vision, or a waking dream? . . . Do I wake or sleep?" [122]

There remains the larger question: If the "shape all light" is a seductress, if she was associated on her appearance with symbols of limited human vision and the terrestrial realm of natural necessity, why does she, after Rousseau has drunk of the cup and seen the vision of evil, suddenly become associated with the morning and evening star and with love? Rousseau's experience, which is fully consistent with Shelley's theory of knowledge, can be clarified by reference to similar events in other poems. As Shelley glosses *Alastor* in the Preface, the Youth is for a time "joyous, and tranquil, and self-possessed," but when his mind seeks to go beyond the natural world, to find in the universe "an intelligence similar to itself," he brings ruin upon himself, for there is in the phenomenal world no prototype of the good, true, and beautiful creation of his own soul. "Blasted by his disappointment, he descends

121 The identity of the "Brescian shepherd" has eluded me, though I suspect that Shelley refers to some specific poet, or lover, or figure in folk-story from the region near Brescia in northeastern Italy. "The favorite song, 'Stanco di pascolar le peccorelle,' is a Brescian national air" (Mary Shelley's note).
122 Keats, "Ode to a Nightingale."

to an untimely grave" (*P.W.*, pp. 14–15). In the Dedication to *The Revolt of Islam* Shelley tells of his own encounter with the Ideal, "when first/ The clouds which wrap this world from youth did pass" (19–20); he came to his initial moral vision ("I will be wise,/ And just, and free, and mild, if in me lies/ Such power") because he grew

> ". . . weary to behold
> The selfish and the strong still tyrannise
> Without reproach or check."
>
> 33–35

With this awakening moral sense—this knowledge of good and evil [123]—there came upon the mind of the young Shelley "a thirst with which I pined" (44–45). Then come these significant lines:

> Alas, that love should be a blight and snare
> To those who seek all sympathies in one!—
> Such once I sought in vain; then black despair,
> The shadow of a starless night, was thrown
> Over the world in which I moved alone. . . .
>
> 46–50

The subsequent lines, telling how Shelley sought unsuccessfully to find "all sympathies in one" until he met Mary, "whose presence on my wintry heart/ Fell, like bright Spring upon some herbless plain" (55–56), are personal history rather than imaginative creation; this biographical record changed somewhat in each poem as Shelley, in his search for the earthly embodiment of the Ideal, became infatuated with Emilia Viviani and Jane Williams. But Shelley's basic philosophical position—that there is not within the phenomenal world any embodiment of even that limited Ideal created by the human imagination—remained unchanged, personal disappointments merely confirming what he knew with his intellect to be a truth of the human condition. Another symbol of the questing human spirit, Pan, who is an earth-god although he is greater than the merely natural world, lacks the unmoved serenity of Apollo ("the eye with which the Universe/ Beholds itself and knows itself divine"), and Pan must, therefore, repeatedly seek in vain for his antitype, must always pursue a maiden and clasp a reed.[124] In *Adonais* Shelley again portrayed himself as the idealist

---

[123] Cf. Shelley to Byron, 21 October 1821: "We are damned to the knowledge of good and evil, and it is well for us to know what we should avoid no less than what we should seek" (Julian, X, 331).

[124] See "Hymn of Apollo" and "Hymn of Pan," *P.W.*, pp. 612–614.

whose fate it was to be ruined through an encounter with the Ideal:

> . . . he, as I guess,
> Had gazed on Nature's naked loveliness,
> Actaeon-like, and now he fled astray
> With feeble steps o'er the world's wilderness,
> And his own thoughts, along that rugged way,
> Pursued, like raging hounds, their father and their prey.
>
> 274–279

To one who had gazed on the naked loveliness of the Good, the True, and the Beautiful that are imbibed from the fount of knowledge and from the "magnificence and beauty of the external world," the realization that there is no fulfillment for human desires in the phenomenal world generates those "thoughts which must remain untold" that eat away the heart of the idealist with the cancer of despair. This experience and these philosophical reflections led to Shelley's ambivalent attitude toward knowledge:

> Lift not the painted veil which those who live
> Call Life: though unreal shapes be pictured there,
> And it but mimic all we would believe
> With colours idly spread,—behind, lurk Fear
> And Hope, twin Destinies; who ever weave
> Their shadows, o'er the chasm, sightless and drear.
> I knew one who had lifted it—he sought,
> For his lost heart was tender, things to love,
> But found them not, alas! nor was there aught
> The world contains, the which he could approve.
> Through the unheeding many he did move,
> A splendour among shadows, a bright blot
> Upon this gloomy scene, a Spirit that strove
> For truth, and like the Preacher found it not.
>
> P.W., p. 569

Shelley's intellectual honesty forced him to reject the traditional arguments for immortality of the soul and for the ultimate triumph of good over evil as "sophisms which disgrace the cause." The desire that these things should be so, the human longing for a morally ordered universe, remained "the strongest and the only presumption that eternity is the inheritance of every thinking being" (P.W., pp. 478–479).

Thus when Rousseau in his thirst for knowledge asked that "beautiful idealism of moral excellence" created by his own imagination to "shew whence I came, and where I am, and why," his vision of that "chasm, sightless and drear" behind the painted veil of limited mortal experience destroyed his appreciation of that veil's transitory beauties. He saw too clearly the apparent meaning-lessness of human endeavors, seemingly destroyed in the inexorable march of natural Necessity that obliterated first the individual human life, then the memory of man's achievements, and finally the race itself.[125] Like the writer of Ecclesiastes (the "Preacher") he saw that "all is vanity" in the realm of "Fate, Time, Occasion, Chance, and Change." Thus bereft of all comfort from Heaven and from Earth, Rousseau's only guide (or that of any intellectually honest idealist, in Shelley's view) was his own epipsychal ideal. Apparently Shelley had made his philosophy clear to Byron, who told Lady Blessington: "He was the most gentle, most amiable, and *least* worldly-minded person I ever met; full of delicacy, dis-interested beyond all other men, and possessing a degree of genius, joined to a simplicity, as rare as it is admirable. He had formed to himself a *beau idéal* of all that is fine, high-minded, and noble, and he acted up to this ideal even to the very letter." [126] Beyond his normative judgment of Shelley, Byron describes the source of Shelley's ethics: "He had formed to himself a *beau idéal. . . .*" In Shelley's mature poetry that ideal created by the human imagina-tion is the only source of ethical values, a unique moral agent in the wilderness of amoral experience:

> "So knew I in that light's severe excess
> The presence of that shape which on the stream
> Moved, as I moved along the wilderness,
>
> .   .   .   .
>
> So did that shape its obscure tenour keep
>
> "Beside my path, as silent as a ghost."
>   424–426, 432–433

Though the Ideal now seems less substantial than the sensory world, the memory of that moment of joyful vision follows the soul of Rousseau (as it had Shelley's soul in *Epipsychidion*) and though "neither prayer nor verse could dissipate/ The night which closed on her," neither could that starless night

---

[125] Besides such poems on the theme of the transitoriness of *gloria mundi* as "Ozymandias" (*P.W.*, p. 550) and "Ode to Heaven" (*P.W.*, pp. 576–577), com-pare Shelley to Peacock, 24 July 1816: "I will not pursue Buffon's sublime but gloomy theory, that this earth which we inhabit will at some future period be changed into a mass of frost" (Julian, IX, 186).

[126] "Journal of Conversations with Lord Byron," *New Monthly Magazine,* XXXV, Pt. 2 (1832), 140.

> . . . uncreate
> That world within this Chaos, mine and me,
> Of which she was the veiled Divinity,
> The world I say of thoughts that worshipped her.
>   *Epipsychidion*, 241–245

The ethical soul is born, according to Shelley, when an individual orients his ideas and attitudes toward a *beau idéal* created by "an imagination inflamed and purified through familiarity with all that is excellent and majestic" both in the external universe and in the records of those "best and happiest moments of the happiest and best minds."

Rousseau, unsatisfied with momentary glimpses of the tempting vision, fell victim to the "cold bright car" of phenomenal life which, with its "savage" and "stunning" music,[127] the "loud million/ Fiercely extolled" (434–438). The later description of the chariot does not refer to the death-like "shape" that the Poet had seen crouching within it. Shelley, I think consciously, designated both that huddled form and the vision of beauty by the same word "shape," expressing the indefiniteness of both creatures—the *beau idéal* and the death-like vision of evil which inevitably accompanies a knowledge of the good.

As the chariot moves in victorious stateliness, above the clouds appears the rainbow, forming a triumphal arch,[128] while "underneath aetherial glory clad/ The wilderness" (442–443); I take these lines to mean that the rainbow colors, produced by the atmosphere's (aether's) diffusion of the Sun's beams, painted all things in their phenomenal hues. Some might say that the rainbow, a traditional symbol of hope, has been distorted into a symbol of evil, but because, for Shelley, the rainbow signified the distortion that reality undergoes when it enters the terrestrial and, thus, the imperfection of human knowledge, it *does* symbolize man's single hope: Beyond the amoral realm of sublunary phenomena, whose ultimate unreality the rainbow represents, there may shine a radiant Reality uniting power (heat) and will for good (light).

Just as parallels and echoes of Dante's *Inferno* underlie the opening phase of "The Triumph," so the account of Rousseau's life

---

[127] Shelley's phrase "stunning music" echoes Milton's "stunning sounds," which occurs during Satan's journey through the Abyss (*PL* II.952).

[128] Cf. *PL* X.298–305: *TL,* 439–441, seems to coalesce this description of the arched bridge between Earth and Hell with the traditional associations of the rainbow (*PL* XI.864–867; cf. Genesis ix.8–17).

is enriched by its numerous echoes of Saint-Preux's pursuit of Julie.
Rousseau's awakening to self-consciousness (308–339) has no exact
parallel in *La Nouvelle Héloïse,* inasmuch as the novel begins, not
with Saint-Preux's birth and childhood, but with the birth of his
passion for Julie. Shelley has, however, drawn certain features of
the setting from a later part of the novel. The description of the
"oblivious valley," with its gentle rivulet, echoes features of Julie's
garden at Clarens called "Elysium" (Part IV, Letter xi).

> En entrant dans ce prétendu verger, je fus frappé d'une agréable
> sensation de fraîcheur que d'obscurs ombrages, une verdure animée et
> vive, des fleurs éparses de tous côtés, un gazouillement d'eau courante
> et le chant de mille oiseaux portèrent à mon imagination du moins
> autant qu'à mes sens. . . . et il me sembloit d'être le premier mortel
> qui jamais eût pénétré dans ce désert.
>
> .   .   .   .
>
> Toutes ces petites routes étoient bordées et traversées d'une eau
> limpide et claire. . . . On voyoit des sources bouillonner et sortir de
> la terre, et quelquefois des canaux plus profonds dans lesquels l'eau
> calme et paisible réfléchissoit à l'œil les objets.
>
> .   .   .   .
>
> Nous descendîmes par mille détours au bas du verger, où je trouvai
> toute l'eau réunie en un joli ruisseau, coulant doucement entre deux
> rangs de vieux saules . . . [*Œuvres,* IX, 275, 280, 282].

In the key incident of Rousseau's experience he asks the "shape
all light" for knowledge, whereupon she offers him a drink from
the crystal glass; in the same way, when Saint-Preux begs Julie for
her love, she grants him in a grove at Clarens a kiss that sets him
on fire with an irresistible passion. Immediately afterward Saint-
Preux writes: "Qu'as-tu fait, ah! qu'as-tu fait, ma Julie? tu voulois
me récompenser, et tu m'as perdu. Je suis ivre, ou plutôt insensé.
Mes sens sont altérés, toutes mes facultés sont troublées par ce baiser
mortel." [129] Again and again throughout the novel Saint-Preux
alludes to the fatal effects of that kiss for which he had longed so
eagerly,[130] and in the relatively realistic novel Julie herself (no
longer simply the ideal that formed the germ of Rousseau's conception) felt the adverse influence of that kiss: "J'appris dans le
bosquet de Clarens que j'avois trop compté sur moi. . . . Un instant,
un seul instant embrasa les miens d'un feu que rien ne put éteindre;
et si ma volonté résistoit encore, dès-lors mon cœur fut cor-
rompu." [131]

[129] Part I, Letter xiv (*Œuvres,* VIII, 111).
[130] See, for example, Part VI, Letter vii (*Œuvres,* X, 258).
[131] Part III, Letter xviii (*Œuvres,* IX, 61).

Soon afterward Saint-Preux, inflamed with his desire for his ideal, Julie, is separated from her by a force beyond the control of both of them; arriving in Paris he writes: "J'entre avec une secrète horreur dans ce vaste désert du monde. Ce chaos ne m'offre qu'une solitude affreuse, où règne un morne silence."[132] But in the midst of the confused wilderness of Parisian society the image of Julie, her picture, recalls him to himself; as Saint-Preux was departing thence she had written to him:

> . . . un amour tel que le nôtre l'anime et la soutient tant qu'il brûle; sitôt qu'il s'éteint, elle tombe en langueur, et un cœur usé n'est plus propre à rien. . . . pourrois-tu te résoudre à traîner sur la terre l'insipide vie d'un homme ordinaire, après avoir goûté tous les transports qui peuvent ravir une âme humaine? . . . tu ne chercheras point l'amour, mais les plaisirs; tu les goûteras séparés de lui, et ne les pourras reconnoître. . . . la tristesse et l'ennui t'accableront au sein des amusements frivoles; le souvenir de nos premières amours te poursuivra malgré toi; mon image, cent fois plus belle que je ne fus jamais, viendra tout à coup te surprendre.[133]

And he confirms her prediction when he writes,

> Je crois, en le voyant, te revoir encore; je crois me retrouver à ces moments délicieux dont le souvenir fait maintenant le malheur de ma vie, et que le ciel m'a donnés et ravis dans sa colère. Hélas! un instant me désabuse; toute la douleur de l'absence se ranime et s'aigrit en m'ôtant l'erreur qui l'a suspendue, et je suis comme ces malheureux dont on n'interrompt les tourments que pour les leur rendre plus sensibles.[134]

Rousseau in "The Triumph" finds himself in a similar state where his remembered vision of an agreeable delusion "glimmers, forever sought, forever lost" (431).

In "The Triumph" Rousseau noticed that the splendor of the victorious chariot flew "far before her" so that, unlike the light of the Sun, which casts shadows even in its diffused terrestrial state, the light from the chariot of earthly life permeated all society and "forbade/ Shadow to fall from leaf or stone" (443–445). The entire "crew," having lost their freedom, seemed to dance in that light like specks of dust within a sunbeam.[135] While Saint-Preux acclimates

---

[132] Part II, Letter xiv (Œuvres, VIII, 386). Cf. TL, 343–350.

[133] Part II, Letter xi (Œuvres, VIII, 377–378).

[134] Part II, Letter xxii (Œuvres, VIII, 468). Saint-Preux has earlier described vividly the beneficial influence of Julie's image: see the conclusion of Part II, Letter xvii (Œuvres, VIII, 428).

[135] Wasserman (The Subtler Language, p. 334) shows that Shelley uses the word "atom" to mean "one of the particles of dust which are rendered visible by light; a mote in the sunbeam" (OED): see Adonais, 179–180; Fragments

himself to life in Paris, he writes several long letters to Julie describing the frivolity and purposelessness of Parisian life and manners.[136] Rousseau in "The Triumph" also observes not only the generally enervating effect of the light from the car of beams but also the particular reactions to that influence. Some of that "crew" [137] played in flowers, content in the blind enjoyment of external nature, until the temporal chariot swept them into oblivion, because, unlike Marvell's suitor, they did not hear at their backs "time's wingèd chariot hurrying near" but were "forgetful of the chariot's swift advance." [138] Others, likewise not directly subservient to the chariot, "stood gazing till within the shade/ Of the great mountain its light left them dim" (451–452). As the speeding vanguard of line 453 makes clear, Rousseau's vision of human life (roughly equivalent to Saint-Preux's account in Part II of *Julie*) is the same one that the Poet viewed at the opening of his vision. The "maidens & youths" (149) become "others" who outspeed the chariot (453). The only group mentioned by Rousseau who were not described by the Poet are those who "stood gazing," and these perhaps include the Poet himself, a mere observer of the pageant. Still others make "circles around it like the clouds that swim/ Round the high moon in a bright sea of air," reflecting the values of the moment emitted by the inconstant, ever changing moonlight of time and reason. Finally, the "more" who "did follow, with exulting hymn,/ The chariot & the captives fettered there" are the same impotent followers whom the Poet imagined as cold and decrepit (164–175). "But all like bubbles on an eddying flood/ Fell into the same track at last & were/ Borne onward." A century

---

Written for *Hellas*, 20; *Epipsychidion*, 477–479, 505; *Scenes from the "Magico Prodigioso" of Calderon* III.167; "Ode to Heaven," 18. Cf. Lucretius, *De Rerum Natura* II.114–122; Milton, "Il Penseroso," 7–8, where, however, the image refers to "vain deluding joyes."

[136] For example, *Julie*, Part II, Letters xiv and xvii. Stawell (p. 128n) mentions these two letters of "the *Nouvelle Héloïse*" as analogues of *TL*, 486ff.

[137] Milton in *Paradise Lost* uses the word "crew" to refer to the fallen angels in Hell (I.51; V.879) and to the evil followers of Nimrod, the first tyrant (XII.38). The last lines of "The Triumph" repeatedly echo the diction and syntax of *Paradise Lost*. For example, *TL*, 447–460, enumerating the varied activities of the "crew" and *TL*, 486–516, cataloguing the types of shadows, partly parallel *PL* II.528–628, describing the diverse amusements and occupations of the devils as they orient and acclimate themselves in Hell (cf. *PL* II.546: "Others more milde" with *TL*, 505–506: "Others more/ Humble").

[138] Marvell's figure closely parallels the temporal aspect of Shelley's symbolic chariot (cf. *Adonais*, 234).

earlier Isaac Watts had used a similar image in one of his greatest hymns:

> Time like an ever-rolling stream,
>   Bears all its sons away;
> They fly forgotten, as a dream
>   Dies at the op'ning day.

But whereas Watts could depend upon "God, our help in ages past," to provide an eternal home for those whom Time thus destroyed, Shelley, for whom not only men but

> Worlds on worlds are rolling ever
>   From creation to decay,
> Like the bubbles on a river
>   Sparkling, bursting, borne away,[139]

for whom the world was but "false & fragile glass" (247), who in the "Ode to Heaven" had represented the voice of the Universe as scorning man's futile pretensions to greatness, and who believed that the deep truth was and must always remain imageless—Shelley needed courage of a higher order, a capacity for hope as infinite as that counseled by Demogorgon at the end of *Prometheus Unbound,* if he was to affirm the value of human moral endeavors.

Rousseau in "The Triumph" admits that, like the historical Rousseau or like Saint-Preux in *Julie,* he was not delayed by the innocent enjoyment of nature [140] or by a solitary life in the shadow of the great mountain (451–452, 462). (The last figure seems to represent the untried lives of those who, remaining under the shadow of the material barrier that separates the antenatal world from the realm of phenomenal incarnation, stand as spectators without actively engaging in the struggles of life and who, thus inexperienced and immature, are easy victims of the chariot's influence.) Nor was he restrained by "the falling stream's Lethean song" of

---

[139] *Hellas,* 197–200.

[140] According to Matthews the image at 461 is "precisely pointed, because Rousseau was a botanist" ("On Shelley's *TL,*" p. 115), but one cannot appreciate the biographical implications without recalling that Rousseau had no interest in botany as a young man, acquiring that enthusiasm only after retiring from the world (see *Confessions,* Book V: "n'ayant alors aucune idée de la botanique, je l'avois prise en une sorte de mépris et même de dégoût; je ne la regardois que comme une étude d'apothicaire" [*Œuvres,* XV, 318]). Shelley's lines derive symbolic overtones from the gardens of Eden, Adonis, and the garden Elysium at Clarens in *Julie,* and, finally, from the "botanizing" of the real Jean-Jacques *after* his withdrawal from the world.
The syntax of *TL,* 461–465, is Miltonic; cf. *PL* IX.41ff.

childhood innocence nor, like the Youth of *Alastor,* by a vain pursuit of "the phantom of that early form" that had enchanted him. Instead, he, like Saint-Preux, plunged "among/ The thickest billows of the living storm" and bared his bosom to the atmosphere of "that cold light" (465–468).[141]

But, Rousseau relates, before he had, in the course of temporal life, ascended the steep of middle age, he beheld a wonder worthy of the rhyme of Dante,[142] whom Love had "led serene" from the "lowest depths of Hell/ Through every Paradise & through all glory" and who had told in words of "hate" (in the *Inferno*) and "awe" (in the *Paradiso*) "how all things are transfigured, except Love."[143] "For," continues Rousseau, "the world," which is "deaf as is a sea which wrath makes hoary," cannot hear the music of Venus, the Third Sphere, "whose light is melody to lovers" (477–479).[144] This extended reference to Dante seems to presage the method of human salvation from the inferno of the Poet's vision as well as from Rousseau's. The literary antecedents of "The Triumph"—the *Trionfi,* the *Commedia, Comus, Paradise Lost, Julie*—end in the protagonist's salvation through love—human

---

[141] "Enfin me voilà tout-à-fait dans le torrent" (Saint-Preux in Paris to Julie, Part II, Letter xvii [*Œuvres,* VIII, 409]).

[142] Stopford Brooke first suggested that the "opposing steep" (470) was "the steep of middle age" (*Poems from Shelley,* p. lviii).

The phrase "Behold a wonder!" occurs at *Paradise Lost* I.777, where Milton describes a similar phenomenon—the flight of Satan's legions and their transformation into tiny, elf-like shapes. A cognate phrase occurs at *PL* XI.733 ("loe a wonder strange!") when Adam and Michael witness the parade of animals entering Noah's ark. The appropriateness of these associations to Shelley's context is obvious. Cf. also Keats's *Endymion* I.893–894.

[143] See "To Death," 18–19: "everything, but Love, destroyed/ Must perish with its kindred clay" (*P.W.,* p. 841); "Fragment: *Amor Aeternus,*" 4–6: "But love, though misdirected, is among/ The things which are immortal, and surpass/ All that frail stuff which will be—or which was" (*P.W.,* p. 549); *Prometheus* II.iv.117–120:

> For what would it avail to bid thee gaze
> On the revolving world? What to bid speak
> Fate, Time, Occasion, Chance, and Change? To these
> All things are subject but eternal Love.

[144] Locock identifies the "sphere" of *TL,* 479, with the Third Heaven, sphere of Venus. Bradley notes that "the Third Heaven, that of Venus . . . according to the astronomy followed by Dante, is the farthest point reached by the shadow of the earth" (p. 445), and he cites the First Canzone of the *Convivio* and *Paradiso* IX.118. Shelley's celebration of Venus, the symbol of love, as the highest goal of man's aspiration obviously depends on a related conception: man cannot know the Sun, the Fourth Sphere, in itself: the Third Sphere is as far into the Heavens as human perception can penetrate, and, therefore, love must remain the guiding star of human activity.

love, or divine love, or both in conjunction, and all of Shelley's earlier works had affirmed the supremacy of love over external circumstance (though some like *Alastor* and *Epipsychidion* had also warned that it might blind the heart of the lover).

Rousseau's allusion to Dante is thematically akin to the progress of Saint-Preux in *Julie,* who, after giving himself over to excesses first in his love for Julie and later in his life among the Parisians, undergoes a purgatorial voyage around the world filled with hardships and then returns to Clarens, scene of his initial passion, where he learns to subject his love to duty. Saint-Preux after passing a number of tests of his virtue (successfully, though as by fire) is admitted first to the garden of *Elysium,* and later to the fellowship of the *Apollo,* an intimate upper dining room in which selected company eat together as equals on special occasions. To Shelley, for whom Apollo and the Sun symbolized the Deity, the significance of Julie's names for her garden and her private dining room could have called forth these associations: *Elysium,* the earthly paradise, symbolized an unfallen natural world; the *Apollo,* with its common table, symbolized a eucharistic preview of the salvation of those who love. Whether or not Rousseau intended that any such significance should be attached to *Elysium* or *Apollo,* these names strike the reader as notably symbolic in otherwise realistic passages of the novel. Shelley, in the passage describing "fountains whose melodious dew/ Out of their mossy cells forever burst" (67–72), had alluded to an earthly garden-paradise, and in the fate of the "sacred few," who had "fled back like eagles to their native noon" (128–137), he implied that some form of super-mundane salvation awaited the great benefactors of humanity.

Following the reference to Dante, Rousseau describes the wonder he encountered: The grove (symbol of the world) grew grey with phantoms, dim forms that seemed to blot out the sun like "a flock of vampire-bats." The source of this effect (though not of the vampire-bat simile) is, as Paul Turner has demonstrated, Lucretius' *De Rerum Natura* (IV.46ff.) where *simulacra* represent the ideas, superstitions, and passions of the men who give them off.[145] In Shelley's version, some seminal concepts beget others "yet unlike themselves" (487–489); some ideas, the products of imaginative minds, eagle spirits, "were lost in the white blaze," returning to the eternal fountain whence they came (489–490); others, folk-super-

---

[145] "Shelley and Lucretius," *RES,* N.S., X (August 1959), 269–282.

stitions, peopled the fields and streams like elves, products of a simple credulity (490–492); still others, more pernicious like apes [146] or vultures, were the shibboleths of monarchies and religious hierarchies that gave imperial power ostensibly to a baby or an idiot [147] but actually to the demonic concepts that rule men's minds (495–505). Others, "like falcons," were used by petty tyrants to rule those under their authority (505–507), or "like small gnats & flies," swarmed about the minds of "lawyer, statesman, priest & theorist," [148] perhaps partly serving their interests and partly clouding their minds (508–510). Finally,

> ". . . Others like discoloured flakes of snow
> On fairest bosoms & the sunniest hair
> Fell, and were melted by the youthful glow
>
> "Which they extinguished; for like tears, they were
> A veil to those from whose faint lids they rained
> In drops of sorrow.—"
>
> 511–516

Although these lines are difficult, certain aspects of the symbolism seem clear: The sufferers, those of "the fairest bosoms & the sunniest hair," are youthful idealists like the young Rousseau—or the young Shelley; the simile comparing the ideas to "discoloured flakes of snow" implies that the concepts, though perhaps pure in their original state, were cold and lifeless (associated with Reason rather than Imagination?) and that the terrestrial atmosphere besmirched them. The passage says, essentially, that phenomenal ideals, further corrupted by the world's slow stain into compromises, fall upon the idealist, cooling and dampening his imaginative ardor even as its fire melts these objections that stand in his way. Melted, the snowflakes become tears symbolic of the frustrations and disappointments that veil the world from the disillusioned idealist.

[146] See *Proposals for an Association of Philanthropists* (1812). Shelley wrote of those who enjoyed the privileges of "the minister, the peer, or the bishop" that "permitting them to reassume the degraded and vilified title of man would preclude the necessity of mystery and deception, would bestow on them a title more ennobling and a dignity which, though it would be without the gravity of an ape, would possess the ease and consistency of a man" (*Prose*, pp. 63–64).

[147] Line 499 may allude to the career of George III, who began his reign before his majority (1760) and ended it (1811–20) in incurable madness.

[148] See *Queen Mab* IV.168–169: "War is the statesman's game, the priest's delight,/ The lawyer's jest, the hired assassin's trade." Shelley's use of "theorist" in "The Triumph" points up his lifelong distrust of abstractions and generalities when compared with the sufferings of living human beings, a distrust that he shared with other liberals of his time who had to struggle against the rationalizations of Paley, the Malthusians, and the laissez-faire economists.

In "The Runaway," which tells of a colt frightened by its first encounter with snow, Robert Frost implies that any younger generation perturbed by the troubles of life should be told, "Sakes, it's only weather." Shelley's simile of falling snow has something of Frost's tone; had Shelley wished to picture these idealists undergoing special persecution, he would have chosen a symbol of less universal experience. The veil of tears prevents these disillusioned idealists from seeing their experiences in a proper perspective and renders them incapable of judging the phenomenal world. Like the Poet, they are likely to cry out that good and the means of good are irreconcilable and, in despair, either to turn their backs on life in misanthropy or else actively to seek death. Vainly they deplore ills, which, if ills, can find no cure from them (*TL*, 224–234, 327–330).

Rousseau gradually "became aware/ Of whence those forms proceeded":

> "From every form the beauty slowly waned,
>
> "From every firmest limb & fairest face
> The strength & freshness fell like dust, & left
> The action & the shape without the grace
>
> "Of life. . . ."
>
> 516–523

The last phrase may provide a clue to the poem's unanswered final question, "Then, what is Life?" As strength and freshness fall from the forms and countenances of all men and they "decay/ Like corpses in a charnel," as "fear and grief/ Convulse [them] and consume [them] day by day," [149] their actions and their shapes were left "without the grace/ Of life." If life possesses grace that it is tragedy to lose, then *life* must have value and not be simply sound and fury signifying nothing. Life distorted, perverted, compromised into hypocrisy, enslaved by self-seeking power, by the meretricious tinsel of worldly gain, by the chains of custom, wasted by a vain pursuit of shadows—such a life is no life at all, but is, as the entire poem represents it, a living death, and such is the life of most men, even those who begin with the ardor and fire of youthful idealism:

> ". . . the marble brow of youth was cleft
> With care, and in the eyes where once hope shone
> Desire like a lioness bereft
>
> "Of its last cub, glared ere it died. . . ."
>
> 523–526

[149] *Adonais*, 348–350.

The shadows that fell away were "numerous as the dead leaves blown/ In Autumn evening from a poplar tree" (528–529), the wind-leaf simile here integrating the seasonal and daily cycles. Each shadow or mask at first resembled "himself"—the person from whom it fell ("each one," 526)—and "these shadows" (528) also were like "each other" [150] until they were distorted, like "clouds moulded by the casual air," by the "car's creative ray" into "all the busy phantoms that were there" in the same way the "sun shapes the clouds," that is, by striking their substance with light which the clouds reflect, thus giving them "shape" to the observer.

Finally, some "weary of the ghastly dance," especially those who had engaged passionately in the pursuit of worldly values, withdrew from the meaningless pageant "and fell, as I have fallen by the way side." This passage resembles another passage from *Julie:*

> A mesure qu'on avance en âge, tous les sentiments se concentrent; on perd tous les jours quelque chose de ce qui nous fut cher, et l'on ne le remplace plus. On meurt ainsi par degrés, jusqu'à ce que, n'aimant enfin que soi-même, on ait cessé de sentir et de vivre avant de cesser d'exister. Mais un cœur sensible se défend de toute sa force contre cette mort anticipée; quand le froid commence aux extrémités, il rassemble autour de lui toute sa chaleur naturelle; plus il perd, plus il s'attache à ce qui lui reste, et il tient pour ainsi dire au dernier objet par les liens de tous les autres.
>
> Voilà ce qu'il me semble éprouver déjà, quoique jeune encore. Ah! ma chère, mon pauvre cœur a tant aimé! il s'est épuisé de si bonne heure, qu'il vieillit avant le temps.[151]

The historical Rousseau withdrew from the dance of Parisian life to the retreat of the Hermitage and tried to gather about him those whom he dearly loved. Shelley had withdrawn from the dance of social life even in England and had more recently left the Pisan circle for Casa Magni. In some such withdrawal as this, not from physical life but from "the world, the flesh, and the devil," Rousseau (already said to be weary [194–198]) dropped exhausted and let that car with its attendant followers roll onward.

When the Poet asks the question, "Then, what is Life?" Rousseau,

---

[150] The syntax of *TL*, 530, is Miltonic: cf. *PL* II.421–422. Locock, who writes in a note to *Revolt* III.xiv (1232–33) that "the use of a plural verb with a technically singular . . . subject is not uncommon in Shelley," cites (besides *TL*, 530) *Queen Mab* VIII.232; *Revolt*, 2151; *Prince Athanase*, 287; "Euganean Hills," 40–43; *Homer's Hymn to Venus*, 1–7; *Epipsychidion*, 473; *Adonais*, 484.

[151] Part IV, Letter i (*Œuvres*, IX, 154–155). The words are those of Julie, not Saint-Preux, but Rousseau divided his own thoughts and desires among the characters of the novel in the interest of realism and gave the wisest and best of his ideas and sentiments to Julie herself.

gazing after the receding chariot, begins, "Happy those for whom
the fold/ Of." The rest is silence, but Matthews' correction of the
final word in line 544 from "gold" to "fold" provides a slight, rather
ambiguous clue to the continuation of this thought, if not of the
poem as a whole. In his late poetry Shelley more and more frequently drew upon the Christian metaphor of the sheepfold as a
symbol of human salvation, usually using in conjunction the symbol
of Venus as Hesperus, the evening star, which, appearing when
the shepherd led his sheep to the fold at the end of the day, Milton
had called the "folding-star." [152] The symbol first appears in *The
Witch of Atlas* in an essentially decorative figure ("Ten times the
Mother of the Months had bent/ Her bow beside the folding-star"
[73–74]), but in *Epipsychidion* and *Hellas* the image takes on important symbolic associations. In the Comet-Tempest passage of
Epipsychidion after the Poet has said to the Comet, "Oh, float into
our azure heaven again!" he goes on to say: "Be there love's folding-
star at thy return" (373–374). In *Hellas* the Christian overtones are
strengthened because in the first use, the passage echoes Milton's
Nativity Ode: "The Powers of earth and air/ Fled from the folding-star of Bethlehem" (*Hellas*, 230–231); there is regret that hills,
seas, and streams were "dispeopled of their dreams," the pagan
deities ("Their waters turned to blood, their dew to tears,/ Wailed
for the golden years" [235–238]), but by the end of the poem, with
the crushing of the Greek rebellion, "Freedom and Peace" must

> . . . flee far
> To a sunnier strand,
> And follow Love's folding-star
> To the Evening land!
> 1027–30

Both the fragmentary Prologue and the end of *Hellas* show that
Christ, representing self-giving love, provides the positive moral
standard and that, therefore, the echo of Milton in the chorus
"Worlds on worlds are rolling ever" is not ironic.[153] Thus Rousseau's declaration beginning "Happy those for whom the fold"
might have continued with an affirmative use of "fold" as the sheepfold into which were gathered followers of the "folding-star" of
Love.

Such speculations, though intriguing, do not carry one far toward an objective comprehension of the poem. What one can

---

[152] "The Star that bids the Shepherd fold," *Comus*, 93.
[153] I. A. Richards pointed out this echo in *Principles of Literary Criticism*,
p. 216.

know about Shelley's theme in "The Triumph of Life" is embodied in the fragment as a whole and in the analogies between this poetic fragment, Shelley's other poems, and his chief models for "The Triumph." Everywhere in "The Triumph" the dark side of human experience is balanced by positive alternatives. Where men wasted their lives struggling meaninglessly along the dusty road, there were fountains of "melodious dew" and "grassy paths, & wood lawns," and thus the faint and thirsting existence was "serious folly" (66–73); whereas some mighty men were chained to the Car of Life, "the sacred few," faced by the same obstacles from within and without, had overcome Necessity to become the saving remnant of humanity. In the tale of his own experience Rousseau does not preach the irreconcilability of "power" and "will," only the great difficulty of maintaining one's integrity in a universe in which a vision of the Ideal makes one dissatisfied with the actual. But Dante in the *Commedia* had told how love could lead man through Hell and Purgatory to Paradise; Petrarch in the *Trionfi* had asserted the triumph of Eternity over all the limitations of man's phenomenal experience; Milton in *Comus* had declared that if one refrains from satisfying his thirst—"the drouth of *Phoebus*"—with any mundane, "orient liquor" but aspires by due steps to reach the Palace of Eternity, he will be guided by a guardian spirit who, "swift as the Sparkle of a glancing Star," will give him safe convoy; J. J. Rousseau in *Julie* had shown how Saint-Preux's love for the Ideal, which in its initial stages overcame his sense of proportion and dedication to duty, in the end redeems him. Lord Bomston writes to Saint-Preux: "Savez-vous ce qui vous a fait aimer toujours la vertu? Elle a pris à vos yeux la figure de cette femme adorable qui la représente si bien, et il seroit difficile qu'une si chère image vous en laissât perdre le goût." [154] And Julie herself in a letter to Claire articulates Rousseau's final judgment of love: "L'amour en lui-même est-il un crime? N'est-il pas la plus pur ainsi que le plus doux penchant de la nature? n'a-t-il pas une fin bonne et louable? ne dédaigne-t-il pas les âmes basses et rampantes? n'anime-t-il pas les âmes grandes et fortes? n'ennoblit-il pas tous leurs sentiments? ne double-t-il pas leur être? ne les élève-t-il pas au-dessus d'elles-mêmes?" [155]

The Rousseau of "The Triumph of Life" had reached the point in his life story at which (if it continued to parallel Saint-Preux's

[154] Part V, Letter i (*Œuvres*, X, 5–6).
[155] Part V, Letter xiii (*Œuvres*, X, 185).

experience) he would begin to feel the redeeming force of the love that had nearly destroyed him. Shelley recognized the danger of pursuing the Ideal; as he wrote to John Gisborne: "I think one is always in love with something or other; the error, and I confess it is not easy for spirits cased in flesh and blood to avoid it, consists in seeking in a mortal image the likeness of what is perhaps eternal" (Julian, X, 401). But he also felt that

> Perhaps all discontent with the *less* (to use a Platonic sophism) supposes the sense of a just claim to the *greater,* and that we admirers of Faust are in the right road to Paradise. Such a supposition is not more absurd, and is certainly less demoniacal than that of Wordsworth, where he says—
>
>
>
> This earth,
> Which is the world of all of us, and where
> *We find our happiness, or not at all.*
>
>
>
> Julian, X, 371

The problem for Shelley, as for all idealists, was to maintain his vision of the Ideal while living effectively within the limitations of the sublunary, actual world. A few days earlier, Shelley had written to Claire Clairmont:

> Some of yours & of my evils are in common, and I am therefore in a certain degree a judge. If you would take my advice you would give up this idle pursuit after shadows, & temper yourself to the season; seek in the daily & affectionate intercourse of friends a respite from these perpetual & irritating projects. Live from day to day, attend to your health, cultivate literature & liberal ideas to a certain extent, & expect that from time & change which no exertions of your own can give you [Julian, X, 365–366; corrected from Jones, II, 400].

He seems to have made these admonitions the guide of his own conduct during his last days at Casa Magni—or did so as much as his ethical imagination would permit, for there he did write "The Triumph of Life."

As I have attempted to show elsewhere [156] Shelley's final withdrawal from attempts to reform the world resulted from the relative failure of his work to reach and influence the public. A number of remarks in his late letters indicate this:

> . . . pray tell me if Ollier has published *Hellas,* and what effect was produced by Adonais. My faculties are shaken to atoms, and torpid. I can write nothing; and if Adonais had no success, and excited no interest what incentive can I have to write? [To Leigh Hunt, 25 January 1822; Julian, X, 351].

[156] "Shelley's 'The Triumph of Life': The Biographical Problem," *PMLA,* LXXVIII (December 1963), 548–549.

Indeed I have written nothing for this last two months. . . . What motives have I to write—I *had* motives—and I thank the god of my own heart they were totally different from those of the other apes of humanity who make mouths in the glass of the time—but what are *those* motives now? [To Leigh Hunt, 2 March 1822; Julian, X, 362; corrected from Jones, II, 394].

I write little now. It is impossible to compose except under the strong excitement of an assurance of finding sympathy in what you write. Imagine Demosthenes reciting a Philippic to the waves of the Atlantic! [To John Gisborne, 18 June 1822; Julian, X, 403–404].

"The Triumph of Life" reflects, however, Shelley's continuing refusal to immerse himself completely in the pleasures of the moment. When he wrote to John Gisborne (18 June 1822), "if the past and the future could be obliterated, the present would content me so well that I could say with Faust to the passing moment, 'Remain, thou, thou are so beautiful'" (Julian, X, 403), he was, as in the "Lines Written in the Bay of Lerici," [157] positing an impossibility: "if the past and the future could be obliterated," if men were angels, if the laws of cause and effect were suspended, if moral considerations and the woes of the entire suffering earth were of no concern to Shelley—then he could wish the present moment of innocent pleasure an eternity. But the still, sad music of humanity reverberating in his soul would not let him completely temper himself to the season, subdue himself to the element that surrounded him, and contribute to the evils he lamented by his hypocrisy.[158]

Such a state of mind provided, perhaps, the motivation for Shelley's final poetic effort, and I have said much already about its meaning and implications. But ideas, according to Shelley's poetic theory, do not become poetry until they are clothed in memorable images and harmonious sounds.[159] "The Triumph of Life" exhibits the poetic art of Shelley at its best not because it differs thematically from his earlier writings, but because—as in "Mont Blanc," "Lines Written Among the Euganean Hills," *Prometheus Unbound, Adonais,* and a handful of the late lyrics— he embodied his vision in striking imagery, coherent symbolism, and tightly woven, melodious verse. Even in its imperfect and fragmentary state "The Triumph" exhibits a high degree of stylistic integrity.

157 See "Biographical Problem," p. 538.
158 See Shelley to Horace Smith, 29 June 1822; Julian, X, 410.
159 Paragraph seven of *A Defence of Poetry, Prose,* p. 280.

CHAPTER THREE

STYLE

PROSODY

Shelley has been acclaimed a master of poetic music, the subtle rhythms of some of his late lyrics being the envy of later nineteenth-century poets. As Milton Wilson has shown, Shelley's prosodic finesse was earned through hard labor, his early efforts in each metrical form paving the way for the stylistic maturity of later work in the same medium: the blank verse of *Queen Mab* for *Alastor* and *Prometheus Unbound,* the Spenserian stanzas of *The Revolt of Islam* for *Adonais,* the early lyrics up through those in *Prometheus* for the choruses in *Hellas* and the lyrics of 1821–22.[1] Shelley's apprenticeship in *terza rima* included the fragmentary "Prince Athanase" (1817), "Ode to the West Wind" (1819), "The Tower of Famine" (1820), the uncompleted "The Woodman and the Nightingale" (?1821),[2] a few poetic fragments that may have been intended to continue in *terza rima,*[3] and translations from Dante's *Inferno* and *Purgatorio* (*P.W.*, pp. 727–731). In addition, of course, many of Shelley's stanzaic poems involve a partially interlocking rhyme-scheme in iambic pentameter verse. *Terza rima* is so difficult to maintain in English, however, that even with this experience Shelley, as the manuscript of "The Triumph" shows, was often hard put to continue the interlocking rhyme without interruption.[4]

Those knowledgeable in Italian and in Dante's versification have contrasted Shelley's *terza rima* with that of the Florentine. Whereas

---

[1] *Shelley's Later Poetry*, pp. 1–19.

[2] *P.W.*, pp. 562–564. See Neville Rogers, *Shelley at Work*, p. 263.

[3] See, for example, *P.W.*, pp. 633, 659.

[4] Dante, of course, divided the *Commedia* into cantos of approximately 130 to 148 lines each.

Dante tends to make the tercet a closed unit like the couplet of Pope, Shelley emphasizes the interweaving of rhymes to develop long periods, the meaning rushing breathlessly from tercet to tercet. In the opening lines (which, in fair copy, are more highly polished than later parts of the poem), the break between the first and second tercets separates the noun "mask" from a necessary modifier ("Of darkness") and from its verb ("fell"). The second tercet again ends with a noun separated from its modifying phrase ("birth/ Of light"). The end of the third tercet divides verb ("unclose") from direct object ("eyelids"); that of the fourth, subject ("incense") from verb ("Burned"); the fifth, auxiliary verb ("did") and one element of a compound subject ("Continent") from the main verb "rise") and from the parallel subjects ("Isle, Ocean, & all things"). Apart from the end of the introductory section (39–40), the first full stop at the end of a tercet appears at line 61, and most of the early tercets are left just as incomplete in meaning as the first five. That this lack of end-stopped tercets was intentional is evident, because most of the full stops do come at the ends of lines, almost invariably the first or second line of a tercet.[5] Whenever Shelley wanted to mark off major breaks within the poem, he could, in the early lines at least, manage to do so at the end of a tercet (39, 73, 106, 175). Both in the rejected openings and in the fair-copy version the syntactical units often counterpoint the *terza rima*'s iambic pentameter and recurring rhymes.

Such a modification of traditional form is not unusual among the Romantic poets, for they could hardly follow slavishly in the steps of their eighteenth-century predecessors, who had perfected the correlation of the formal pattern and the syntactical unit. The young Keats declaimed against Pope and his rocking-horse metrics,[6] but Shelley had a more mature sense of the relation of his work to that of his great predecessors. To Byron, who was bitter toward Keats (now dead) for his attack on Pope, Shelley wrote: "I did not know that Keats had attacked Pope; I had heard that Bowles had done so, and that you had most severely chastised him therefor. Pope, it seems, has been selected as the pivot of a dispute in taste, on which, until I understand it, I must profess myself neuter. I certainly do not think Pope, or *any* writer, a fit model for any succeeding writer; if he, or they should be determined to be so, it

---

5 E.g., lines 4, 8, 20, 42, 51, 59, 65.

6 "Sleep and Poetry," 181–187; see also *The Letters of John Keats: 1814–1821*, ed. Hyder Rollins, I, 141.

would all come to a question as to under *what forms* mediocrity should perpetually reproduce itself; for true genius vindicates to itself an exemption from all regard to whatever has gone before. . . ." [7]

Beyond differences between the English and Italian languages and beyond what may have been Shelley's desire to avoid imitating the stylistic peculiarities of Dante or of the English neoclassicists, the theme and development of "The Triumph of Life" required prosodic treatment quite different from the *Commedia*. The first word ("Swift"), the first verbal ("hastening"), and the first verb ("sprang") set a rapid pace which, though broken in the immediately succeeding lines (which describe the slower response of terrestrial creatures to the swift advent of their celestial father [8]), resumes with the vision of the rushing chariot and its dancing worshipers. Shelley's basic stylistic problem was to reinforce his meaning through the prosody without violating the basic pattern of his adopted metrical form; he had to speed up the lines without falling into anapestic or dactylic rhythms and without resorting to internal rhymes (as he had in "The Cloud" to achieve a similar sense of speed). He relied, therefore, on subtler manipulations of varied weight of accent, pauses within lines, and patterned assonance to achieve this desired end.

George Young rightly distinguishes metrical *stress* from both verbal *accent* (the emphasis given to one or more syllables of an isolated multisyllabic word) and sentence *emphasis*.[9] Young declares that "within a foot verse stress must not contravene accent" but, he continues, "not that every accented syllable must be stressed, nor that every stress must find some syllable with an accent. It is enough if in the same word the accented syllable is not left unstressed, while one unaccented is stressed." The relation between *stress* of the verse and rhetorical *emphasis* within a sentence is somewhat more difficult to determine, since the poet's intended metrical stress is usually deduced in part through analysis of his rhetorical intention, but there are certain obvious cases where a poet's metrical stress will counterpoint his rhetorical emphasis.

It is not surprising that Shelley, admiring Milton more than any other English poet, should have adopted some of Milton's freedom

---

[7] 4 May 1821 (Julian, X, 265–266). See also Julian, X, 285, 371.

[8] E.g., "unclose/ Their trembling eyelids" (9–10), "Burned slow" (13).

[9] *An English Prosody on Inductive Lines*, pp. 6–8.

in the use of the five-stress line.[10] One can come to grips with the metrics of "The Triumph" most easily by analyzing selected passages according to the interrelations of *accent, emphasis,* and *stress.* Since, as Young remarks, "monosyllables can have no accent" (p. 7), and since monosyllables predominate in "The Triumph," one can simplify the process by scanning the first sentence of "The Triumph" for both *accent* and *emphasis* in one operation (an acute accent mark ['] indicates a syllable of heavy accent, or emphasis, a grave mark ['] denotes a secondary accent, or emphasis, and an [x] identifies an unaccented, unemphasized syllable):

> Swift as a spirit hastening to his task
> Of glory & of good, the Sun sprang forth
> Rejoicing in his splendour, & the mask
> Of darkness fell from the awakened Earth.

In none of these lines are there five syllables of heavy accent and emphasis; but rather three in line 3 and four in each of the other three lines. When a mind familiar with the metrical norm of English decasyllabic verse imposes the iambic pattern upon Shelley's lines, there is a very slight shift in the sound; "forth" (2), which receives secondary emphasis before the participle, is reinforced by its position in the line and receives the primary *stress,* in turn reducing the weight of "sprang" to a secondary stress: "the Sun sprang forth." The "&" in line 3 would, likewise, profit from the combined weight of its position following a pause (indicated by Shelley's comma) and its position in the line to receive at least a secondary stress but probably a primary one; line 3 would then be read: "Rejoicing in his splendour, & the mask," raising the number of stresses to four as in the other three lines. In the first line, "to" could receive a secondary stress. There are no other words in these lines that can possibly be stressed if the sentence is to be read with meaning; for example, "from" in line 4 could conceivably receive emphasis if it did not immediately follow "fell," which is both heavily stressed and emphasized. The effect of extreme swiftness of these opening lines is achieved by the simple expedient of reducing the number of stresses from five to four per line, while maintaining the effect of iambic pentameter by strictly observing the decasyllabic norm and by stressing the final syllable in each line.

---

[10] One should recall that G. M. Hopkins based his "Counterpoint Rhythm" in part on Milton's practice in the choruses of *Samson Agonistes.* See *Poems of Gerard Manley Hopkins,* ed. W. H. Gardner, 3rd ed., p. 7.

Shelley varied the number of stresses to create quite different effects. A poet must state his metrical norm early in the poem so that there can arise in the reader's mind a pattern of expectancy against which all variations will be measured. Though Shelley took advantage of the traditional expectations that ten-syllable lines arouse in readers of English poetry to speed up his verse in the opening lines of "The Triumph," he could maintain the effectiveness of his verse only by establishing the norm within his poem as well. This he does in the remaining lines of the introduction (5–40). For example, after one has balanced verbal accent, rhetorical emphasis, and metrical stress, lines 5 to 8 scan as follows:

> The smokeless altars of the mountain snows   5
>   Flamed above crimson clouds, & at the birth
> Of light, the Ocean's orison arose
>   To which the birds tempered their matin lay.

Line 5 contains only four stresses, but though there is no stress on the sixth syllable (some readers might give "of" a secondary stress), the other stresses are where one would expect them in regular iambic pentameter verse. Lines 6 and 8 contain five primary stresses apiece, one foot being reversed in each line; line 7 is perfectly regular except for the lighter secondary stress in "orison." Lines 9–20 scan thus:

> All flowers in field or forest which unclose
>   Their trembling eyelids to the kiss of day,   10
> Swinging their censers in the element,
>   With orient incense lit by the new ray
> Burned slow & inconsumably, & sent
>   Their odorous sighs up to the smiling air,
> And in succession due, did Continent,   15
>   Isle, Ocean, & all things that in them wear
> The form & character of mortal mould
>   Rise as the Sun their father rose, to bear
> Their portion of the toil which he of old
>   Took as his own & then imposed on them;   20

Lines 9 and 10 maintain the generally regular pattern of stress established in the previous sentence; line 11, containing two lighter stresses, pushes the stress forward to give almost the effect of dactyls, an impression that supports the "swinging" decribed by the line. But Shelley's metrical finesse shows to best advantage in lines 12 and 13. Here the flowers, in contrast to the swift, hastening, springing Sun of lines 1–4, "burned slow & inconsumably." If Shelley intended that sound should reinforce meaning, these lines must move slowly. As the scansion of these lines shows, rhetorical emphasis requires that the last two syllables in line 12 be stressed, and Shelley follows this by placing two important monosyllables at the beginning of line 13; two preceding unstressed syllables ("by the") almost demand that "new" be given a full stress, and "Burned," occupying a weak position in the iambic pattern, is more important to the meaning than "slow." Besides these four consecutive stresses, Shelley has added an eleventh syllable to line 12 (in "orient"), has placed five reasonably heavy stresses in line 13, and has arranged his syntax and emphasis to produce a long pause at the end of line 12 and a short pause after "inconsumably" in line 13. After these two heavy lines, the verse returns to fairly regular iambic pentameter through line 20.

Lines 22–24 repeat the effects of alternating speed and slowness. One must pronounce the line describing the Poet's nervous insomnia relatively quickly, the syntax hurrying one on without a pause at the end of the line, which has only four primary stresses: "Had képt as wákefúl as the stars that gém/ The cóne of níght." But, the next two lines, which tell of the Poet being overcome with drowsiness and preparing to sleep, move slowly:

> The cóne of níght, now they were laíd asléep,
> Strétched my faint límbs beneath the hóary stém.

Besides two full pauses, line 23 contains at least five primary stresses and a secondary one: "now" must be stressed after the pause and emphasized for meaning, while the other words in the adverbial clause are important syntactically.

Although it is dangerous to pursue this study into later sections of the poem that Shelley himself did not revise, let us examine a few lines where the text is not open to much question:

> The wíld dánce máddens in the ván, & those   138
> Who leád it, fléet as shádows on the gréen,
> Outspéed the cháriot & without repóse   140
> Míx with eách óther in tempéstuóus méasure

Compare, with the rapid dance of the maidens and youths, these lines:

> Is spént upon the désert shóre.—Behínd   164
> Old mèn, and wómen fóully disárrayed
> Sháke their gréy haír in the insúlting wínd. . . .

Or compare these,

> Without the opportunity which bóre
> Hím ón íts eágle's píniŏn tŏ thĕ péak
>   221–222

with these:

> Frŏm whìch ă thóusañd clímbĕrs háve bĕfóre
> Fáll'n ăs Năpóleŏn féll."—Ì félt mў chéek
> Áltĕr tŏ seé thĕ greát fórm páss ăwaý
>   Whŏse grásp hăd léft thĕ gíant wórld sŏ wéak
> Thăt évĕrý pígmў kícked ĭt ăs ĭt laý—
>   223–227

The fluid movement of lines 221–222, containing at most four firm
stresses apiece, gives place to the heavily stressed, regular, patterned
march of the giant world enchained by pygmy tyrants. From this
point the lines become more and more weighted with emphases
that demand equal pronunciation with regularly stressed syllables:

> Ănd múch Ì'grieved tŏ thínk hòw pówer ěˣ wíll
> Iñ óppósítiŏn rúle òur mórtăl dáy—
>   Ănd whý Gód máde îrrécŏncílăblè
> Goód ěˣ thĕ meáns ŏf goód. . . .
>   228–231

Shelley has secured an additional primary stress in line 230 by
placing "God" between two words that also demand stresses and an
extra secondary stress by employing "-able" as the rhyme syllable.
(This weak rhyme is, in turn, supported by being between the strong
"will" and "fill" in the rhyme-pattern.)[11]
Although Shelley uses the tercet as a plastic, nonrestrictive unit,
and although he modulates the iambic pentameter norm, speeding
or slowing it to support the meaning of the lines, by conforming to
the ten-syllable line and to masculine rhymes he prevents the verse
of "The Triumph" from losing either its firmness or energy. Not
only are there no feminine rhymes in the forty-eight fair-copy lines,
but of the 548 lines in the fragment, only thirty-nine lines have
feminine endings.[12] There is only one imperfect rhyme in the first
forty-eight lines ("forth / Earth / birth"—lines 2, 4, 6), and though
later in the draft imperfect rhymes abound, in all but one instance
(290, 292, 294) at least two of the three words rhyme exactly.
Of the eight instances of *rime riche* (an exact repetition of the
phonetic syllable) in "The Triumph" some may be attributed to

11 Cf. lines 228–30–32.
12 The feminine rhymes are: 120–2–4; 141–3–5; 156–58–60; 201–3–5; 255–7–9;
261–3–5; 290–2–4; 359–61–63; 362–4–6; 416–18–20; 437–39–41; 473–5–7; 479–81–83.

Shelley's difficulties in developing his poem within the limitations of the *terza rima* pattern (e.g., "light / chrysolite" [412, 414] and "clime / climb" [467, 469]), but some instances are not accidental. In the long simile that compares the approach of the car of light to the new moon with the old moon in its arms, there is the triple rhyme "form / storm / deform" (84, 86, 88) and much later in the poem, where Rousseau tells how he, not delayed by the memory of his vision of the "shape all light," plunged into "the thickest billows" of sensual experience, the same pattern of rhyme is repeated ("form / storm / deform" [464, 466, 468]). In the first passage the word "form" refers to the old moon: "the ghost of her dead Mother, whose dim form" (84); in the second instance, the word refers to the now-unseen "shape all light": "the phantom of that early form" (464). Using quite different evidence I have attempted to show how the "shape all light" was, in a real sense, the "mother" of Rousseau's vision of evil; since the experience of Rousseau and the Poet are, presumably, parallel, the "form" of line 84 would be exactly analogous to the "form" of line 464, the "old moon" analogous to the mortal embodiment of the ideal, the "ghost" (84) equivalent to the "phantom" (464). In line 86 the "silent storm" of the chariot's "rushing splendour" would be associated with, though distinct from, the "living storm" of people under the power of life (466). The "Shape," crouching like the shadow of the old moon in the crescent of the chariot, "sate within as one whom years deform" (88), and Rousseau bared his bosom to the clime of "that cold light, whose airs too soon deform" (468). When one finds in *MS* clear evidence that Shelley worked hard to make "deform" the rhyme-word of line 468, even though the middle of the line was not quite perfected, the evidence seems to indicate that, just as it was no accident that the word "shape" is used for both the vision of evil within the car of light and the "shape all light" or that Iris, the rainbow, is associated both with the beautiful vision of the "shape all light" (356–357) and with the "new Vision" (434, 439–441), so it is part of Shelley's method of relating the vision of evil with the vision of good to repeat the same rather unusual (*rime riche*) rhyme pattern in two apparently unrelated passages.

Though "The Triumph" contains eight other instances where the same three rhyme-words appear in two different tercets, only once are the three rhyme-words repeated in the same order: both lines 57, 59, 61 and 386, 388, 390 end in "beneath / death /

breath." [13] Here again the apparent coincidence, when examined closely, proves to be an especially fortunate one, for although the two contexts do not, at the surface, seem to be related to one another, once the nature of the "shape all light" is understood, one can correlate the two passages. The first (56–61) describes those lost souls whom the Poet saw wandering aimlessly before the advent of the cold, bright chariot. Some "pored on the trodden worms that crawled *beneath";* others walked in the gloom of their own shadows "and called it *death*"; still others fled from their shadows, "half fainting in the affliction of vain *breath.*" In the later context (386–392) Rousseau tells how, at the approach of the "shape all light," "all the gazer's mind was strewn *beneath*/ Her feet like embers"; as the nonspiritual men trod on the worms, the lesser physical creatures, beneath their feet, so the limited, human vision of ideal beauty destroyed the lesser spiritual visions in the mind of the beholder. As the lost men mistakenly called their own shadows *"death,"* unaware that without a spiritual ideal their higher natures are already dead, so the "shape all light" tramples the sparks of Rousseau's mind "into the dust of *death*"; finally, the "vain *breath*" of those unforeseeing multitudes is contrasted to "the *breath* of darkness" that will reillumine "even the least/ Of heaven's living eyes." The contrast is clear enough to one who remembers that Shelley customarily divided humanity into three main categories: the many who lead meaningless lives, the disillusioned idealists, and the humanitarians, suffering servants of their fellow men.[14] The blind multitude of the early lines destroy both themselves and others through their insensitive, purposeless activity; the visionary of the later passage is overwhelmed by the blinding vision of the quasi-ideal being that he has imaged to himself. The death of "those whose hearts are dry as summer dust" is permanent; their breath is forever expended in vain. The death of the visionary's Heaven-given flame is temporary or even illusory, merely awaiting the returning "breath of darkness" before it once again shines forth.

> Dust to the dust! but the pure spirit shall flow
> Back to the burning fountain whence it came,
> A portion of the Eternal, which must glow
> Through time and change, unquenchably the same.
> *Adonais,* 338–341

[13] The other repeated tercet-rhymes are: 32–4–6 and 353–5–7; 60–2–4 and 431–3–5; 78–80–82 and 210–2–4; 365–7–9 and 395–7–9; 449–51–53 and 497–499–501; 455–7–9 and 530–2–4.

[14] See Preface to *Alastor, P.W.,* pp. 14–15.

Though the pressure exerted on "The Triumph" by the exigencies of *terza rima* are evident in the draft, one must admit that Shelley, whose technical powers were at their height, managed for the most part to avoid weakening his verse to express his meaning. The reduplication of the rhymes in lines 273–282 ("reign / strain / vain / pain" and "melody / I / misery / company") marks the only obvious place where Shelley was unable to compel the unwilling dross to the likeness of the beauty he imagined. One must observe that Shelley, in his efforts to shape the verbal materials to his purpose, sometimes found the meaning itself taking a turn that he had not originally intended, but that he was not mastered by the difficulties of his chosen medium is clearly shown by the organic structure in which the poem was developing.

I undertake close study of the phonetic effects of Shelley's verse with a realistic awareness of its difficulties. Since Shelley's pronunciation must remain somewhat conjectural—even to a linguist of Henry Higgins' skill who might postulate the accent of a Sussex-born, Eton-and-Oxford-bred Englishman of 1822 who had lived in Italy for four years—I have chosen to analyze the effects of assonance and alliteration in "The Triumph of Life" in twentieth-century Standard American English. Although individual sounds may differ from Shelley's pronunciation, the relations between them should not be too much distorted.

Shelley's use of recurring sounds in assonance and alliteration is interesting because the echoes of sound prove in many cases to reinforce the meaning in some significant way. For example, in the first line of the poem two important words are assonant and partly alliterative, "Swift" and "spirit," the first of which modifies the second (figuratively); both words, in turn, alliterate with the most important word of line 2, "Sun," to which both are closely related; "sprang" alliterates exactly with "spirit" (to which it relates through the comparison of the simile) and partially with "Sun," its subject; "splendour" (3) alliterates with "sprang," replacing one liquid consonant (r) with another (l) while retaining the nasal at the end of the accented syllable. In line 2 the syntactical parallelism of "glory" and "good" is echoed in their alliteration. The opening lines are dominated by the fricatives, nasals, and liquids: for example, in line 5, "The smokeless altars of the mountain snows"; here the first stressed syllable in the line ("smoke-") is assonant and alliterative with the last ("snows"); as in the case of the interrelations between the sounds of "Swift—spirit—Sun—sprang" (1–2), there is a relation between "smokeless" and "snows" in meaning as well as sound, for although syntactically "smokeless" modifies "altars," since "altars" is a metaphor for "mountain snows," the latter word is the one really modified by "smokeless."

I suggest, then, that by subtly repeating and slightly modifying certain sounds, Shelley integrates his verse, causing line to flow into line, without making his use of assonance and alliteration too bald or overwrought, and second, that by frequently introducing these phonetic echoes in pairs or groups of words that have some rather significant syntactical or logical relation to one another, Shelley underlines these relationships, helping the auditor of his poem to understand it. Here are several other examples from the first twenty lines: line 7, "Ocean's orison arose" ("Ocean's" and "arose" are assonant; "orison" contains no consonant not present in one of the other two words); lines 7–8, "light" / "lay" (arrival of the first, which is celestial, produces the second, terrestrial); line 8, "matin lay" (assonant); line 9, "flowers" / "field" / "forest" (the obvious alliteration—picking up that of the verbs "fell" and "Flamed" of 4, 6—is reinforced by liquids [l, r] and by alveolar fricatives [s] and stops [d, t]); lines 10–13 are tied together by a pattern of assonance in "trembling," "censers," "element," "incense," "sent"; "kiss," "swinging," and "lit," three key words of lines 10–12, are assonant; in line 14 the contrast between the earthly flowers and the sun-drenched air is emphasized in the assonance of "sighs" and "smiling"; in line 17, not only do "mortal" and "mould" alliterate, but "mortal" is assonant with "form," and these "mortal" "forms" bear their "portion" (19), while the Sun "rose" (18), "took toil" (20, 19) as his "own" and "imposed" it on them (20). There is, without doubt, much natural assonance and alliteration lurking in almost everything one writes—as there is in the sentence I am writing now —but the difference between accidental and poetic consonance is that chance phonetic similarities are random and unsustained, whereas the truly poetic is functional without being obtrusive.[15] Let

[15] Keats, who like Shelley was very conscious of sounds, employs a great deal of alliteration and assonance, but even in his greatest poems the repetition of sounds tends to become—as it does in many of Shelley's lyrics—a bit heavy-handed: I am thinking of "Ode to a Nightingale," 15–20, or, in the same poem, "self-same song" (65) and "sole self" (72). On the other hand, Keats certainly uses sounds functionally; in "Ode to a Nightingale," for example, he employs fricatives (particularly "f's") to begin key words describing both the sordid real world from which the Poet attempts to escape ("fever," "fret," "few, sad, last

us consider for a moment one other passage from "The Triumph of Life":

> . . . Like the young moon
> When on the sunlit limits of the night
> Her white shell trembles amid crimson air
> And whilst the sleeping tempest gathers might. . . .
>
> 79–82

Several patterns of vowel and consonant sounds run through the passage. The diphthong [ɑɪ], begun in "icy" and "light" (the first and last accented words of line 78), is taken up in "Like" (79), and "night" (80), "white" (81), "whilst" and "might" (82), each time strongly accented. Moreover, there are interrelations among the consonants of the same words: "light" and "Like" alliterate and both end with voiceless stops; "white" rhymes with the rhyme pattern "light / night / might" and alliterates with "whilst," which also ends in "t." The voiceless stops "t" and "k" are reinforced in these lines by the recurrence of the voiceless labial stop (p) in "sleeping tempest" (82) and the voiced labial, dental, and velar stops (b, d, g) in "trembles amid" (81) and "gathers" (82); these voiced consonants appear in verbs that contrast with the "sleeping" of the "tempest." [16] The first accented words in lines 80, 81, 82 are "When," "white," and "whilst." The vowel sound of "When" (80) is repeated in "shell trembles" and "tempest." But a vowel sound equally prominent is the [ɪ] sound, the second half of the [ɑɪ] diphthong that dominates these lines: "sun*lit* lim*i*ts" (80), "am*i*d cr*i*mson" (81).

In this connection it is important to note how Shelley balances his use of sound to prevent its degeneration into monotonous patter. In line 80 Shelley coined the adjective "sunlit." [17] Earlier he had coined "sunlight" as an adjective ("Euganean Hills," 82) but to introduce another [ɑɪ] diphthong—and an internal rhyme— would have been too heavy-handed; moreover, there is a syntactical relation between "sunlit" and "limits," its noun, whereas all the words with the [ɑɪ] diphthong relate, not to the sun but to the

---

gray hairs") and the dream world that also fails him ("Flora," "Full," "Fade far," "forget," "fly," "Fays," "flowers," "Fast fading," "foam," "faery lands forlorn," "Forlorn!" "fancy," "fam'd," "fades," "Fled"), thus relating them in their common failure to sustain human aspirations.

16 The verbs that follow ("doth . . . bear" [83] and "bends" [85]) echo this pattern of voiced stops, liquids, and nasals.

17 See *OED*.

"li*ght*" of the moon that, though "wh*i*te" and possessing "m*i*ght," is "*i*cy" and related to the "n*i*ght" in Shelley's symbolic universe. Similarly, whereas voiceless consonants relate to "noon" (77), "Sun" (79), and "sunlit," the "cold glare" of the moon "obscured" the "Sun as he the stars." [18]

One could examine other passages in the same detail, but perhaps the reader believes that I have already oversubtilized Shelley's poetry, reading relations between sounds beyond the poet's ken and interest. Let us turn to a reported dialogue between Shelley and Byron on Shakespeare's poetry:

Shelley. . . . Is not a line, as well as your outspread heroics, or a tragedy, a whole, and only as a whole, beautiful in itself? as, for instance, "How sweet the moonlight sleeps upon this bank." Now, examining this line, we perceive that all the parts are formed in relation to one another, and that it is consequently a whole. "Sleep," we see, is a reduplication of the pure and gentle sound of sweet; and as the beginning of the former symphonizes with the beginning *s* of the latter, so also the *l* in moonlight prepares one for the *l* in sleep, and glides gently into it; and in the conclusion, one may perceive that the word "bank" is determined by the preceding words, and that the *b* which it begins with is but a deeper intonation of the two *p*'s which come before it; sleeps upon this slope, would have been effeminate; sleeps upon this rise, would have been harsh and inharmonious.

Byron. Heavens! do you imagine, my dear Shelley, that Shakspeare had any thing of the kind in his head when he struck off that pretty line? If any one had told him all this about your p's and s's, he would just have said, "Pish!"

Shelley. Well, be that as it may, are there not the coincidences, I suppose you would call them, that I showed in the line?

Byron. There are. But the beauty of the line does not lie in sounds and syllables, and such mechanical contrivances, but in the beautiful metaphor of the moonlight sleeping.

Shelley. Indeed, that also is very beautiful. In every single line, the poet must organize many simultaneous operations, both the meaning of the words and their emphatic arrangement, and then the flow and melting together of their symphony; and the whole must also be united with the current of the rythm.

Byron. Well, then, I'm glad I'm not a poet! It must be like making out one's expenses for a journey, I think, all this calculation!

Shelley. I don't say that a poet must necessarily be conscious of all this, no more than a lady is conscious of every graceful movement. But I do say that they all depend upon reason, in which they live and move, and have their being; and that he who brings them out into the light

[18] According to this analysis, Mary Shelley's insertion of "bl*i*nding" in line 78 was a perfect choice.

of distinct consciousness, beside satisfying an instinctive desire of his own nature, will be more secure and more commanding. But what makes this metaphor beautiful? To represent the tranquillity of moonlight is the object of the line; and the sleep is beautiful, because it gives a more intense and living form of the same idea; the rythm beautifully falls in with this, and just lets the cadence of the emphasis dwell upon the sound and sense of the sweet word "sleep;" and the alliteration assimilates the rest of the line into one harmonious symmetry. This line, therefore, is it not altogether a work of art? [19]

Shelley, it would seem from these remarks, was not an advocate of the "rapt bard" method of poetic composition. Indeed, his whole discussion of Shakespeare and particularly *Hamlet* is an attempt to demonstrate that Shakespeare's art was equal to his genius. All these effects and relations of thought, image, and sound, whether the products of conscious or subconscious activity, "depend upon reason" and "he who brings them out into the light of distinct consciousness . . . will be more secure and more commanding."

SIMILE, METAPHOR, AND SYNAESTHETIC IMAGERY

We have seen in the explication of "The Triumph" how Shelley's imagery integrates his symbolic universe with a consistent natural scene—probably one modified slightly from an actual scene near Casa Magni. The various types of light in the poem—even the cold glare of the moon-like chariot—all have their origin in the Sun, but "the one Spirit's plastic stress" is refracted, distorted into a thousand unimagined shapes by the recalcitrance of the "unwilling dross that checks its flight." [20] Shelley has utilized the key symbolic pattern of *Adonais*—the refraction of sunlight by the earth's atmosphere [21]—and has integrated this with more graphic

[19] From "Byron and Shelley on the Character of Hamlet," *New Monthly Magazine and Literary Journal*, XXIX, Pt. 2 (1830), 330–331. W. E. Peck reprints a slightly abridged and occasionally inaccurate version of the conversation in *Shelley: His Life and Work* (II, 421–432); Peck's conjecture that Thomas Medwin was the "Eye Witness" is probably incorrect, in the opinion of Professor Ernest J. Lovell, Medwin's biographer, with whom I have corresponded on this problem. The sentiments put in Shelley's mouth are, on the other hand, unquestionably his; they agree in substance with the discussion of organic form in *A Defence of Poetry* (written early in 1821 but unpublished until 1840). The specific words attributed to Shelley, however, no doubt include some of the anonymous author's substitutions for what was probably Shelley's more exact diction.

[20] *Adonais*, 381–385.

[21] Wasserman has discussed Shelley's use of this figure in *Adonais* (*The Subtler Language*, pp. 339–342).

symbols: the dusty road and triumphal procession of the *Trionfi,* the crystal glass of *Comus,* the *simulacra* of *De Rerum Natura,* the damned souls of the *Inferno.* But while examining the meaning of "The Triumph," I gave inadequate attention to Shelley's use of figurative language.

According to Milton Wilson, Shelley developed an "increasing fondness" for similes in his late poetry, particularly in "The Triumph," a development that Wilson attributes to the influence of Italian poetry.[22] I am not sure that there is statistical evidence that in Shelley's later poetry as a whole the simile did gain at the expense of metaphor, but certainly in "The Triumph" simile is the dominant figure of speech; this I take to be in part yet another evidence that Shelley saw his poem as an epic structure and that he was following stylistically in the steps of Homer, Dante, and Milton.[23] Various critics have attempted to analyze the qualitative differences between simile and metaphor and to explain why in Romantic poetry the simile seems to predominate,[24] but although I am not prepared to generalize about the Romantic poets, I believe that the conventional explanations fail to include the main reason why Shelley throughout his poetry used the simile so extensively: He wanted to make quite clear, in many cases, that he was not *equating* two things but merely suggesting a *likeness* at one specific point of comparison or—as in extended, "epic" similes— at several specific points. He was, in other words, attempting to avoid the vagueness and impressionism that some critics seem determined to find in his poetry.

For example, in the first stanza of "Hymn to Intellectual Beauty" (1816) Shelley describes the evanescent brilliance of "the awful shadow of some unseen Power" in a series of similes, each comparing this imageless mystery, which generates hope and a spirit of delight in the human heart, to a natural phenomenon that has

[22] *Shelley's Later Poetry,* p. 289.
[23] The three epic poets, according to paragraph 28 of *A Defence of Poetry* (*Prose,* pp. 290–291). See Shelley to Byron, 16 July 1821: "I still feel impressed with the persuasion that you *ought*—and if there is prophecy in hope, that you *will* write a great and connected poem, which shall bear the same relation to this age as the 'Iliad,' the 'Divina Commedia,' and 'Paradise Lost' did to theirs; not that you will imitate the structure, or borrow from the subjects, of any of these, or in any degree assume them as your models" (Julian, X, 285). Shelley would have maintained his epic intention without following the structure or subjects of earlier epics, but he, I think, would not have avoided epic similes.
[24] See, for example, R. A. Foakes, *The Romantic Assertion* (New Haven, 1958), pp. 23–38.

both "grace" and "mystery." In the second and third stanzas of
the "Hymn" a similar series compares the effects of certain beautiful phenomena with the ability of the "Spirit of BEAUTY" to
give "grace and truth to Life's unquiet dream." Shelley refused to
equate the spirit of the unknown, transcendental Power with the
transitory forms like cloud and rainbow, which had for him quite
different symbolic values. When in famous metaphors in *Adonais*
Shelley calls himself "a pardlike Spirit beautiful and swift . . . a
dying lamp, a falling shower,/ A breaking billow," he intends that
the reader should derive from the equations all the implications
and overtones that these terms carry in his symbolic vocabulary;
on the other hand, in a subsequent simile his "branded and en-
sanguined brow" is *"like* Cain's or Christ's" only in that its mark
isolates him from his fellow men, for good or ill; he *is* neither a
Cain nor a Christ, nor are *they* equated.

In "The Triumph" the relation between simile and metaphor is
fairly clear-cut. Shelley introduces an important symbol with a
simile to establish within very precise limits its value for the poem.
Thereafter, he may express the same relation in metaphor. The
Sun, a symbol of the Absolute that is not in itself comparable to
any creature, is compared only in regard to its speed: "Swift as
a spirit," the words "glory and good" supplying a value for the
Sun and discouraging readers from confusing the benevolent Sun
with his dangerous daughter, in spite of their family resemblance.
The next simile occurs in line 22, where the Poet says that he has
been kept "as wakeful as the stars"; certainly the Poet has none
of the serenity, permanence, or brilliant light of the celestial stars,
but he is associated with them in the only way he can be: He,
too, has been awake all night. When the chariot appears it is compared to the moon in a long epic simile (79–90) that precisely
establishes its value. The comparison between the chariot and its
train and a Roman triumph is developed in detail through another
epic simile (111–116). At least some of the "sacred few . . . fled
back *like* eagles to their native noon," the simile applying a value
to these individuals partly in terms of a metaphor ("native noon"),
the value of which has been established by the poem's first simile.

Early in the Poet's vision the members of the crowd that follow
the chariot were said to be "numerous as gnats" (45–46), borne by
the crowd as are dead leaves (50–51), and made wilder by the approaching chariot "as the woods of June" by the South wind (75–76);
before the end of the poem's first movement (175) they rage

"like clouds upon the thunder blast" (109), outspeed the chariot as "fleet as shadows" (139), go to their destruction "like moths" (153) or "like two clouds . . . that . . . die in rain" (155–157), and are so totally destroyed that no trace can be found "but as of foam after the Ocean's wrath" (163). In part, of course, these similes establish the value of the devotees of lust, but to a greater degree, perhaps, they establish the value of the terrestrial symbols for the poem. When these same phenomena reappear in similes in Rousseau's story, this time associated with the beautiful "shape all light," they serve as an index of her nature without making it necessary for Rousseau to attribute sinister qualities to her. Obviously the young Rousseau at the time of his encounter believed her to be perfectly good; it was only after she had faded, bringing the new vision of evil, that he became aware of her limitations. Through employing the same terms in two sets of similes, Shelley is able to embody numerous clues to the destructive potential of the apparently beneficent vision and to point out the close relation between the "shape all light" and the darker "shape." Moreover, Rousseau and the Poet can both remain ignorant of the precise nature of the relation between the two visions (as both apparently are to the end of the fragment) while the reader can, as in a well-ordered mystery novel, work ahead of the detectives by recognizing the clues left by the author.

That the chief function of the similes lies in establishing such values and relations between the Poet's vision in the first movement and Rousseau's vision in the third movement can be seen from the distribution of similes within the fragment. In the introductory section (1–40) there are but three similes: "Swift as a spirit . . . Sun" (1–2); Poet, "wakeful as the stars" (21–23); and vision "came through as clear as . . . evening hills" through a "veil of light" (30–33); each of these similes establishes the value of a kind of light and/or the Poet's relation to it. In the first phase of the vision (41–175) there are, on the other hand, fifteen similes—several of them quite long and involved, especially the comparison of the chariot with the moon (79–87), the comparison of the pageant with a Roman triumph (111–116), and the cloud-lightning simile (155–158). In the next movement of the vision (176–308), where Rousseau appears to identify some of the captives chained to the chariot, there are only five similes, two of which are quickly turned into metaphors: Dominion followed Aristotle and Alexander "as tame as vulture in a chain" (261–262), but immediately Alexander

is described as having wings and being one of the "flock of conquerors," all, presumably, vultures in Shelley's symbolic universe;
later "Gregory & John and men divine" are said to rise "like
shadows between Man & god," but immediately the simile becomes
the metaphorical "eclipse" that quenched the "true Sun" (288–292).
The other similes of the section (196–197; 269–270; 280–281) are
briefer, though functional. In this section Shelley does not need
so many similes because in discussing human beings whose careers
were well known he could use a more direct method of establishing their values: "Their power was given/ But to destroy" (292–
293). In sharp contrast to the preceding section, Rousseau's account
of his own experience is filled with similes, in the end becoming
almost a series of direct comparisons. Only three similes occur
between the beginning of Rousseau's story and the appearance of
the "shape all light" (308–348), but the "shape" herself and her
effects on Rousseau (348–393) are described in no less than nine
similes; the passage in which Rousseau drinks from the "crystal
glass" and the "shape all light" subsequently fades (401–433) contains six rather elaborate and interrelated similes; the brief description of the pageant with its triumphal chariot (434–468) and account
of the "wonder worthy of the rhyme" of Dante (469–543) include
four and eighteen similes respectively. In this last major section of
the fragment, the formless *simulacra* are assigned values through
comparisons with various animals: The entire vision blots out the
Sun as does a "flock of vampire-bats" and individual groups of the
shadows are "like" eaglets, elves, apes, vultures, falcons, gnats and
flies, and flakes of snow; in many cases the similes are followed immediately by metaphors that exploit the similarity first established
through the simile ("others like elves/ Danced in a thousand unimagined shapes" [490–491]; "others . . . sate like vultures, others
. . . made their nests . . ." [497–500]). Shelley uses simile primarily, then, to establish the value of the characters and phenomena
of the poem by drawing points of likeness between them and natural creatures and objects that possess recognizable symbolic
significance.

Metaphor, on the other hand, serves to develop the implications
of comparisons already articulated through simile, or to relate the
scene described not to such particularized aspects of natural creation as leaves, flowers, or specific animals, birds, or insects, but
rather to larger, more generalized concepts. For example, the striking conclusion to the first movement, "And frost in these performs

what fire in those" (175), *summarizes* the contrast between those who raced before the chariot and the impotent laggards, but *develops* it very little, merely restating in terms of primary sense impressions the implications already spun out in the previous lines. Again, within the simile comparing the pageant with a Roman triumph occurs the line "Imperial Rome poured forth her living sea" (113), a metaphor neither strikingly original nor depending chiefly on its own implications for its value, since not only do there appear later in the poem several similes attaching a malevolent significance to the sea, but the simile of which this metaphor is a part clearly establishes the value of the entire image. In a few instances (e.g., "Janus-visaged Shadow" [94], "grim Feature" [190], "star that ruled his doom" [256], and "flower of Heaven" [257]) the force of metaphors depends on recognition of their literary sources; in other words, their value is already established in a literary context outside of Shelley's poem. Metaphors of this kind both link "The Triumph" to the tradition out of which it grows and reinforce the similes that establish symbolic values within the poem by bringing to bear the associations of entire works (Plato's epigram) or large portions of them (Milton's myth of Sin and Death).[25]

The third type of figurative language that seems particularly significant in "The Triumph" is the synaesthetic imagery frequently contained within the structure of metaphor or simile. For example, at the opening of the poem the scent of the flowers that are stimulated by the rising Sun is referred to as "odorous sighs" (14), a figure in which metaphorical "sighs" is modified by an adjective that is literally descriptive of the sensory impression. Other synaesthetic phrases include "melodious dew" (67), "emerald fire" (348), "silver music" (355), "breath of darkness" (390–391), and the series of comparisons between the fading light of Lucifer at dawn and a series of collateral sensory impressions—"the scent of a jonquil," the "soft note" of the Brescian shepherd, and "the caress/ That turned his weary slumber to content" (419–423). R. H. Fogle has suggested that Shelley's synaesthetic imagery is intellectual rather than sensuous and that it "is the poetical expression of a conscious, intellectual quest after a cosmic and psychic unity. . . ."[26] But

---

[25] Some of Shelley's metaphors in "The Triumph" lie in the shadowland between figurative language and dead metaphor: e.g., "stream of people" (44–45).
[26] *The Imagery of Keats and Shelley*, p. 137.

Shelley uses synaesthetic imagery to explore the problem of unity and multiplicity in much the same way that he employs the rainbow: Just as the multiple colors of the rainbow are aspects of a single, white radiance, so the impressions of sight, hearing, smell, and touch are qualities of one Reality that expresses itself in a variety of sensations. The Sun, father of all things, rises to receive the multiform worship of his numerous creatures, which praise him through reflected light, odors, and sounds. Love, symbolized in the planet Venus, manifests itself to mortals through light, odor, music, and a sweet caress. Why should Shelley employ only four of the five senses in these synaesthetic passages? Probably because whereas sight, hearing, smell, and touch are avenues to knowledge of the external world, taste has traditionally been employed metaphorically as the sense of subjectivity: *"De gustibus non est disputandum."* [27] Shelley employs figures of speech involving taste to describe subjective experience, whereas his synaesthetic imagery involving the other four senses, like his rainbow symbolism, records the effort of men to describe their apprehension of the One through impressions of the Many, attempts that must always end in some measure of failure.

In poems like "To a Skylark" or "Hymn to Intellectual Beauty" Shelley uses synaesthesia not in a vain quest for unity, or even in an attempt to express the inexpressible, but simply to record the failure of expression, to delineate the limitations of both words and the sensuous world of simple impressions that gives birth to human "ideas."

> What thou art we know not;
>   What is most like thee?
> From rainbow clouds there flow not
>   Drops so bright to see. . . .[28]

Why should Shelley demonstrate the inadequacy of earthly counterparts to describe the ineffable reality symbolized in a "skylark" that never was a bird? For the same reason that the sceptical philosopher attempted to discover and define the limits of human reason. If Shelley demonstrated the inadequacy of a wealth of images to express some attribute of the Absolute, then perhaps the reader

---

[27] Cf. G. M. Hopkins' sonnet "I wake and feel the fell of dark, not day": "God's most deep decree/ Bitter would have me taste: my taste was me" (9–10; *Poems*, p. 110).

[28] "To a Skylark," 31–34 (*P.W.*, p. 602).

would discover that the whole is greater than its parts, that the Divine and the human are, in fact, eternally incommensurate, and that all anthropomorphism serves but to obscure the "Unknown God."[29] Shelley's synaesthesia seems to me always functional to his philosophic position and often, as in "The Triumph," functional to the poem's symbolic development. Rousseau's encounter with the "shape all light" (who participates in the divine nature even if she is only an aspect of it) is described in terms of a multiplicity of sensuous similes that at once associate the "shape" with terrestrial creation and explore her nature through numerous inadequate parallels. Like many spiritual experiences—such as Saul's on the Damascus road—the event itself so overpowers "Rousseau" that he spends the rest of his life trying to rationalize it, to define it in terms of his ordinary experience. But words, and even symbolic actions themselves, are often inadequate to articulate and communicate fully the interior dimensions of such an experience. Several Christologies have been erected firmly upon different and partially contradictory statements by St. Paul, who was trying to set forth the meaning of his own experience of Christ. Shelley attempts to prevent an oversimplification of the experience he describes by graphically demonstrating the inadequacy of mere words to convey the revelation.

Such a method is "Platonic," but it does not imply that words are unimportant. Words can precisely articulate ordinary human concepts and can then go on to explore the limits of verbal expression, just as reason can define its areas of competence, or human beings can recognize their own finiteness. A "hard, dry" poetic style may not necessarily imply, as T. E. Hulme thought,[30] that a poet recognizes man's limited nature. The arrant dogmatist can describe anything in "hard, dry" terms; he can disclose the will of God or can deny God's existence with extreme precision. Shelley's exploration of the limits of language is an aesthetic analogue to the humility that prevented him from dogmatizing on ontological matters, even about questions upon which he felt a psychological need for certainty, and synaesthetic imagery is often the vehicle of that exploration.

[29] *Hellas*, 211, 735.
[30] "Romanticism and Classicism," *Speculations: Essays on Humanism and the Philosophy of Art* (London, 1924). For a full critique of Hulme's relation to Romanticism, see Frank Kermode, *Romantic Image*.

RHETORIC

Besides organically harmonizing the meter, figures of speech, and symbols in "The Triumph," Shelley utilizes some rather more obvious rhetorical techniques. One is his very effective use of the climactic sequence in which Rousseau reveals his identity (204) only after very full descriptions of his external appearance by the Poet (180–188) and his spiritual condition by Rousseau himself (188–204).[31] The contrast between Rousseau and Napoleon is emphasized both by the general parallelism of their introductions and by repetition of certain key words: Whereas Rousseau "bore" a spark (207), "opportunity bore" a passive Napoleon (221); whereas "a thousand beacons" lit from Rousseau's spark "yet . . . rise" (206–207), Napoleon and "a thousand climbers" "fell" (223–224).[32]

A subtle dramatic shift in the value of words can be seen in a phrase that occurs quite early in the Poet's vision: the Poet first bemoans the ignorance of the crowd: "none seemed to know/ Whither he went, or whence he came, or why/ He made one of the multitude" (47–49). After he beholds more of the vision, the Poet begins to doubt his own powers and, feeling as bewildered as those lost masses, he exclaims:

> "And what is this?
> Whose shape is that within the car? & why"—
> I would have added—"is all here amiss?"
> 177–179

The grim shape of Rousseau warns him of the danger in his "thirst of knowledge" (194–196), and that the lore of the Wise "Taught them not this—to know themselves" (212), but the Poet continues to demand knowledge: "First who art thou?" (199), "And who are those chained to the car?" (207), "Who is he with chin/ Upon his breast . . . ?" (215–216). After he has seen the spirit of Napoleon, however, the Poet himself is revolted by the knowledge he has gained, knowledge that seems to lead merely to disillusionment, and for a time he "half disdained" to view the pageant (224–234). At this point Rousseau forces him to "behold . . . those spoilers spoiled" (234–235) and to "mark . . . The mighty phantoms of an

---

[31] The same method is used in the description of Napoleon, lines 215–224.

[32] Whereas Rousseau's self-description (199–207) centers around images of fire, the symbol of spiritual vitality, the description of Napoleon—like those of Aristotle and Alexander—rests upon animal imagery. Note also that Napoleon's "grasp" (226) is a moral as well as a physical metaphor.

elder day" (252–253). The Poet, still heartsick at the apparent hopelessness of the pageant, turns back to his original questioning of Rousseau ("First who art thou?"), echoing in his questions the fatal ignorance of those lost on the dusty road:

> "Whence camest thou & whither goest thou?
> How did thy course begin," I said, "& why?"
>   296–297

Rousseau himself cannot answer the most important questions ("Why this should be my mind can compass not;/ Whither the conqueror hurries me still less" [303–304]), "But," he continues,

> "follow thou, & from spectator turn
> Actor or victim in this wretchedness,
>
> "And what thou wouldst be taught I then may learn
> From thee—"
>   305–308

The "wretchedness" for which the Poet had earlier asked Heaven's mercy (181) must be his if he is to know the answers to his own questionings. But the very quest for experiential knowledge is self-defeating, for as Rousseau tells his story, his defeat was brought about through a similar thirst for knowledge: "Shew whence I came, and where I am, and why—" (398). The "shape all light" had replied, "Arise and quench thy thirst," but besides leaving Rousseau as ignorant as ever, the drink of Nepenthe lost him the vision of beauty in the surrounding world. The Poet's final question "Then, what is Life?" may reflect his recognition that the Tree of Knowledge is not the Tree of Life.[33]

---

[33] See Byron's *Manfred* I.i.12.

CHAPTER FOUR

THE TREE OF KNOWLEDGE

Shelley's attitude toward the search for knowledge, as I have tried to show above, was a complex one. Man had to know a great deal about the world in which he lived in order to ground his ethical system firmly. Perhaps Shelley's sharpest criticism of Wordsworth grew out of what Shelley regarded as the Lake Poet's unwillingness to look beneath the natural phenomena that he found metaphysically comforting. In *Peter Bell the Third* Shelley wrote:

> . . . from the first 'twas Peter's drift
>   To be a kind of moral eunuch,
> He touched the hem of Nature's shift,
> Felt faint—and never dared uplift
>   The closest, all-concealing tunic.
>
> She laughed the while, with an arch smile,
>   And kissed him with a sister's kiss,
> And said—"My best Diogenes,
> I love you well—but, if you please,
>   Tempt not again my deepest bliss.
>
> " 'Tis you are cold—for I, not coy,
>   Yield love for love, frank, warm, and true;
> And Burns, a Scottish peasant boy—
> His errors prove it—knew my joy
>   More, learnèd friend, than you."
>
> 313–327

Peter is, at this point in Shelley's satire, in a position similar to that of Rousseau during his encounter with the "shape all light" (394–404) but he responds quite differently:

> . . . 'twixt love and fear,
> He looked, as he no doubt felt, queer,
>   And in his dream sate down.
>
> 335–337

110

Rousseau had approached the "shape" "as one between desire and shame/ Suspended," but he responded to her invitation by rising and drinking from the cup she proffered. Thus his troubles began, whereas Peter's difficulties commenced when he "sate down" and thereby refused to gaze on "Nature's naked loveliness." [1] He who failed to know "whither he went, or whence he came, or why/ He made one of the multitude" (48–49) was damned, and he who feigned a "morn of truth," "deep night caught" "ere evening" (214–215).

"Then who shall be saved," one may ask, "if ignorance is not bliss and if the wisdom of this world is become moral folly?" Shelley in his most important metaphysical statement, the "Essay on Life," has in part answered both this and the Poet's final question in "The Triumph": "What is life? Thoughts and feelings arise, with or without our will, and we employ words to express them. We are born, and our birth is unremembered, and our infancy remembered but in fragments; we live on, and in living we lose the apprehension of life. How vain is it to think that words can penetrate the mystery of our being! Rightly used they may make evident our ignorance to ourselves, and this is much" (*Prose,* p. 172). Those who, blindly leading the blind, rise "like shadows between Man & god" (289) are defeated by life; only the man who is willing to remain agnostic upon the ultimate questions (who can say, as Shelley did in a note to *Hellas,* "that there is a true solution of the riddle, and that in our present state that solution is unattainable by us, are propositions which may be regarded as equally certain" [2]) can avoid falling prey to either the Scylla of dogmatism or the Charybdis of cynicism. "Philosophy, impatient as it may be to build, has much work yet remaining as pioneer for the overgrowth of ages. It makes one step towards this object: it destroys error and the roots of error. It leaves, what it is too often the duty of the reformer in political and ethical questions to leave, a vacancy. It reduces the mind to that freedom in which it would have acted but for the misuse of words and signs, the instruments of its own creation" ("Essay on Life," *Prose,* p. 173).

Thus Shelley's philosophy returns full circle to the moral efficacy of freedom. Like Kierkegaard and Berdyaev, Shelley found in the presumptions of dogmatism, either idealistic or materialistic, religious or scientific, chains that enslaved man and made him an au-

[1] *Adonais,* 275.
[2] *P.W.,* p. 478.

tomaton rather than a free moral agent. But the freedom for which Shelley worked did not dissociate one from other human beings or from the system of the universe; on the contrary, in reason's search for its own limits it carried the individual to the inevitable conclusion that, contrary to all "common sense" conceptions, the individual probably had no independent existence:

> The view of life presented by the most refined deductions of the intellectual philosophy is that of unity. Nothing exists but as it is perceived. The difference is merely nominal between those two classes of thought which are vulgarly distinguished by the names of ideas and of external objects. Pursuing the same thread of reasoning, the existence of distinct individual minds, similar to that which is employed in now questioning its own nature, is likewise found to be a delusion. The words *I, you, they* are not signs of any actual difference subsisting between the assemblage of thoughts thus indicated, but are merely marks employed to denote the different modifications of the one mind [*Prose*, p. 174].

But, Shelley adds quickly, he, the writer, does not presume that he *is* that one mind (as would a solipsist) but only a "portion of it." "The words *I* and *you* and *they* are grammatical devices invented simply for arrangement. . . . It is difficult to find terms adequate to express so subtle a conception as that to which the Intellectual Philosophy has conducted us. We are on that verge where words abandon us, and what wonder if we grow dizzy to look down the dark abyss of how little we know" (*Prose*, p. 174).

Shelley never implies that we can live our everyday lives as though "*I* and *you* and *they*" were "totally devoid of the intense and exclusive sense usually attached to them." [3] As he has already stated, this admission "establishes no new truth" but rather frees one from the confining categories of old dogmatisms; "it destroys error and the roots of error"; [4] it disperses the eclipse which men worship, so that they can once again seek the Sun that glows beyond the atmosphere of our mortal limitations (cf. *TL*, 288–292). The practical mode of our existence is unchanged, and in the theoretical realm one merely recognizes that the answer to the great mystery is, in our present state, unattainable by us. Shelley says of the world of our ordinary experience, "The relations of *things* remain unchanged, by whatever system. By the word *things* is to be understood any object of thought—that is, any thought upon which any

[3] *Prose*, p. 174.
[4] *Prose*, p. 173.

other thought is employed with an apprehension of distinction. The relations of these remain unchanged; and such is the material of our knowledge" *(Prose,* p. 174). It is at this point that Shelley, an adherent of the sceptical "intellectual philosophy," joins Kierkegaard, Berdyaev, and the religious existentialists of our own day. The events of experience constitute our only reality and all systems developed by finite human minds to explain them are limited postulates that can be tested only in the fires of experience. One must commit himself to a course of action, one must choose among possibilities, but the choice is "free" in the sense that the choice is for its own sake and not for the sake of certain known consequences, foreseen rewards or punishments.

Thus, the answer to the questions posed by the Poet in his dialectical search for truth with the spirit of "Rousseau" (a figment of his own creative imagination) is that there is no answer. One must rest content in the knowledge that neither he nor any other man can answer the ultimate questions, even though the knowledge one does have points in certain directions.

> What is the cause of life? That is, how was it produced, or what agencies distinct from life have acted or act upon life? All recorded generations of mankind have wearily busied themselves inventing answers to this question; and the result has been—Religion. Yet, that the basis of all things cannot be, as the popular philosophy alleges, mind, is sufficiently evident. Mind, as far as we have any experience of its properties, and beyond that experience how vain is argument! cannot create, it can only perceive. . . . It is infinitely improbable that the cause of mind, that is, of existence, is similar to mind [*Prose,* pp. 174–175].

Shelley experienced moments of communion with the universe

> . . . in which the burthen of the mystery,
> In which the heavy and the weary weight
> Of all this unintelligible world,
> Is lightened.[5]

In experiences like that he recorded in "Lines Written Among the Euganean Hills," he *felt* that man was greater than he *knew.*[6] But such moments of calm clarity in which his soul was mastered by the spirit of delight came more rarely in his later years, and even when he was under their spell he would not categorically declare

[5] Wordsworth, "Lines Composed a Few Miles Above Tintern Abbey . . .," 38–41.
[6] Wordsworth, "Afterthought" to *The River Duddon.*

that their source was something beyond the realm of ordinary human experience:

> Be it love, light, harmony,
> Odour, or the soul of all
> Which from Heaven like dew doth fall,
> Or the mind which feeds this verse
> Peopling the lone universe.
> "Euganean Hills," 315–319

"The Triumph of Life" probably never would have provided a categorical answer to the Poet's last question, not because Shelley was weak-minded, or was having trouble with his love life, or had lost his gift for poetry, but because the philosophy that underlies "The Triumph"—and, I think, all of Shelley's mature poetry— held that it was not only futile to seek the answer to the question but immoral to pretend to have found it: "And for the morn of truth they feigned, deep night/ Caught them ere evening" (214– 215). But even though Shelley did not pretend to have solved the great riddle, to have learned "what none yet ever knew or can be known," [7] he would probably have ended "The Triumph of Life," as he had *Prometheus Unbound*, *Adonais*, and *Hellas*, on a note of affirmation, for he believed that it was "the province of the poet to attach himself to those ideas that exalt and ennoble humanity" without dogmatizing on those subjects, "concerning which all men are equally ignorant." [8] Knowing full well that the *beau idéal* that he followed in his personal life was partial and limited, and without attempting to impose it as a rule of life on other men, he never in his career as a poet went against the best light he had, this vision that united "all of wonderful, or wise, or beautiful, which the poet, the philosopher, or the lover could depicture." [9]

"It seems to me," Shelley wrote to Horace Smith nine days before his death,

> that things have now arrived at such a crisis as requires every man plainly to utter his sentiments on the inefficacy of the existing religious, no less than political systems, for restraining and guiding mankind. Let us see the truth, whatever that may be. The destiny of man can scarcely

[7] "The Boat on the Serchio," 33 (*P.W.*, p. 655).
[8] Note to *Hellas*, *P.W.*, p. 478.
[9] Preface to *Alastor*, *P.W.*, p. 14.

be so degraded that he was born only to die—and if such should be the case, delusions, especially the gross and preposterous ones of the existing religion, can scarcely be supposed to exalt it. If every man said what he thought, it could not subsist a day. But all, more or less, subdue themselves to the element that surrounds them, and contribute to the evils they lament by the hypocrisy that springs from them— [10]

The truth that Shelley saw was, on the negative side, man's own ignorance—his inability to answer the ultimate metaphysical questions. But on the positive side, one could know in poetry "the best and happiest moments of the happiest and best minds." In the moral realm, where the "sad reality" [11] that "is" has no jurisdiction over the "ought" of the ethical imperative, man has as his guides the eagle spirits of the past, those "sacred few who could not tame/ Their spirits to the Conqueror" (128–129):

> . . . it exceeds all imagination to conceive what would have been the moral condition of the world if neither Dante, Petrarch, Boccaccio, Chaucer, Shakespeare, Calderon, Lord Bacon, nor Milton had ever existed; if Raphael and Michael Angelo had never been born; if the Hebrew poetry had never been translated; if a revival of the study of Greek literature had never taken place; if no monuments of ancient sculpture had been handed down to us; and if the poetry of the religion of the ancient world had been extinguished together with its belief.[12]

In the poet's "beautiful idealisms of moral excellence" lay man's hope for whatever temporary improvements in his life could be wrested from the powerful forces of "Fate, Time, Occasion, Chance, and Change." In the moments of his highest energy, when, as in fifth-century Athens or in the Renaissance of Western Europe, the realm of the spirit made its influence felt throughout an entire society, "the world's great age" could begin anew,

> And leave, if nought so bright may live,
> All earth can take or Heaven can give.[13]

To remain in doubt of man's relation to the underlying fabric of the Universe, and yet to live in hope and love, giving oneself unstintingly to the service of one's fellow men, to set for one's task the possible impossibilities of Demogorgon's final speech in *Prome-*

[10] 29 June 1822 (Julian, X, 410).
[11] Dedication to *The Cenci, P.W.,* p. 275.
[12] *A Defence of Poetry, Prose,* pp. 292–293.
[13] *Hellas,* 1088–89 *(P.W.,* p. 477).

theus Unbound [14]—this was to find true humanity and true brother-hood with the noble dead who had brought fire from Heaven and lit beacons on the earth.

Within the technical finesse of "The Triumph of Life"—its in-cisive rendering of character, its coherent symbolism, its subtle music—lies a vision of the dark human dilemma that has been excelled by no modern poet. But "The Triumph" contains some-thing far more meaningful than simply a realistic portrayal of the complexities of phenomenal existence: a moral vision of the po-tential dignity and worth of the human individual that renders the grotesque panorama not "absurd" but truly tragic. In "The Triumph of Life" Shelley shows himself to be a poet for tough-minded men who are willing to "see the truth, whatever that may be" and yet unwilling to forsake a vision of the possibilities of the human spirit; a poet for those who are not afraid to accept all the knowledge that science can give us, who do not fear that in the analysis of the rainbow all poetry will be lost; [15] a poet for those who are not afraid to gamble their pleasures, their fortunes, their reputations, and their lives on the possibility that the ideals of moral excellence espoused by Jesus and Socrates, by the greatest poets and creative spirits of the ages, are ultimately true as well as beautiful.

[14] To suffer woes which Hope thinks infinite;
    To forgive wrongs darker than death or night;
      To defy Power, which seems omnipotent;
    To love, and bear; to hope till Hope creates
    From its own wreck the thing it contemplates;
      Neither to change, nor falter, nor repent;
    This, like thy glory, Titan, is to be
    Good, great and joyous, beautiful and free;
    This is alone Life, Joy, Empire, and Victory.
                    P.W., p. 268

[15] See Benjamin Robert Haydon's account of the "Immortal Dinner" (28 December 1817) when Lamb and Keats agreed that Newton "had destroyed all the poetry of the rainbow by reducing it to the prismatic colours" (quoted from Sidney Colvin, *John Keats*, p. 247). Cf. also Keats's "Lamia," 229-238.

PART TWO

"THE TRIUMPH OF LIFE": A TEXTUAL STUDY

KEY TO ABBREVIATIONS OF TEXTS AND
TEXTUAL STUDIES

MS	Bodleian MS Shelley adds. c. 4, ff. 19–58.
PP	*Posthumous Poems of Percy Bysshe Shelley.* London, 1824.
C_1	*The Poetical Works of Percy Bysshe Shelley,* ed. Mrs. Shelley. 4 vols. London, 1839.
C_2	*The Poetical Works of Percy Bysshe Shelley,* ed. Mrs. Shelley. 3 vols. London, 1847.
C	Agreement of C_1 and C_2.
R_1	*The Poetical Works of Percy Bysshe Shelley,* ed. William Michael Rossetti. 2 vols. London, 1870.
WR	[Mathilde Blind]. "Shelley," *Westminster Review,* N.S., XXXVIII (July 1870), 75–97.
F	*The Poetical Works of Percy Bysshe Shelley,* ed. Harry Buxton Forman. 4 vols. London, 1876–77.
R_2	*The Complete Poetical Works of Percy Bysshe Shelley,* ed. William Michael Rossetti. 3 vols. London, 1878.
R	Agreement of R_1 and R_2.
W	*The Complete Poetical Works of Percy Bysshe Shelley,* ed. George Edward Woodberry. 4 vols. Boston, 1892.
H	*The Complete Poetical Works of Shelley,* ed. Thomas Hutchinson. Oxford, 1904.
MLR i	A. C. Bradley. "Notes on Passages in Shelley," *Modern Language Review,* I (October 1905), 25–42.
L	*The Poems of Percy Bysshe Shelley,* ed. C. D. Locock. 2 vols. London, 1911.
MLR ii	A. C. Bradley. "Notes on Shelley's 'Triumph of Life,'" *Modern Language Review,* IX (October 1914), 441–456.
J	*The Complete Works of Percy Bysshe Shelley,* eds. Roger Ingpen and Walter E. Peck. Julian Edition. 10 vols. London and New York, 1926–30.
C omnia	This symbol, used in the historical collations, indicates that the reading is followed by *C* and all texts derived from *C* (or *PP*): *R, F, W, H, L, J.*
TLS	G. M. Matthews. "The 'Triumph of Life' Apocrypha," *London Times Literary Supplement,* 5 August 1960.
SN	G. M. Matthews. "'The Triumph of Life': A New Text," *Studia Neophilologica,* XXXII (No. 2, 1960), 271–309.
RES	G. M. Matthews. "Shelley and Jane Williams," *Review of English Studies,* N.S., XII (February 1961), 40–48.
T	The text of this edition.

CHAPTER FIVE

HISTORY OF THE TEXT

MARY SHELLEY'S EDITIONS

The basic text of "The Triumph of Life," upon which all editions before 1960 ultimately depended, appeared in Mary Shelley's edition of Shelley's *Posthumous Poems* (1824). Of her labor in preparing that text Mrs. Shelley wrote: " 'The Triumph of Life' was his last work, and was left in so unfinished a state, that I arranged it in its present form with great difficulty" (p. vii). In a footnote to her "Note on Poems Written in 1822" in the four-volume *Poetical Works* (1839) Mrs. Shelley said of her editing of the *Posthumous Poems:* "Did any one see the papers from which I drew that volume, the wonder would be how any eyes or patience were capable of extracting it from so confused a mass, interlined and broken into fragments, so that the sense could only be deciphered and joined by guesses, which might seem rather intuitive than founded on reasoning. Yet I believe no mistake was made" (IV, 226). Nevertheless, the errata leaf included in some copies of *Posthumous Poems* corrected one line of "The Triumph" (96), and in her first collected edition (1839) Mrs. Shelley made several changes that most textual scholars, including Charles H. Taylor, Jr., in *The Early Collected Editions of Shelley's Poems*, have assumed were corrections from the MS. G. M. Matthews has shown (*SN*, pp. 272–273) that in five of the seven major differences between *PP* and C_1, *PP* is closer to *MS*,[1] while in two instances C_1 is more nearly correct.[2] At least three of the five cor-

---

[1] Lines 78, 173, 238, 260, and 505.

[2] Lines 84 and 167–168. Matthews lists a third instance in which C_1 corrects *PP:* He says that a change of " 'vesture' for 'verdure' in line 447 [*sic*]" might have resulted "from a return to the MS" (p. 272). Neither Taylor nor any editor of Shelley records "verdure" as a reading in *Posthumous Poems*, and in the nine-

ruptions of the text that occur between *PP* and C_1 are the kind of change that Mrs. Shelley might have authorized to make the poem seem less fragmentary even though she knew she was departing from the MS: In line 78 she removed the brackets from "blinding" (editorially inserted in *PP*); in line 238 she altered "name the world" (*PP*) to "names which the world" (*C*); in line 260 she changed "near walk" (*PP*) to "near him walk" (*C*) in a metrically incomplete line. The change in line 505 of "make" (*PP*) to "made" (*C*) could represent either an unnoticed compositor's error (and thus tell nothing about Mary Shelley's use of *MS*) or an effort by Mrs. Shelley to bring the tense into conformity with the preceding verbs. On the other hand, the change of "work" to "part" in line 173 seems to me evidence that Mary Shelley probably did consult *MS* on this line, for although *"part"* is canceled in *MS* (f. 27r), it is written more clearly than "work", its uncanceled replacement. Since, according to *SN*, one correction (167–168) *"must* have resulted from a return to the MS," and one other ("form" for "frown" in 84) *"might* have so resulted" (p. 272), there is no reason to suppose that Mary Shelley did not return to *MS* to check a number of lines that had puzzled her in 1824 or that might afterward have seemed incongruous. Nevertheless, Matthews is correct in asserting that "Mrs. Shelley . . . never read the draft through after 1824" (p. 272), and until his text appeared, *Posthumous Poems* provided the most accurate rendering of Shelley's poem; earlier editors erred in assuming that the collected editions were more authoritative than *PP*.

Besides the significant changes cited by Matthews, there are forty-seven variants between *PP* and C_1. Most of these changes seem to have been authorized by Mrs. Shelley, although at least two variants in punctuation, the addition of a dash after "cheek" in line 224 and a single quotation mark after "behold" in line 234 (corrected in the second edition of 1839), and one change in spelling, "sate" to "sat" in line 506 (the word remains "sate" elsewhere in the text), must be regarded as compositor's errors. Because the text of C_1 has been conventionalized in spelling [3] and in details of punctuation, it appears

---

teen copies of *PP* that I have checked or that others have checked for me, line 449 reads: "The grassy vesture of the desart, played," (the nineteen copies were those of the British Museum; Cambridge University Library (2); Bodleian Library, Oxford (2); Duke University Library; Harvard University Library (2); Huntington Library; University of Illinois Library; Library of Congress; McGill University Library; New York Public Library (2); Pierpont Morgan Library; University of Texas Library (2); Yale University Library; and my own copy).

[3] For example, in lines 92, 164, 224, 236, 398, 407, 499, and 504.

more correct than *PP;* most of its new readings are, however, farther from *MS.*

The text of Mary Shelley's three-volume edition of 1847 (C_2), the last revision published during her lifetime, is farther from *PP* than is C_1. Of the thirty-four variants between C_1 and C_2 two punctuation variants in C_2 (93, 190) represent significant corrections of *PP* and C_1, while two others (224, 234) correct typographical errors in C_1, returning to the readings of *PP*. On the other hand, the only three verbal variants (222, 241, 336) are typographical errors in C_2. In thirty cases where C_1 and C_2 differ, *PP* agrees with C_1, and, as might be expected, *MS* supports *PP* and C_1 rather than C_2 in a majority of these instances. The text of C_2 represents a further sophistication of punctuation but is less authoritative than *PP* or C_1.

ROSSETTI, BLIND, AND FORMAN

Entering a lively exchange of correspondence in *Notes and Queries* on the text and meaning of Shelley's poetry on 28 March 1868, W. M. Rossetti began to discuss principles of editing the Shelley canon. At the outset he declared that, while he quite agreed with those who disliked the " 'cobblering and tinkering' of the verses of deceased poets," he believed that Shelley's poetry had suffered from numerous printers' errors that ought to be corrected. His subsequent "Notes and Emendations on Shelley" [4] showed such detailed knowledge of Shelley's text that Moxon chose Rossetti to reedit Shelley's poetical works. One can see from Rossetti's remarks in *Notes and Queries* that he felt free to emend the text of "The Triumph of Life": "This poem—of lurid magnificence and overpowering enthralment—is, as I have already observed, so far from being completed that it ought to be printed among the 'Fragments.' We must not, therefore, be surprised if some passages are imperfectly intelligible or only half constructed. Still, we may fairly try to elicit a meaning where we find, as the poem stands printed, only a blurred suggestion." [5] In his two-volume edition of 1870 (R_1) Rossetti altered the punctuation, spelling, and other accidental features of the poem at will, and even emended words freely, according to his principles, correcting "errors" in sense, grammar, and meter. Although his wholesale departures without authority from Mrs.

[4] *N & Q,* 4th Ser., I (11, 18, and 25 April 1868), 333–336, 357–360, 384–387.
[5] Fourth Series, I (25 April 1868), 386.

Shelley's texts brought a storm of protest from the reviewers and although in some instances he did mistake Shelley's intention, his poetic sense was keen enough to enable him to correct errors and point out inadequacies in previous editions of "The Triumph." For example, even while he damaged the flow of the verse by greatly increasing the number of full stops in the text, he was the first editor (the only one before Matthews) to print the poem in tercets with alternate lines indented to indicate the rhyme scheme. In his notes Rossetti explained his textual emendation of ten lines [6] and pointed out problems or suggested additional emendations in eight lines.[7] Besides those changes Rossetti recorded in notes, he silently corrected line 184. Of these proposed variants from Mrs. Shelley's editions, five agree in substance with the present text (T) and two others agree with SN.[8] For two lines (401, 404) there is no MS available to check Rossetti's suggestions, and in other instances (131–135, 168, 175, 475, 534) changes in the text have since been made on the basis of MS evidence, though not in ways suggested by Rossetti. Rossetti's poetic sensitivity was so acute that without the aid of the MS he was able to correct the text and to point out legitimate problems. Although his example was repudiated by most later editors and though his practice is very dangerous, his emendations in "The Triumph" not only stimulated interest in the poem's textual problems, but clarified several difficult passages.

The most valuable immediate fruit of Rossetti's editorial labors came forth in Mathilde Blind's review article of the edition in the *Westminster Review*.[9] In this essay (WR) Miss Blind published eighteen substantive additions or changes in the text of "The Triumph of Life" that had been supplied to her by Richard Garnett, who had apparently gleaned them from MS while editing "Lines Written in the Bay of Lerici" for his *Relics of Shelley* (1862). Besides presenting for the first time Discarded Opening "A" (*TLDO*-"A") and the words of line 281 and part of line 282, Miss Blind included verbal corrections for fourteen other lines.[10] One emendation (363) was misprinted in WR but corrected in F, while still another (322) was so ambiguous that, though Rossetti incorporated the

---

[6] Lines 84, 103, 168, 205, 320, 472, 475, 496, 510, and 530.

[7] Lines 132, 134, 175, 190, 401, 404, 515, and 534.

[8] Those agreeing with T are in lines 84, 184, 472, 496, and 510; the additional two that agree with SN are in 205 and 320.

[9] N.S., XXXVIII (July 1870), 75–97.

[10] Lines 63, 70, 109, 112, 158, 202, 296, 311, 361, 377, 475, 486, 497, and 534 (475 and 534 correcting suggestions by Rossetti).

change in R_2, its significance was misunderstood by most later editors.

Harry Buxton Forman's four-volume edition of 1876–77 (F) marked a conservative reaction to Rossetti's practice of free emendation. Although Forman made some independent changes in spelling [11] based on his study of Shelley's diction and spelling habits (on which he commented at the end of each volume in an appendix, "On Certain Words Used by Shelley . . ."), he followed Mary Shelley's editions in his text of "The Triumph," using PP as his copy text but incorporating most substantive changes from C_1.[12] Forman also incorporated Miss Blind's list of emendations (even correcting line 363 for the first time); he did not, however, acknowledge his indebtedness to her article but cited the MS in his notes as though he himself had consulted it.

Forman's notes to "The Triumph" include copious commentary on Rossetti's treatment of the text: F follows R_1 in emending lines 205, 480, and 496, and Forman agrees that line 401 is metrically faulty. (In two lines [93, 190] where Forman credited Rossetti with substantive changes in punctuation, the changes had first appeared in C_2.) In his disagreements with the text and notes of R_1, Forman was correct in seven instances,[13] but was wrong in rejecting five of Rossetti's emendations or criticisms.[14] While basing the text itself essentially on the authority of MS (as it was then known through Mrs. Shelley and Garnett), Forman in his notes made original observations on substantive features of eight lines or passages; subsequent study of MS has shown him essentially correct in five cases and wrong in three.[15]

Though Forman's editorial principles were basically much sounder than Rossetti's, the latter reigned in the popular market through his one-volume Moxon's Popular Poets edition (based on R_1) and his three-volume redaction of the text in 1878 (R_2), which was reprinted at various dates to the end of the century. Although R_2 retained most of the basic features of R_1, a few differences require comment. In R_2 Rossetti incorporated the list of corrections from

11 In lines 64, 85, 92, 442, and 502.

12 Like Rossetti, Forman followed PP in reading "work" in 173 instead of "part" (C_1).

13 Lines 102–103, 142, 190 ("Feature"), 320, 362, 515, and 530.

14 Lines 84, 133, 168, 184, and 510. At 472 Forman returned to PP (and MS) whereas SN and T follow Rossetti's emendation.

15 Forman was correct in 142, 235, 265, 276–282, and 293; wrong in 133, 252, and 464.

WR, even correcting line 322 in spite of WR's ambiguity on this line. The notes to R_2 omitted two emendations proposed in R_1 (175, 190) but added two other proposals.[16] In one substantive (238) and several accidentals, R_2 returned to the readings of PP where R_1 had followed C.[17] Rossetti retained most of R_1's excessively heavy punctuation in R_2 but, as though to counteract the choppy effect of this pointing, pushed the tercets together into "verse paragraphs" which emphasize the flow of meaning but indicate the *terza rima* only by the indentation of alternate lines.

DOWDEN, WOODBERRY, HUTCHINSON, LOCOCK, AND THE JULIAN EDITORS

In the popular Macmillan Shelley (1890) Edward Dowden based his text primarily on F, occasionally modifying spelling and punctuation. Dowden's text, which I have collated, is not sufficiently independent to deserve space in the record of variants; I mention it here only because of Dowden's important work on Shelley and because his edition circulated widely.

Although George Edward Woodberry's four-volume Centenary Edition of 1892 (W) brought new MS evidence to bear on other poems, it introduced no significant changes into the text of "The Triumph." Woodberry's greatest contribution was his insistence upon the necessity of recording all the substantive variants from earlier editions, for, as he wrote: "The personal judgment of the editor counts for so much in any edition that a variorum text is the only just and perfect rendering of his [Shelley's] poetry that is now possible" (I, vii). He did not, however, carry either his theory or his practice to the length of recording variants in spelling (which he Americanized) or punctuation (which he emended freely). He introduced for the first time fifty minor changes in the text of "The Triumph of Life"—fifteen new spellings and thirty-five changes in punctuation, several of them minor variations from R.

In 1904 Thomas Hutchinson edited Shelley's poetry for the Clarendon Press. In 1905 this text (H) was reset as the Oxford Edition and, again entirely reset in demy 8vo format in 1934,[18] it

---

[16] In R_2 Rossetti proposed "Conqueror" for "conquerors" in 129 and "fate" for "hate" in 475; the first suggestion was right and the second wrong, according to MS.

[17] E.g., 136, 149, 283, and 368.

[18] In the text of "The Triumph of Life" these three printings of the edition are identical.

remains in the Oxford Standard Authors series the most readily available of the important editions. Hutchinson contributed very little to the text of "The Triumph of Life." *H* depends heavily though not slavishly on *F*, following *F* in all substantive matters but breaking away in minor details on the authority of other editions.[19] Of the three capitalizations he introduced for the first time (line 268 and two in line 333), the latter two have been substantiated by *MS.* *H* also agrees with *T* in omitting punctuation at the end of line 364, though in *H* this may have resulted from a compositor's oversight. *H* introduced minor innovations in spelling or punctuation at lines 28, 92, 178, 179, 269, 368, 415, and 442.

In 1911 C. D. Locock, who had earlier published *An Examination of the Shelley Manuscripts in the Bodleian Library* (1903), reedited Shelley's poetry in two volumes for Methuen (*L*). Locock made valuable contributions to the text of "The Triumph of Life" through the aid of Richard Garnett, who communicated additional information, apparently from notes taken during his earlier examination of *MS.* There is no evidence that Garnett studied the MS of "The Triumph" after 1870: The notes he supplied to Locock do not deal with the lines debated by Rossetti and Forman or questioned by explicators of the poem, and Locock wrote in a note to line 134 that "failing a rediscovery of the lost manuscript, the construction of the sentence seems beyond remedy" (II, 481). On Garnett's authority Locock added three-and-a-half lines to the end of the poem (544–548) and three words to line 133, corrected words in lines 134 and 475 (this latter mistake had been perpetuated by *WR*), bracketed "quickly" (283) and "chiefs" (285) because they are not in *MS,* and noted that lines 439–450 (actually 438–450) appear on the back of a letter cover with a postmark dated May 15. Although Garnett also informed Locock of *WR*'s confusion of line 322, Locock, who was "reluctant to disturb the text reading, now generally accepted," retained *F*'s reading in his text while recording the correct one in a note.

Locock also had at his disposal A. C. Bradley's "Notes on Passages in Shelley" (*MLR i*) and carefully collated the earlier editions, but he relied ultimately on his own understanding of the poem for his readings. *L* follows Bradley's punctuation of line 190 (a reading retained in *SN* and *T*), and in a note suggested the change of "tips"

[19] For example, *H* follows C_2 at 34; R_2 at 109; *PP* and R_2 at 368; *C* and others at 449, 499; *PP* and *W* at 503.

to "tops" in line 309 (adopted in *T* on *MS* authority). On the other hand, *L* replaced *"where"* of line 161 with the conjectural *" 'Ware,"* and in the notes conjectured changes in lines 103, 151, 237–238, 333, and 406 that *MS* has not substantiated. In accidentals *L* tends to be liberal rather than conservative, often following *R* in opposition to *PP, C, F,* and *H*.

Finally, among the critical editions of "The Triumph of Life" depending basically on Mrs. Shelley's reading of *MS* (slightly emended from Garnett's notes) is that in the fourth volume of the Julian Edition (*J*). The Julian editors had been preceded by able editors of two schools—those like Forman and Hutchinson who introduced almost no changes not authorized by *MS* and those like Rossetti and Locock who, after careful study, emended the text in an attempt to clarify what they took to be Shelley's intended meaning; unfortunately, the Julian editors, having at their disposal the accumulated information and judgments of a century, produced the worst text of "The Triumph of Life" in any historically significant edition. First, *J* followed C_2 as its copy text,[20] a mistake in judgment avoided by all previous editors and one that should have been avoided by anyone who collated C_2 with C_1. Second, *J* failed to correct the text in five [21] of the eighteen places corrected by *WR*. Third, *J* conjecturally emended two words in line 494.[22] Fourth, *J* follows the "Robert S. Garnett MS. leaf" (actually part of *TLDO*-"D"), which Peck, who had published a rough transcription of the leaf as an appendix to *Shelley: His Life and Work,* had already identified as "the first draft of these lines," [23] as the authority for four verbal variants in lines 37–38 and a virtually new 40, this despite the fact that one change left line 37 an unrhymed line. Moreover, *J*'s uncritical eclecticism resulted in such aberrations as the punctuation of lines 149 (after C_2) and 150 (after *PP*), in which "As their feet twinkle" is caught between two semicolons. *J* also contains such compositor's errors as the end punctuation of line 190 and the spacing of line 404. In short, the text of "The Triumph

[20] This can be seen from the collations of lines 31–35, 53, 146, 149, 295, 302, 349, 351, 392, 418, and 529.

[21] Lines 70, 112, 361, 363, 377.

[22] Rossetti and Locock had, of course, also conjecturally emended the text, but in almost every instance their emendations occurred at difficult cruxes that required clarification before one could understand the poem as a whole, whereas the Julian editors' change of "On vulgar hands" to "In vulgar bands" serves no similar purpose.

[23] II (Boston, 1927), 278, 402–404.

of Life" in the most recent critical edition of Shelley's poetry (and the only edition of Shelley's works that attempts to be complete) was both conceived on erroneous principles and shabbily executed.

MATTHEWS AND THE PRESENT TEXT

In the *Times Literary Supplement* of 5 August 1960, G. M. Matthews published an article entitled "The 'Triumph of Life' Apocrypha" (*TLS*) in which he printed some rejected passages from "The Triumph" MS and two of the four discarded openings of the poem, together with notes and commentary. In *Studia Neophilologica,* No. 2, 1960, appeared " 'The Triumph of Life': A New Text" (*SN*), in which Matthews published a text of the poem and the other discarded openings based on *MS.* Finally, in *Review of English Studies* (1961) Matthews published "Shelley and Jane Williams" (*RES*), in which he provided a new text of "Lines Written in the Bay of Lerici." Although Matthews utilized different editorial methods suitable to his media of publication, the three studies taken together provide the most complete analysis of the evidence of "The Triumph" MS that has appeared. As the first published text since *PP* to be based directly on *MS, SN* corrected many errors in *PP,* as well as several corruptions that had entered the text since 1824. *SN* contains, according to Matthews, "104 *verbal* variants from *Posthumous Poems,* counting each associated group as one variant" (p. 273). In addition, Matthews introduced such significant changes as that in line 281, where the end of the line is punctuated as the Poet's speech rather than as part of Rousseau's.

A few of Matthews' editorial principles require comment inasmuch as they explain a number of the variants in accidentals between *SN* and *T.* Of Shelley's punctuation Matthews wrote: "Those all-purpose signals, dots and dashes, are no longer very acceptable and can often be advantageously replaced; but in this poem, as in 'Julian and Maddalo', both devices contribute to the characteristic method and movement, and I have retained a number of them" (p. 274); on Shelley's spelling: "Shelley's idiosyncrasies and archaisms ('thier', 'althose', 'sate', 'kist', 'desart', etc.) would only matter if the poem relied on such things for dignity or atmosphere, which it does not. . . . The spelling here is modernized, though all the old forms are, of course, noted; this has involved 22 modifications of the MS" (pp. 274–275). He treats Shelley's use of capitals as a different matter from his idiosyncrasies of spelling, a capital letter usually implying "some special relation, however slight, transient, or local, between the poet and the object named," but he discards eleven of Shelley's capitals that "belong to entities . . . whose importance in the poem, it seems to me, is incommensurate with that of the Sun and its analogues, Life and its analogues, and the Earth" (p. 275).

Matthews thus follows the example of Mrs. Shelley in that he attempts to polish and conventionalize what Shelley wrote, modernizing spelling and punctuation and altering capitals to accord with his interpretation of the poem. Such revisions of Shelley's text might be necessary for a popular edition of the poem, but in a scholarly text returning to the MS such liberal treatment of accidentals is a questionable practice. Nevertheless, Matthews corrected the text of "The Triumph of Life" more than any other single editor of the poem, and his readings must be carefully considered by all future editors of Shelley.

The text of the present edition (*T*), which was begun in 1958, has benefited greatly from G. M. Matthews' publications. Though Matthews worked with the aid of Mrs. Shelley's editions and Garnett's few corrections, no single redaction from a manuscript that in places deserves the appellation "chaotic" could solve the textual problems of "The Triumph of Life." *T* differs from *SN* on 211 accidental matters in 177 lines; these variants result chiefly from differences in editorial principles, for though *SN* departs from *MS* much more frequently than *T*, these departures often agree with *PP* or *C*. Much more significant are the substantive differences between *SN* and *T*: seventy-one variants in fifty lines. *T* returns to *PP*'s readings in eighteen [24] of the 104 lines in which there are verbal variants between *SN* and *PP*, and *T* introduces new verbal readings in thirty lines.[25] Compare with these figures the number of variants between *T* and *PP*: 395 accidental variants in 298 lines and 161 substantive variants in 113 lines (besides final lines omitted from *PP*); between *T* and C_1: 417 accidentals in 312 lines and 161 substantives in 115 lines (besides final lines omitted); and, finally, between *T* and *H*: 415 accidentals in 311 lines and 144 substantives in 100 lines (besides final lines omitted).

[24] Lines 150, 169, 251, 271 ("The"), 276, 282 ("he"), 320, 354 ("invisible"), 359, 369, 372 ("moist"), 421, 465, 468, 502, 522, 529, and 534.

[25] Lines 103, 115, 117, 127, 137, 143, 154, 158, 167, 191, 194, 205, 237, 265, 267, 272, 309, 311, 318, 340, 347, 366, 373, 381, 386, 408, 435, 463, 494, and 526.

CHAPTER SIX

EDITORIAL PROCEDURES

This edition of "The Triumph of Life" follows Shelley's holograph as closely as the unfinished state of that draft will permit. Because every departure from the MS opens the possibility of obscuring the poet's intention, the text (with three minor exceptions noted below) departs from exact transcription of Shelley's words and pointing *only* to add minimal punctuation where the unfinished state of the draft demands an editorial judgment to provide continuity to the poem.

Though the text is conservative, it is no mere record of jumbled words and phrases, as the draft sometimes is. Following the example of Mrs. Shelley and G. M. Matthews, I have attempted to determine Shelley's intention both from the physical evidence of the MS and from the prosodic laws of *terza rima*. Sometimes, for example, changes in ink or the sharpness of the quill can be used to determine the order in which certain alternatives were written, thus revealing Shelley's latest preference; occasionally one must include in the text lines once canceled but, apparently, mentally reinstated by the poet as he continued his composition; sometimes one must include a canceled word or omit a nonessential uncanceled word to maintain the pentameter line. By using such evidence and the elementary rules of grammar and syntax, one can solve by far the greater number of problems in the text, filling out most lines and leaving only one real problem of continuity in the rhyme scheme.

This text represents the accumulation of one editor's inductions and judgments, and individual points are, of course, open to question. I have provided, therefore, full textual apparatus: a variorum collation of variants from earlier critical editions and from *MS*, with emphasis on *MS* and the two authoritative editions, *PP* and *SN;*

exact transcription of crucial passages of *MS;* and notes in which I discuss debatable editorial decisions. This apparatus should enable future editors and explicators of the poem to exercise their own judgments on those points where genuine doubt exists.

Since even the fragment of "The Triumph" that we possess was still very much in a state of flux, we can be sure that, had Shelley lived, he would have revised and corrected the draft extensively, as was his custom, before publication. Some of the canceled words and phrases that we, by necessity, include in the text would have been replaced by others more completely fulfilling the poet's intention. Within these broad limits, however, the following text, with its accompanying transcriptions, collations, and notes, reveals Shelley's version of this poem when he laid it down for the last time.

PRINCIPLES OF EDITING

Cancellations and Doubtful Readings

In the collations and notes, words canceled in *MS* are printed in italics. (Italicized words from other editions, of course, indicate italics.) When long canceled passages are interesting in themselves or may help to elucidate the text of the poem, I have endeavored to transcribe complete sections of *MS*. Sometimes these transcriptions include doubtful or even conjectural readings, but I believe that a complete transcription of the relevant passage—even though imperfect in certain points—will be of aid to future editors who wish to compare my readings with *MS*.

Occasionally Shelley superimposed words upon earlier readings; I have recorded such occurrences in my transcriptions thus: ${Yet \atop But}$ the higher word is the later word and is superimposed upon the lower. Illegible words are indicated thus: [?]; doubtful readings thus: ?dreary or *?spark*. Where it is undetermined how many separate words are contained in an illegible passage, the following sign is used: [? *?* ?], with one question mark for each word I believe to be present. Italic question marks indicate *canceled* illegible words; Roman question marks indicate uncanceled illegible words.

Alternatives

Where genuinely debatable alternative readings appear in *MS,* a transcription of the relevant section and a note will clarify the relationships.

Punctuation

In the first forty-eight lines I have retained all of Shelley's punctuation and have added only what seems absolutely necessary to convey the obvious sense of the words. In the rough-draft portions I have been somewhat more liberal in adding punctuation but have refrained from altering Shelley's own pointing unless *MS* indicates clearly that the poet's intention changed after the punctuation was recorded.

Following the practice of other editors, I have supplied quotation marks to the text, for the holograph contains none, but I have recorded each addition as a variant from *MS,* as well as all variants between my usage and that of each other edition. Shelley often used a dash (—) to indicate the beginning or end of a quotation; I have retained these dashes (even though editorial addition of quotation marks somewhat obscures their original function), for they still indicate the length of the pause within the line.

Inasmuch as Shelley's punctuation is often inconsistent with modern British or American usage, establishing Shelley's own preferred punctuation does not in itself solve all interpretive problems. The editor's duty is to provide for explicators a text that conforms as nearly as possible to the author's intention; the explicator must then compare the practice in the text with that of the author in other authoritative texts (in Shelley's case, his fair copy holographs and those volumes that he himself saw through the press) to determine the significance of the orthography, punctuation, diction, and syntax.

Thomas Hutchinson pointed out what seems to me the chief value of Shelley's somewhat unorthodox practice: "Shelley's punctuation, so far as it goes, is of great value as an index to his metrical, or at times, it may be, to his rhetorical intention—for, in Shelley's hands, punctuation serves rather to mark the rhythmical pause and onflow of the verse or to secure some declamatory effect, than to indicate the structure or elucidate the sense" (*H,* p. iv). One piece of corroborative evidence is Shelley's frequent omission of necessary punctuation, particularly commas, at the ends of lines of verse. I believe that to Shelley's ear the normal pause at the end of a line equalled the pause given for a comma. Since Shelley apparently voiced his lines as he composed and wrote his poetry to be read aloud, he would not feel it necessary to insert commas at the ends of lines.

That Shelley composed aurally, a practice common among poets,

explains some imperfections of this draft. The editor must occasionally include lines now canceled in *MS* and, less frequently, omit
uncanceled lines and words; had the poet relied chiefly upon the
visual impression of the page, he would surely have recopied lines
once canceled but later mentally reinstated in the text. To test
this hypothesis of Shelley's composition—especially as it influenced
his habits of punctuation—one should take up a piece of Shelley's
prose that he is known to have supervised through the press (the
preface to *The Revolt of Islam, The Cenci,* or *Adonais* in its first
edition, for example) and read it orally, with the length of pause
determined by the mark of punctuation. What is unorthodox and
confusing in appearance becomes clear and logical when read aloud.

Spelling

Shelley's idiosyncrasies of spelling (as Forman pointed out eighty
years ago) are quite likely to be significant for pronunciation, meaning, or both. To change the spelling of "sate" to "sat," for example,
is to corrupt the sound of the word, for—as a glance (in the Shelley
Concordance) at Shelley's use of "sate" and "sat" as rhymes will
show—Shelley pronounced "sate" to rhyme with "hate" and "sat" to
rhyme with "that." In some instances I have been unable to discover any reason for variant spellings in Shelley's MS; indeed, in
a few cases it is difficult to determine which vowel Shelley has
written where. But wherever I have been able to determine, or even
suspect, that Shelley may have had a reason for an unusual spelling,
I have retained his orthography in the text. In other instances I
have recorded my departures from *MS*.

I have consistently followed Shelley's use of "and" and of the
ampersand (&) in my text. Inasmuch as all previous editors have
changed Shelley's ampersands to and's, I have not recorded these
variants in my collations. It is understood that where *T* has an
ampersand, all other editions read "and."

Terminology

To avoid misunderstandings I have employed the following terms
in my textual notes to indicate various relationships among words
or phrases in the manuscript:

(a) *"sprung"* changed to "sprang": One or more letters of the first
    word have been altered so as to form the second word.

(b) "his" superimposed on *"their"*: The first word, written later, is superimposed on the second, in whole or in part.

(c) "his" above "their": The first word has been written slightly higher on the page than the second word. (No chronological order implied.)

(d) "his" below "their": The first word is written slightly lower on the page than the second word. (No chronological order implied.)

(e) "his" before *"their"*: The first word is written to the *left* of the second. (No chronological order implied.)

(f) "his" after *"their"*: The first word is written to the *right* of the second. (No chronological order implied.)

(g) "his" earlier than "their": Chronology established.

(h) "his" later than "their": Chronology established.

(i) ?Mankind: Doubtful reading.

(j) [?]: Illegible word.

(k) ⟨e⟩ : Editorially added letter.

(l) $\begin{Bmatrix} \text{Yet} \\ \text{\textit{But}} \end{Bmatrix}$: Higher (later) word superimposed on lower (earlier) word.

CHAPTER SEVEN

"THE TRIUMPH OF LIFE": A VARIORUM EDITION

f. 19r   Swift as a spirit hastening to his task
        Of glory & of good, the Sun sprang forth
    Rejoicing in his splendour, & the mask

        Of darkness fell from the awakened Earth.
    The smokeless altars of the mountain snows   5
        Flamed above crimson clouds, & at the birth

    Of light, the Ocean's orison arose
        To which the birds tempered their matin lay.
    All flowers in field or forest which unclose

        Their trembling eyelids to the kiss of day,   10
    Swinging their censers in the element,
        With orient incense lit by the new ray

    Burned slow & inconsumably, & sent
f. 19v   Their odorous sighs up to the smiling air,
    And in succession due, did Continent,   15

        Isle, Ocean, & all things that in them wear
    The form & character of mortal mould
        Rise as the Sun their father rose, to bear

    Their portion of the toil which he of old
        Took as his own & then imposed on them;   20
    But I, whom thoughts which must remain untold

        Had kept as wakeful as the stars that gem
    The cone of night, now they were laid asleep,
        Stretched my faint limbs beneath the hoary stem

  4 Earth— *PP*
  7 light *SN*   ocean's *SN*   arose, *PP*
14 air *MS*
     air; *PP*
15 And, *PP*   Continent *MS*
                  continent, *PP, SN*
16 ocean, *PP, SN*
17 mould, *PP*
18 sun *PP*
19 toil, *PP*
20 them: *PP*
23 asleep *PP*

7   *PP* and *SN* retain some of Shelley's capitalization but alter other capitals to lower case, a practice that depends, as Matthews admits (p. 275), on personal estimation of the significance of the words in question. Shelley's capitalization of "Ocean's" must be retained unless it can be demonstrated that either: (1) the word is not actually capitalized in *MS;* or (2) Shelley's pen slipped and the capitalization does not represent his intention. In this fair-copy portion of the holograph, where Shelley transcribed from an earlier state of the text (where the word was also capitalized), neither of these possible objections is defensible. Shelley consistently capitalized "Ocean" (see 16, 38) and certain other words in *TL* (see "Continent", 15).

14 Following earlier editors, I have supplied punctuation after "air" to separate two independent clauses; cf. the even heavier stop in *DO*-"D" (see Appendix B).

15, 16 "Continent," "Ocean": see note to 7 above.

17 Shelley probably began to write a capital "F" before he wrote "form".

18 *SN* reads "Sun" in *MS,* and "Sun" is certainly capitalized in the rough draft versions (see Appendix B). Shelley, by capitalizing "Continent", "Isle", and "Ocean" and then referring to the sun as father of all mortal things, seems to attribute to it more than naturalistic implications.

Which an old chestnut flung athwart the steep   25
    Of a green Apennine: before me fled
The night; behind me rose the day; the Deep

    Was at my feet, & Heaven above my head
When a strange trance over my fancy grew
    Which was not slumber, for the shade it spread   30

Was so transparent that the scene came through
f. 20r   As clear as when a veil of light is drawn
O'er evening hills they glimmer; and I knew

    That I had felt the freshness of that dawn,
Bathed in the same cold dew my brow & hair   35
    And sate as thus upon that slope of lawn

Under the self same bough, & heard as there
    The birds, the fountains & the Ocean hold
Sweet talk in music through the enamoured air.
    And then a Vision on my brain was rolled . .   40

———————

As in that trance of wondrous thought I lay
    This was the tenour of my waking dream.
Methought I sate beside a public way

    Thick strewn with summer dust, & a great stream
Of people there was hurrying to & fro   45
    Numerous as gnats upon the evening gleam,

25 chesnut *PP*
27 deep *PP, SN*
28 heaven *SN*   head, *PP*
                    head; *SN*
31 transparent, *PP*
34 dawn *MS*
35 hair, *PP, SN*
36 sat *SN*
37 self-same *SN*
38 birds *MS*   fountains, *SN*   ocean *PP, SN*
39 air, *PP*
40 vision *PP*   rolled. *PP*
                   rolled . . . *SN*
41 lay, *PP*
42 dream:— *PP*
    dream: *SN*
43 sat *SN*
45 fro, *PP*
46 gleam *MS*

27, 28   "Deep", "Heaven": see note to 7 above.

28   The comma or full stop after "head" that has been supplied by *PP, SN,* and all other editors prejudices the meaning of the passage and cannot be justified on textual grounds. The "strange trance" is, in Shelley's fair copy, more intimately related to the dawning day and to the situation of the Poet with "the Deep" at his feet and "Heaven" above his head than is conveyed by the altered pointing.

30   "shade" above *"rest".*

31   "so" above *"too".*

32   "As" was superimposed on a slightly longer, illegible word *("?Was"),* then canceled, and finally written again above the line; "drawn" after *"spread".*

34   The added comma after "dawn" conventionalizes the pointing of the series of verbs depending on "I had".

35   "cold" above *"sweet"* which is, in turn, superimposed on *"rain"* (perhaps only "rain" was canceled, leaving "sweet" as an uncanceled alternative); "brow" above *"eyes".*

36   "that" superimposed on *"this"*; "dawn" changed to "lawn". I retain *MS* spelling of "sate", which is consistent throughout. Shelley pronounced "sat" and "sate" differently: He rhymed "sat" with "that" (*Sensitive Plant* III.114–115) and "sate" with "state" (*Revolt* V.xxx.8–9), "weight" (*Revolt* VI.xxxiii.1, 3), and "gate" (*Rosalind,* 1054, 1056).

37–40   The variants introduced into these lines by the Julian editors on the "authority" of the R. S. Garnett MS leaf represent extreme editorial irresponsibility: The Garnett leaf was so obviously part of an earlier, rejected version of the opening lines (as Peck admits elsewhere: see *Shelley,* II, 279ⁿ) that only one willing to sacrifice Shelley's intention for the sake of novelty could have considered such changes in the text.

38   "Ocean": see note to 7 above; Shelley customarily did not punctuate before conjunctions that coordinate members of a parallel series: Here, as elsewhere in *MS,* he neglects all separation, perhaps indicating that pauses in oral reading of the line should be no greater than those achieved by the normal grouping of each noun with its definite article.

39   "music" after *"the".*

40   "Vision": see note to 7 above; Shelley's suspension points indicate important breaks or divisions in the thought of the poem; below 40 are two short, heavy horizontal lines with scribbling between them.

41   *"This was the"* above "As in that".

43   "sate": see note to 36 above.

45   "there" superimposed on *"thus".*

45–47   Depending on where one supplies commas in these lines, the phrase "All hastening onward" can modify "steam/ Of people" or "gnats". I follow *SN* in retaining this ambiguity.

All hastening onward, yet none seemed to know
Whither he went, or whence he came, or why
f. 21r   He made one of the multitude, yet so

Was borne amid the crowd as through the sky   50
One of the million leaves of summer's bier.—
Old age & youth, manhood & infancy,

Mixed in one mighty torrent did appear,
Some flying from the thing they feared & some
f. 21v   Seeking the object of another's fear,   55

And others as with steps towards the tomb
Pored on the trodden worms that crawled beneath,
And others mournfully within the gloom

Of their own shadow walked, and called it death . . .
And some fled from it as it were a ghost,   60
Half fainting in the affliction of vain breath.

But more with motions which each other crost
Pursued or shunned the shadows the clouds threw
Or birds within the noonday ether lost,

47   onward *MS*
49   yet] and *PP*
50   crowd; *MS*
      crowd, *PP*
51   *the MS*   *of* summers *bier MS*
                              bier; *PP*
                              bier: *SN*
52   *Old age & youth, manhood & infancy, MS*
                              infancy *PP*
53   appear *MS*
54   *Some MS*   feared, *PP, SN*
55   *an*other's *MS*   fear *MS*
                              fear; *PP*
56   tomb, *PP*
59   walked *PP*   death; *PP*
61   breath: *PP*
      breath; *SN*
62   more, *SN*   motions, *PP*   crost, *PP*
                                              crossed, *SN*
63   shunned] spurned *PP*   threw, *PP*
64   noon-day *PP*

48   This final line of fair copy is at the bottom of f. 20r; f. 20v is blank; f. 21r
     contains a number of canceled lines and line fragments before 48 appears
     again (in rough draft). For an earlier, rough draft version of the lines
     written to follow 46, see Appendix C.

49   Matthews says *"too"* changed to "so"; this is possible though not certain.

50–51   *MS:*

> Was borne amid the crowd; as *like* through the
> sky

>> *the million*
> One of *an army* of *autumnal* leaves.—

>> *leaves* million   summer's
>>> leaves *of autumns bier*

The semicolon after "crowd" seems to have been written before Shelley
decided to add the simile; the period and dash after *"autumnal* leaves" in
the original version of 51 show where he finally decided to place the full
stop.

52   This line, completely canceled in *MS,* must be included to maintain the
     rhyme-scheme.

53   "torrent" above *"impulse".*

54   There is no legible alternative for *"Some";* an uncanceled word above
     "Some" may be "By" or "Or", while an illegible word below it may, as *SN*
     suggests, be a second "Some".

55   I retain the first two letters of *"another's"* on metrical grounds.

57   *MS:*

> *Dragging his weary limbs   intent*
>> *Watched* Pored on
> *And others so*   trodden   beneath,
>> *Watching,* the *mangled* worms that crawled *below*

"Poured" (R_1) was a typographical error: see Rossetti's letter to Garnett,
16 January 1870 (*Letters About Shelley,* p. 34).

59   "walked," above *"sate,";* "death . . .": see note to 40 above.

60   *Orig.: "But many more or slow or swift pursued".*

61   *MS* does not support *PP* and *SN's* weakening of the stop after "breath"; had
     Shelley's intention changed, he could easily have changed his period to a
     colon or semicolon.

63   "the clouds" above *"of pale".*

64–65   The comma after "lost" may indicate that the adverbial phrase and
     clause "Upon . . . grew" modifies "Pursued or shunned" rather than
     "threw" and "lost".

Upon that path where flowers never grew;   65
    And weary with vain toil & faint for thirst
Heard not the fountains whose melodious dew

    Out of their mossy cells forever burst

f. 22r   Nor felt the breeze which from the forest told
    Of grassy paths, & wood lawns interspersed   70

With overarching elms & caverns cold,
    And violet banks where sweet dreams brood, but they
Pursued their serious folly as of old . . . .

    And as I gazed methought that in the way
The throng grew wilder, as the woods of June   75
    When the South wind shakes the extinguished day.—

And a cold glare, intenser than the noon
    But icy cold, obscured with   light
The Sun as he the stars. Like the young moon

65   grew, *PP, SN*
66   thirst, *PP*
67   fountains, *PP*   dew. *MS*
68   thier *MS*   for ever *PP*   burst; *PP*
                                  burst, *SN*
70   paths *PP*   wood, lawn-interspersed, *PP*
                    wood-lawns interspersed *SN*
71   over-arching *PP*   elms, *SN*   cold *MS*
73   old. *PP*
      old . . . *SN*
74   gazed, *PP*
76   south *PP, SN*   day, *PP, SN*
77   glare *MS*   noon, *PP, SN*
78   with [blinding] light *PP*
      with light *SN*
79   sun, *PP, SN*

65ff.   *MS* does not support the change of semicolon to comma (*PP, SN*); see note to 68 below.

66   *Orig.:* "And faint for thirst & weary with vain toil". Shelley underlined the two elements and used a metathesis sign to indicate the proper order of this line.

67   *MS:*

                         whose
         Heard not the fountains *of* melodious dew.

         The change from "*of*" to "whose" introduced a clause that necessitated discarding the period after "dew".

68   *MS:*

                     cells
              mossy *caves* forever
         Out of thier *ivied caverns ever* burst

         "their" sometimes appears in *MS* as "thier"; because it is often difficult to determine the actual order of the vowels, I have consistently used "their" in the text but have recorded each instance where *MS* clearly has "thier". No comma is necessary at the end of 68: The clause begins at 66; "they" (understood) controls two verbs, "Heard" (67) and "felt" (69), which are negated in nonparallel constructions because of metrical limitations.

69   *Orig.* (bottom of f. 21v): "*Nor saw the landscape on which ?May ?had perish[?ed]*"; "told" above "*brought*"; below this line is written: "*News of soft beds*".

70   Both *H* and *L* indicate in notes that C_1 read "wood-lawn-interspersed"; all copies of C_1 (and C_2) that I have examined follow *PP* in reading "wood, lawn-interspersed,". Either *L* followed *H* in an error or there are two states of C_1 which have hitherto gone undifferentiated. *J* fails to incorporate *WR*'s correction of "lawn" to "lawns". The text follows Shelley's practice in *MS* by omitting the hyphen between "wood" and "lawns" (see "mountain snows", 5).

73   "old . . . .": see note to 40 above.

74–76 This sentence, which has a single word ("methought") for both subject and verb of its main clause, begins with an adverbial clause starting "as" and ends with a simile that uses "as"; the verb of "woods" is "do" (understood).

75–76 *MS:*

         There came a   as the woods of June
                          waves & woods
         The throng grew wilder, *like the forest tops*
         When *the heat* the South wind *turns Heaven*
                              makes the sad Heavens grey
                              shakes the extinguished day.—

         The punctuation of this line is unmistakably clear: Shelley probably intended to separate 74–76, where the Poet witnesses an effect upon the crowd, from 77–79, where he first discovers the cause of the disturbance.

77   "glare" above "*light*"; "noon" after "*Sun*"; a comma must be supplied after "glare" to complement the comma after "cold" (78).

78   "obscured with" above "*with fascinating*"; Mrs. Shelley apparently inserted "blinding" to fill out the meter.

79   *MS:*

         Pierced Heaven & covered earth   Like   young
                              filled the earth; *and* like the moon
              The Sun as he the stars.

When on the sunlit limits of the night   80
　Her white shell trembles amid crimson air
　　And whilst the sleeping tempest gathers might

Doth, as a herald of its coming, bear
f. 23r　　The ghost of her dead Mother, whose dim form
　Bends in dark ether from her infant's chair,   85

　So came a chariot on the silent storm
Of its own rushing splendour, and a Shape
　So sate within as one whom years deform

81   air, PP
82   might, PP
83   a] the PP
84   her] its PP   mother, PP, SN   form] frown PP
85   infants chair MS
　　infant's chair,— PP
88   sat SN   within, PP   deform, PP

79–85 As *R, W,* and *H* punctuate these lines, the construction beginning "Like the young moon" is a clause, with "moon" the subject and "Doth . . . bear" its verb. *MS* gives no special sanction to this reading: It seems possible to me that the construction is a phrase with a dependent adjectival clause which begins rather unusually with "When", has "shell" as its subject, and has "trembles" and "Doth . . . bear" as its verbs. Such a reading not only accords with the evidence of *MS* but also eliminates three grammatical solecisms: As I read the passage (1) "Like" is a preposition rather than a conjunction; (2) "its" (83) refers to "shell", the subject of "Doth . . . bear", rather than to "moon", which is referred to as "her" in 81 and 84–85; (3) the adverbial clause in 82 beginning "whilst" takes on significance and no longer seems a truncated, unsuccessful attempt to parallel the "When" construction. The "When" clause is adjectival because it describes a state of the moon, its appearance as a new moon. This reading does, however, introduce one difficulty: Why should the simile of the main clause beginning "So came . . ." emphasize the similarity in *action* more than that of *state of being* between "moon" and "chariot"?

80 "sunlit limits of the night" below *"limits of the day and n";* the *OED* cites this as the first use of the word "sunlit", which Shelley probably coined not only because of its assonance with "limits" but because his earlier-coined "sunlight" ("Euganean Hills," 82) would have produced an awkward internal rhyme.

83 "herald" above *"token";* a doubtful, uncanceled word above "bear" that *SN* read "[s]hape" was added in different ink after the rest of the page was complete.

84–85 *MS:*

                    the old moon
              ?her dead
      The ghost of *its old* Mother, whose dim form
      Bends in dark *air*   her infants
                    ether   from *the silver* chair

"her" (84) is probable, though the word is very faint.

86 "silent" above *"invisible".*

87 "rushing" above *"roy"* (of "royal"?).

88 "as" above *"like";* "sate": see note to 36 above.

Beneath a dusky hood & double cape
>Crouching within the shadow of a tomb,   90
And o'er what seemed the head, a cloud like crape,

>Was bent a dun & faint etherial gloom
Tempering the light; upon the chariot's beam
>A Janus-visaged Shadow did assume

The guidance of that wonder-winged team.   95
>The Shapes which drew it in thick lightnings
Were lost: I heard alone on the air's soft stream

89 cape, *PP*
90 tomb *MS*
91 oer *MS*   head a cloud like crape *MS*
                    head a cloud-like crape *PP*
                    head a cloud, like crape, *SN*
92 bent, *PP, SN*
93 light *PP*   chariots beam *MS*
                    chariot beam; *PP*
94 a *MS*   shadow *PP*
95 team; *PP*
96 shapes *PP, SN*   drew it in] drew in *PP*
                            drew it, in *PP errata leaf*
97 lost:— *PP*   airs *MS*

90 *MS:*

        Crouching *within beneath*
      Sitting within the shadow of a tomb
            in shadow, [?]
        For all over it was bent in
         Bending behind
      Crouching within the shadow of a tomb

"within" was canceled and reinstated by underlining.

91 *MS:*

      oer what seemed the head a cloud like
   And *over it, like a widows veil of* crape

There are three possible ways of reading 91–93, those rendered by *PP* and *SN* in which "crape" or "cloud" respectively is the subject of "was bent" ("gloom" in either case being in apposition to the subject) or a third possibility:

      And o'er what seemed the head, a cloud like crape,
        Was bent a dun & faint etherial gloom
      Tempering the light; . . .

In this case, "a cloud like crape" (or, "a cloud-like crape", see note to 70 above) is in apposition to "head", while "gloom" is the subject of "Was bent" in an inverted word order ("Tempering" modifying "gloom"). In the original version, "like a widow's veil of crape" obviously does not provide a subject for "Was bent", leaving "gloom" as the only possibility. One must either follow *PP* (which adds only one hyphen and one comma to the text) or else, assuming that 92 was completed before 91 was changed, set off "a cloud like crape" as parenthetical and retain "gloom" as the subject of "Was bent" (as I have done in the text).

93 *MS:*

  Softening Tempering
    Obscure amid the light . . . the ?cars
    Amid the light; *out* upon the chariots beam

F and *L* credit emendation of punctuation to *R*, but *R* (who does not mention this line in his notes) merely modified the change introduced in Mrs. Shelley's later editions.

94–97 *MS:*

    Sate There sate a Janus-visaged Shadow did assume
                 whirlwind
               wonder-
       guidance of that *lightning* winged team.
     The *rule of the*
    { *?For* }   in thick lightnings
    { *?But* } *those* who drew it *lost in the ?thick light*
    The Shapes which
    { Were }   alone on
    { *Each* } lost: I heard *upon* the airs *slow* stream
               soft

"The Shapes which" and "alone on" added after page completed and quill sharpened.

f. 23v   The music of their ever moving wings.
          All the four faces of that charioteer
                    Had their eyes banded . . . little profit brings   100

          Speed in the van & blindness in the rear,
                    Nor then avail the beams that quench the Sun
          Or that his banded eyes could pierce the sphere

                    Of all that is, has been, or will be done.—
          So ill was the car guided, but it past   105
                    With solemn speed majestically on . . .

  98   ever-moving *PP, SN*   wings *MS*
 100   banded; *PP*
 101   blind*ness MS*   rear *MS*
 102   sun *PP*
          Sun, *SN*
 103   his] with *PP*   *could MS*   *the sphere MS*
                    their *SN*
 104   been *PP*   done; *PP*
                    done, *SN*
 105   guided *MS*   passed *SN*
          guided— *PP*
          guided; *SN*
 106   on. *PP*

99   *"The Janus vi"* above *"And* the four"; "All" below *"And"*.

100–101   *MS:*

> *Were bound*
> > *Had all their eyes banded*
> > *And* Had their eyes banded . . . *?ill*

> > > > *light   brings*
> > > > *profit springs*
> > > > *little good*

> Speed in the van & blind $\begin{Bmatrix} ness \\ ed \end{Bmatrix}$ in the rear

The grammar of this clause is a problem; "brings", the rhyme-word and a singular verb, has two subjects ("Speed" and "blindness"). In *MS* "brings" replaces *"springs"* and the second syllable of "blindness" is superimposed on *"-ed"*; perhaps Shelley once intended to make "profit" the subject of the sentence, "springs" the verb, and add "From" to the beginning of 101.

102–104   *MS:*

> *Yet so was*   *the?m*
> > *And* $\begin{Bmatrix} the \\ that \end{Bmatrix}$ *light is round ?him ?cast*
> > Nor then avails *there is light around*
> > > > beams that quench the Sun

> *Or sight within its pierce*
> > $\begin{Bmatrix} these \\ the \end{Bmatrix}$ *pierce*
> Or that   *eyes* banded eyes *could scan the sphere*
> > *his*

> *Of the to come the present & the past*
> *So was that chariot guided—*
> Of all that is, has been, or will be done.—

The muddled syntax of these lines is but another evidence of the unfinished state of the poem. When 102 read: "Nor then avail that light is round them cast", the noun clause paralleled that in 103–104, both "that" clauses being subjects of "avail". To maintain the rhyme-scheme, however, Shelley altered 102, introducing a relative clause to modify "beams" and changing his original *"that"* to "the"; *PP* tried to make 103–104 parallel to the new "that" clause by substituting "with" for "his" in 103. Perhaps Shelley might eventually have phrased the lines in some manner such as this:

> Nor then avails that those beams quench the Sun
> Or that his banded eyes could pierce the sphere
> Of all that is, has been, or will be done.—

103   Matthews writes that Shelley "first wrote 'Or that the eyes', then cancelled *the eyes*, but converted *the* into 'these' . . . . Finally . . . he emphasized the first e of 'these' and added ir underneath, to make 'their' ". However, the "ir" that *SN* finds is immediately below—even slightly to the left of—"th". Changes in ink show that the word below the line was written earlier than "the" was changed to "these". Although this word below the line is hard to read, I believe it to be "his" with the upstroke of the "h" rather faint, the "i" and "s" hastily stroked together without the openness of Shelley's usual final "s". Had Shelley wished, he could simply have canceled "these" and written "their" either above or below it.

104   *PP* and *SN* both weaken the punctuation after "done.—" against the clear evidence of *MS;* Shelley here sets off the Poet's commentary on the futility of the chariot (100–104) from the more objective statement that follows (105–106); cf. 224–234.

The crowd gave way, & I arose aghast,

f. 24r   Or seemed to rise, so mighty was the trance,
And saw like clouds upon the thunder blast

The million with fierce song and maniac dance   110
Raging around; such seemed the jubilee
As when to greet some conqueror's advance

Imperial Rome poured forth her living sea
From senatehouse & prison & theatre
When Freedom left those who upon the free   115

Had bound a yoke which soon they stooped to bear.
Nor wanted here the true similitude
Of a triumphal pageant, for where'er

f. 24v   The chariot rolled a captive multitude
Was driven; althose who had grown old in power 120
Or misery,—all who have their age subdued,

107   aghast *MS*
108   trance *MS*
109   saw, *PP*   thunders blast, *PP*
                         thunder-blast *SN*
111   around *MS*
      around— *PP*
      around: *SN*
112   greet] meet *PP*   *conquerors MS*
114   senate house, and forum, *PP*   theatre, *PP, SN*
      senate-house and prison *SN*
115   *When Freedom left those who MS*
      When [   ] upon the free *PP*
      When   upon the free *SN*
116   yoke, *PP*
117   true] just *PP, SN*
118   where'eer *MS*
119   rolled, *PP, SN*
120   driven;— *PP*   althose] all those *PP, SN*
      driven: *SN*
121   have] had *PP*   thier *MS*   subdued *PP, SN*

107   "aghast" above *"in haste"*; below this line is: *"So mighty was the Vision"*.
109   "thunder blast": see note to 70 above; "thunder" corrected by *WR*.
110–111   *MS:*

with fierce song
The million *in a fierce* and maniac dance
Raging around
Followed And And headlong joy around the charioted
Rushing behind it, and a moving arch
Such as the rainbow ?moulds, in its advance
it methought the jubilee
such seemed the

112   There is no replacement for *"conquerors"*; "greet" corrected by *WR*.
114   *Orig.: "Of senators & gladiators and slaves"*; "senatehouse" written as one
      word in *MS*.
115   *MS:*

When Freedom left those who would not be free
upon the free

PP and *SN* include the first word of the canceled line (*"When"*) but omit
the remaining four words necessary to complete the line and the sense of
the passage.
116   "Had bound" above *"Imposed"*; the change seems to clarify the antecedent
      of "they" (116), which is "those" rather than "free" (115): this change
      from past to past perfect makes it clear that "left" (115) and "stooped"
      (116) were contemporaneous, whereas the "free" had been bound earlier.
117   *MS:*

likeness
Nor wanted here the *semblance more express*
?first true similitude

PP and *SN* read as "just" the word I believe to be "first"; I have preferred
the clear, uncanceled alternative "true".
119   In the draft Shelley often neglects to set off introductory adverbial clauses;
      the sense is clear whether or not one supplies an editorial comma.
120–122   *MS:*

Mitred or sceptred or arrayed in arms
in golden arms &
Follow
Arrayed & swords which
Was driven; althose who had grown old in power
Or misery,—all who have { thier } *world* subdued,
{ the } age
On
And whom the world had looked to their last hour
Or whom the world had
and
By action or by suffering, *or* whose hour

Line 120 contains a full stop and at least eleven syllables; perhaps Shelley
purposely contracted "all" and "those" to "althose" to indicate a rapid,
elided pronunciation.

By action or by suffering, and whose hour
Was drained to its last sand in weal or woe,
    So that the trunk survived both fruit & flower;

All those whose fame or infamy must grow   125
    Till the great winter lay the form & name
Of their own earth with them forever low,

    All but the sacred few who could not tame
Their spirits to the Conqueror, but as soon
    As they had touched the world with living flame 130

Fled back like eagles to their native noon,
    Or those who put aside the diadem
Of earthly thrones or gems, till the last one

    Were there;—for they of Athens & Jerusalem
Were neither mid the mighty captives seen   135
    Nor mid the ribald crowd that followed them

124   flower;— *PP*
127   thier *MS*   ?own *MS*   their own] this green *PP*   for ever *PP*
                                                 their fair *SN*
      low *MS*
      low;— *PP*
128   —All *SN*
129   Thier *MS*   *spirits MS*   conquerors— *PP*
130   flame, *PP*
131   noon *MS*
133   gems, till the last one] gems [   ] *PP*
                         gems—till the last one *SN*
134   For *MS*   there: *SN*   *they MS*   Jerusalem, *MS*
      Were there, of Athens or Jerusalem, *PP*
135   *seen MS*
      seen, *PP, SN*
136   them . . . *MS*
      them, *PP, SN*

120–124   The verb tenses in these lines shift from past perfect ("had grown")
to present perfect ("have . . . subdued") to past ("was drained", "survived"). The shift to "have . . . subdued" in 121 is not a blemish if "age"
means "era" (*MS:* "age" below "*world*"). These "great" and "unforgotten"
(cf. 208–215) "have subdued" their respective eras, which in the annals of
history are embalmed in an eternal "present perfect" state of completion;
"hour" (122) is not a synonym for "age" but rather is contrasted with it—
the individual's hour, "the world's great age". (Cf. *Concordance:* "age",
"hour").

125   Above this line is written: "*Who have enjoyed & suffered all hi*".

127   *MS:*

> Of the   green ?own
>   green
> Of thier *green* earth *in deep darkness;*
>   with them forever low   ,

SN (note): "['fair' is uncertain, and might be e.g. 'living' or even 'busy' . . .].''
Agreeing that the uncanceled word replacing "*green*" is difficult to read,
I believe that it is "own", hastily written and with a less pronounced final
downstroke on the "n" than is characteristic of Shelley; the comma after
"low" may be only a drop of ink.

128–129   *MS:*

> All but the   cannot
> *Except those* sacred few who*m* could not tame
>   Conquerors   as
>   Thier *spirits* to the *yoke, but soon*

I prefer "could not" to "cannot" in 128 because of the use of the past
perfect in 130 ("had touched"); 129 once read: "Thier spirits to the Conquerors yoke, but soon"; it seems probable that Shelley, noting the incongruous metaphor, first canceled "spirits", and looked for something more
easily yoked, but later canceled "yoke" and changed the intended possessive
("Conquerors") to the objective case, added "as" to fill out the meter, and
mentally reinstated "spirits".

132–134   *MS:*

> Or those who *kept ?lay their spirits*
>   put aside the diadem till the last one
>   Of earthly thrones or *jewels* gems, *till the last swoon;*
>   *The ?two*   Were there;—
>   *For they*   of Athens & Jerusalem,
>   For   crowd
>   *Were not among the crew—loud was the rage*

Shelley, as *SN* notes, "forgot that the grammar of 120 onwards would eventually require a main verb for those enslaved to the chariot"; "Were there"
was inserted to serve this function and "*For they*" canceled to make
metrical room; finally "For" was rewritten, indicating reinstatement of
"*For they*", so necessary to the sense of what follows; the line, though an
Alexandrine, now fulfills the meaning.

         Or fled before . . Now swift, fierce & obscene
         The wild dance maddens in the van, & those
f. 25v   Who lead it, fleet as shadows on the green,

            Outspeed the chariot & without repose   140
         Mix with each other in tempestuous measure
            To savage music . . . . Wilder as it grows,

         They, tortured by the agonizing pleasure,
            Convulsed & on the rapid whirlwinds spun
         Of that fierce spirit, whose unholy leisure   145

            Was soothed by mischief since the world begun,
         Throw back their heads & loose their streaming hair,
f. 26r   And in their dance round her who dims the Sun

         Maidens & youths fling their wild arms in air
            As their feet twinkle; they recede, and now   150
         Bending within each other's atmosphere

            Kindle invisibly; and as they glow
         Like moths by light attracted & repelled,
            Oft to new bright destruction come & go.

137   Swift *MS*   Nor those who went before fierce and obscene. *PP*
                        Nor those who went before . . . Fierce and obscene *SN*
139   it— *PP*
140   chariot, *PP*
142   *savage music* . . . . *MS*
      savage music, wilder *PP*
      savage music . . . Wilder *SN*
143   the] their *PP, SN*
144   Convulsed, *SN*
145   Spirit *SN*
146   begun; *MS*
147   hair *MS*
      hair; *PP*
148   sun, *PP*
150   twinkle; now they recede, and now, *SN*   recede *MS*
151   others *MS*
152   invisibly— *PP*   glow, *PP*
154   new] their *PP, SN*   go, *PP, SN*

136–137 *MS:*
>   Nor mid the [?] ribald crowd that followed them . . .
>   The *dance grew wilder*
>   *Meanwhile   the dance grew wild, & more obscene*
>   *And The youths & maidens near the rushing car*
>   The   *near the car appeared*
>   With   melancholy
>   *Seemed* [?] *?and lay a*
>   *Caught* Or fled before . . Now Swift   *?more*
>   fierce & obscene
>   *Nor those who went before . . . the ?dance*

"Or fled before . ." superimposed on a canceled phrase beginning *"Caught"*; "Now" (superimposed on an illegible word) was added to fill out the meter after "Swift" had been written as the first word of a new sentence. Correction of this line eliminates the need for commas after 135 and 136, because "followed" and "fled" are the compound verbs of "that"; "Were . . . seen" governs the parallel construction "neither mid . . . nor mid". Note the sudden, yet carefully prepared for, shift from past to present tense in the Poet's narration.

139 "fleet" above *"swift".*

140 "the" superimposed on *"wild".*

142 Matthews gives "Wilder" in his text but believes that the word in *MS* begins with a lowercase "w"; I read *MS* as having a capital "W". Four, not three, suspension points precede "Wilder": the significance (if any) of the varying number of suspension points (cf. 100, 106, 137) is a problem for the explicator.

143 *"Thier"* changed to "They"; *"thier"* changed to "the": The change from *"thier"* to "the" clarifies the parallelism of the three participles ("tortured", "convulsed", "spun") in 143–144; "the agonizing pleasure" is not so much a possession of the "Maidens & youths" as something imposed or inflicted on them by "that fierce spirit".

144 "rapid" above *"ceaseless"; "mighty"* below *"ceaseless"; "spun"* below *"?tried".*

145 Above is the half-line *"Of this dark spirit whose";* "fierce" (in pencil) above *"stormy"* (canceled in pencil); Matthews' capitalization of "spirit" does not accord with his punctuation of the ensuing relative clause as a restrictive one; Shelley's punctuation, we must remember, is often unconventional (according to modern usage at least) and sound, not sense, determines much of the pointing in *MS.*

150 *SN* (note): "[150 is emended in pencil . . .; 'they', in 150, was added afterwards between the first 'now' and 'recede', partly obscuring the former]"; although Matthews' analysis of *MS* is correct, one need not add an extra word that gives a line eleven syllables (besides a full stop); inasmuch as "they" partly obscured the first "now", *PP's* reading probably represents Shelley's final intention.

154 "?new" (pencil) below *"the";* because no letters in the word rise higher than the last two and there is no dot for an "i", it is unlikely that the word is "their" (*PP* and *SN*); one of the two horizontal lines that cancel *"the"* was probably mistaken for the cross of a "t".

Till like two clouds into one vale impelled   155
    That shake the mountains when their lightnings
        mingle
And die in rain,—the fiery band which held

f. 26v   Their natures, snaps . . . ere the shock cease to
        tingle
One falls and then another in the path
    Senseless, nor is the desolation single,   160

Yet ere I can say *where* the chariot hath
    Past over them; nor other trace I find
But as of foam after the Ocean's wrath

    Is spent upon the desert shore.—Behind,
f. 27r   Old men, and women foully disarrayed   165
    Shake their grey hair in the insulting wind,

155   Till— *SN*
156   mingle, *SN*
157   rain— *PP, SN*
158   *ere MS*   *cease MS*
      snaps—the shock still may tingle; *PP*
      snaps . . . while the shocks still may tingle *SN*
160   Senseless Nor *MS*   single *MS*
      Senseless—nor *PP*
161   *I MS*   *where— PP*
             where, SN
162   Passed *SN*   them— *PP*
163   Oceans *MS*
      ocean's *PP, SN*
164   desart shore;— *PP*   behind *MS*
                      behind, *PP*
165   men *PP, SN*   disarrayed, *PP*
166   hairs *PP*   wind *MS*

155 *MS:*

> *Ere* Till
> *Embrace*
> *Then* like two clouds into one vale impelled

"*Ere*" canceled in pencil; "Till" written in pencil (the dash in *SN* may be justified by this late change in the text of the line).

157 *Orig.: "And weep their strength in raindrops".* "That" (156) is the subject of "shake" (156) and "die"; "clouds" (155) is the antecedent of "That".

158 *MS:*

> Their natures, *in a leash while*   still may
>   snaps . . . *ere* the shock *cease* to tingle

Shelley canceled "*while*" in pencil, showing that his last inclination was to the lower reading: Earlier he canceled "*ere*" and partly canceled "*cease*" in ink, but did not touch "to"; this inconsistency may indicate that Shelley wavered between choosing the version beginning "*while*" and that beginning "*ere*"; Shelley eliminated one earlier objection to the "*ere*" reading when he canceled the "*Ere*" in 155 (f. 26r) and replaced it (in pencil) with "Till", probably at the same time he canceled "*while*" (158) (cf. the sound-echo "Their"/"ere" in 158 with "ere"/"where" in 161). The word "shock" is singular: Shelley's "k" always has an extra loop or flourish (cf. "rocking" and "mocking", f. 26v *reverso*).

159 "path" after "*dust*".

160 *MS:*

> *And the cold desolation is not single*
> Senseless
> *And* Nor is the desolation single

"Senseless" was inserted to fill out the meter.

161 "Yet" superimposed on "*?But*"; "can" (pencil) above "*I could*" (canceled in pencil).

162 "I find" (pencil) above "*remained*" (canceled in pencil).

163 This line corrected in pencil; 164–175 composed in pencil except for some corrections in ink.

164 The first of the penciled words between 163–164 that *SN* reads "Jane & I" seems to me to be "Sun" (below "*?rainbows*") and the ampersand, if it is one, is not the same kind Shelley used elsewhere in *MS*. The bottom of f. 26v contains four sketches of boats and the word "Ricetti" written four times. Immediately below 164 and written *reverso*, in ink (probably before Shelley began to use folios 25–26 for "The Triumph"), are five lines of a lyric (see Appendix D).

165 Matthews removes the comma after "men" on the grounds that " 'Old' must qualify both men and women, since both have grey hair, so despite Shelley's firm comma 'foully disarrayed' must also qualify both nouns." Such reasoning begs the question: The textual editor must follow Shelley's clear intention, leaving the significance of the punctuation to the judgment of the explicator; the comma may indicate nothing more than a slight pause in oral reading.

166 "insulting" below "*?dishonoured*".

Limp in the dance & strain with limbs decayed
    To reach the car of light which leaves them still
Farther behind & deeper in the shade.

    But not the less with impotence of will   170
They wheel, though ghastly shadows interpose
    Round them & round each other, and fulfill

Their work and to the dust whence they arose
    Sink & corruption veils them as they lie
And frost in these performs what fire in those.   175

f. 27v   Struck to the heart by this sad pageantry,
Half to myself I said, "And what is this?
    Whose shape is that within the car? & why"—

---

167   Limp] Grasp *SN*   decayed, *PP*
      Limp in the dance &] To seek, to [   ], to *PP*
168   to *MS*
      To reach the car of] Limping to reach the *PP*
169   Far*ther MS*
      Far behind, *SN*
171   wheel *MS*   interpose, *SN*
172   fulfil *PP, SN*
173   work, *PP, SN*   to] in *PP*
      whence they arose] from whence they rose *PP*
174   Sink, *PP, SN*   lie, *PP, SN*
175   those *MS*   And past in these performs what [   ] in those. *PP*
176   pageantry *MS*
177   said, and *MS*   this *MS*
      said—And *PP*
178   whose *MS*   &] And *PP*   why— *MS, PP*
           and *SN*   why—" *SN*

167   The first word (which *SN* reads "Grasp") is either "Limp" or "Drop":
      Shelley's capital "G" is made with a long loop below the line (cf. *"God"*,
      181, f. 27v; "God" and "Good", 230–231, f. 30r; "Gregory", 288, f. 37v;
      "Glided", 363, f. 41v; "Glimmers", 431, f. 45r; "Grew", 481, f. 49r); "Limp"
      is the more likely. (*C₁* read the first two words ["Limp in"] as "Limping".)

167–168   *MS:*

> And *follow in the dance, though*
>   *with steps to find*
> And *dance behind* & seek strain
> To seek to reach ?the ?*chariot* with limbs decayed
>   Limp in the dance car of light
>   car
> *Seeking* to reach the *chariot* which leaves them still

These lines are manifestly in a state of flux and remain doubtful.

169   Matthews removes the canceled syllable "-ther" on critical grounds (which
      I find unconvincing), but subjective interpretation must here yield to
      objective prosody: *SN's* line has but nine syllables.

171–172   *MS:*

>   ?thirsty
> *They shake ?their fleshless bones without repose*
> *The mocking youth with vain & ?wanton skill*
> *And frost in these performs what fire in the*
>   wheel   those
> They *dance* though ghastly shadows interpose
> And   move
> *Mocking ?the [?] youthful band*
> Round them & round each other, and fulfill

The text follows *PP* in retaining an ambiguity of *MS* that was eliminated
in *SN*, which adds a comma after "interpose". According to *PP* "Round
them . . . other" can modify "interpose"; in *SN* this adverbial phrase must
modify "wheel"; the position of the adverb would favor *PP's* version.

173–174   Although *PP* and *SN* supply commas after "work", "Sink", and "lie",
      Shelley commonly omits commas before "and" in a parallel series of verb
      phrases. (The comma after "other" [172] concludes a parenthetical
      dependent clause.)

175   Rossetti (*R₁*) suspected "past" of being a misreading. This line, although
      difficult to read, repeats a canceled line that appears above, about midway
      on the same folio. (See transcription 171–172 above.)

177–178   *MS:*

> Half to myself I said, and what is this
>   is
> *And who, is the mistress of the mystery?*
>   is *she*
> *And who she   , and a voice made reply*
>   *And a voice said—Life!—*
>   And who *the mistress of the mystery*
>   *is*
>   *And a voice ?said Life!—*
>   *Life And life* . . .
>   *And said* . . .
>   *And who is she*
>   *And* whose shape is that within the car? & why—

I would have added—"is all here amiss?"
    But a voice answered . . "Life" . . . I turned &
    knew
(O Heaven have mercy on such wretchedness!)   181

    That what I thought was an old root which grew
To strange distortion out of the hill side
    Was indeed one of that deluded crew,

And that the grass which methought hung so wide   185
f. 28r   And white, was but his thin discoloured hair,
And that the holes it vainly sought to hide

    Were or had been eyes.—"If thou canst forbear
To join the dance, which I had well forborne,"
    Said the grim Feature, of my thought aware,   190

"I will now tell that which to this deep scorn
    Led me & my companions, and relate
The progress of the pageant since the morn;

179 added is *MS*   amiss? *MS*
     added—is *PP*   amiss?— *PP*
180 answered— *PP*   Life . . . *MS*   turned, *PP*
     answered: *SN*   "Life!"— *PP*
181 (Oh Heaven, *PP*
183 side, *PP*
184 that] those *PP*   crew *MS*
185 grass, *PP*
186 hair *MS*
187 hide, *PP*
188 Were, or had been, *SN*   eyes.—if *MS*   canst, *PP*
                                  eyes:—"If *PP*
189 forborne *MS*
     foreborne!" *PP*
     forborne", *SN*
190 Feature *MS, PP*   thought aware *MS*
                             thought: "Aware, *PP*
191 I *MS*   now tell] unfold *PP*
                             tell all *SN*
192 companions; *MS*
193 *the* pageant *MS*   morn *MS*

179 *"murmured"* after *"said"; "*added*" above "murmured".*
180 *MS:*

>   *I saw* I turned & *saw*
> But a voice answered . . Life . . . *and then I ?kn saw . .*
>   knew.

181 "Heaven" above *"God".*
182 "what" superimposed on *"?where".*
184 "degraded" above "deluded"; "[?]" after "degraded". (Rossetti conjectured
     the change of "those" to "that" [*N & Q*].)
185 Shelley first canceled this entire line (except "hung" above *"grew")* and then
     reinstated it by underlining.
186 Final "s" of "hair*s*" firmly canceled; "hairs" after *"hair"* and below *"locks".*
187 *MS:*

>   *they*
> And $\begin{Bmatrix} \text{that} \\ \text{two} \end{Bmatrix}$ *great* the holes *they* it vainly sought to hide
>   it

Forman's conjectural "he" has no foundation, for the pronouns refer to
"hair", "locks", or "hairs".
188 *MS:*

> Were or had been eyes.—
> *Had once been eyes and,—if thou canst forbear*

189 *"have"* changed to *"had";* "well" above *"not".*
190 "Said" after *"Said he";* "F" superimposed on *"f".*
191–193 *MS:*

>   *from the*
>   how *to this car*
>   I will *relate by what*   *depth of scorn*
>   I *?hardened fell, and all the passage*
>   *now tell*   which
>   I will *relate all*   that   to   this deep̊   scorn
>   ∧
>   relate
>   Led me & my companions; and *will tell*
>   *fortune prog*
>   The *passage of the* pageant since the morn
>   progress of

191 *"now tell"* originally replaced *"relate",* was canceled when *"will tell"*
     was used in 192, and was reinstated when "relate" superseded *"will
     tell"* in 192; *"all"* was separately canceled to make room, metrically,
     for "which".

"If thirst of knowledge doth not thus abate,
Follow it even to the night, but I   195
  Am weary" . . . Then like one who with the weight

Of his own words is staggered, wearily
f. 28v He paused, and ere he could resume, I cried,
"First who art thou?" . . . "Before thy memory

"I feared, loved, hated, suffered, did, & died,   200
And if the spark with which Heaven lit my spirit
  Earth had with purer nutriment supplied

"Corruption would not now thus much inherit
  Of what was once Rousseau—nor this disguise
Stained that within which still disdains to wear it.—

194 If *MS*   doth not thus abate *MS*
        shall not then abate, *PP*
        shall not thus abate, *SN*
195 even] thou even *PP, SN*
196 weary . . . then *MS*
  weary."—Then *PP*
  weary" . . . then *SN*
198 paused; *PP* cried *MS*
        cried: *PP, SN*
199 First *MS*   thou . . . before *MS* memory, *PP*
  "First, *PP, SN*   thou?"—"Before *PP*
200 I feared loved hated suffered, did, & died *MS* did *PP*
201 *spi*rit *MS*
202 Earth had] Had been *PP* nutriment] sentiment *PP*   supplied, *PP*
203 Corruption *MS*
204 Rousseau,— *PP*
205 Stained that which ought to have disdained to wear it; *PP*
  Stain that which ought to have disdained to wear it; *SN*

194–195 *MS:*

                           like the

    If *thy ?thirst ?thy ?wis*   shall   then

        that thirst of knowledge doth not thus abate

              it   ?ever   even to

    Follow *its wheels into* the night, but I

    194 "doth" is underlined (not canceled) in *MS,* suggesting that it was Shelley's latest choice; in any event, "doth" goes with "thus" and "shall" with "then" as paired alternatives.

    195 *PP* and *SN* read "?ever" as "thou": Although very small and virtually illegible, it may be "?more", "?car", or "?even"; in any case, it is superfluous to both sense and meter and may safely be dismissed ("even to" was added later than the doubtful word).

200–202 *MS:*

        feared

        loved *&* hated

    I *did acted, suffered,* suffered, did, & died

      And if the *flame which*

                spark with which Heaven lit my   *sp*irit

              had with with purer nutriment   *soul*

    Had from a purer flask   *oil*

    Earth *from a purer*   *flask had* ᴧ supplied

203 "thus" above *"so"*.

204–205 *MS:*

    Of what was once Rousseau—*I leave*

                    nor this disguise

           within which still disdains

    Stained *the pure*

         that *which should disdain* to wear it.—

           which ought to have disdained to wear [?]

The text retains "Stained" (with "have" understood) as a natural construction emphasizing the implied temporal constrast between the corruption that "now" inherits (203) the soul that had (in the past) been stained by a disguise that it "still" disdains to wear. There is some *MS* basis for preferring the line-ending of the text over the alternative in *PP* and *SN:* "it.—" is clear (and punctuated) only in the higher version; "within which still disdains" is written smaller, probably with a newly sharpened quill, and thus later than "which ought to have disdained to wear [?]".

"If I have been extinguished, yet there rise   206
A thousand beacons from the spark I bore."—
"And who are those chained to the car?" "The Wise,

"The great, the unforgotten: they who wore
Mitres & helms & crowns, or wreathes of light,   210
f. 29r   Signs of thought's empire over thought; their lore

"Taught them not this—to know themselves; their
     might
Could not repress the mutiny within,
And for the morn of truth they feigned, deep night

"Caught them ere evening." "Who is he with chin   215
     Upon his breast and hands crost on his chain?"
"The Child of a fierce hour; he sought to win

"The world, and lost all it did contain
Of greatness, in its hope destroyed; & more
     Of fame & peace than Virtue's self can gain   220

206   *If I have been extinguished, yet there ?then rise MS*
207   *A thousand beacons from the spark I bore.— MS*
                              bore"— *PP*
                              bore." *SN*
208   And *MS*   car? The *MS*   Wise *MS*
                       car?"—"The *PP*   wise, *PP, SN*
209   The great the unforgotten they who wore *MS*
      unforgotten,— *PP*
210   wreaths *PP, SN*   light *MS, SN*
211   thought's] thoughts *MS*   thought;] thought— *PP*
212   Taught *MS*   this, *PP*
213   mutiny] mystery *PP*
214   *And for the morn of truth MS*
215   Caught *MS*   evening Who *MS*
                          evening."—"Who *PP*
216   breast? . . . and *MS*   crossed *SN*   chain? *MS*
      breast, *PP, SN*   chain?"— *PP*
217   The *MS*   He *MS*
218   The *MS*   all it] all that it *PP*
219   destroyed, *SN*
220   Virtues *MS*
      virtue's *PP, SN*

206–211 *MS* (f. 28v):

> *If I have been extinguished, yet there ?then rise*
> *A thousand beacons from the spark I bore.—*
> *And then the shape turned that which mi*
> *what might be its eyes*

And $\left\{ \begin{array}{c} \text{who} \\ I \end{array} \right\}$ are those chained to the car? The Wise

they who wore

great   the unforgotten *the supreme*
The *mighty the immortal*
       are
Such were they called; and their wisdom
   Mitres & helms & crowns, or wreathes of light
   Signs of
Of the soul   thoughts empire over thought,

208   The "W" of "Wise" is probably a capital, though this is not beyond question. (Matthews in his collation says it is a capital.)
210   Shelley's spelling of "wreathes" may derive from Milton (*Paradise Lost* VI.58); cf. *Revolt* IX.ii.4.
211   ";their lore" appears at the top of f. 29r.

213 *MS:*

repress

Could not restrain the *rebels in their heart*
mutiny within,

Although *SN* was the first edition to correct "mystery" to "mutiny" a Bodleian assistant pointed out the error in the catalogue to a 1958 exhibit: *Notable Accessions: Guide to an Exhibition Held in 1958* (Oxford: Bodleian Library, 1958), p. 52.

215   "chin" after *"his stern"*.

216–219 *MS:*

captive

Upon his breast?...   *The latest victim hero*
he decks the triumph well.—

A slave who sought and hands *folded in* sorrow
A willing slave who sought   crost on his chain?
his

   The latest victim
      That is Napoleon
      He   The last is he: a crown he sought to win
         This is a   he
      This was The Child of a fierce hour; He sought to win
         And lost

all   did

The world, and lost *more than* it *doth* contain
   Of glory, in the birth of its new dawn
   Of greatness, *in a tyrant*
in its hope destroyed; & more

217   "The" (superimposed on an illegible word) may be a late addition to the line: Perhaps, therefore, the capital "C" of "Child" does not represent Shelley's final intention.
218   Although this line is metrically imperfect, "that" (*PP*) does not appear in *MS*.

220   "fame & peace" above *"peace & fame";* "can" above *"could"*.

"Without the opportunity which bore

f. 29v   Him on its eagle's pinion to the peak
From which a thousand climbers have before

"Fall'n as Napoleon fell."—I felt my cheek
Alter to see the great form pass away   225
Whose grasp had left the giant world so weak

f. 30r   That every pigmy kicked it as it lay—
And much I grieved to think how power & will
In opposition rule our mortal day—

And why God made irreconcilable   230
Good & the means of good; and for despair
I half disdained mine eye's desire to fill

With the spent vision of the times that were
And scarce have ceased to be . . . "Dost thou
behold,"
Said then my guide, "those spoilers spoiled, Voltaire,

"Frederic, & Kant, Catherine, & Leopold,   236
Chained hoary anarch, demagogue & sage
Whose name the fresh world thinks already old—

221   Without *MS*
222   eagles *MS*   pinions *PP*
      eagle *PP*
224   Fall'n *MS*   fell—I *MS*
      "Fall'n, *PP*
225   Alter, *PP*   *the MS*   great form] shadow *PP*
226   weak, *PP*
227   lay; *PP*
      lay, *SN*
229   day, *PP, SN*
232   eyes' *PP*
234   be.— *PP*   dost thou behold *MS*
235   Said my *PP*   guide those *MS*   Voltaire *MS*
236   Frederic & Kant *MS*
      "Frederic, and Paul, *PP*
      "Frederick, and Kant, *SN*
237   anarch *MS*   demagogues *MS*
      And hoary anarchs, demagogues, and sage— *PP*
      Each hoary anarch and demagogue and sage *SN*
238   ———name the world thinks always old, *PP*   old, *SN*

222   *MS:*

Napoleon on an eagle's flight stormy speed
Even to the height from which he fell.—he

swore

     To *that*   its   *brink*
     Him on *the an* eagles pinion to the *verge*

peak

224   *"I felt my cheek"* below *"I dare not speak".*
225   *"great form"* above *"mighty shadow"; "pass away"* superimposed on *"[?] glide".*
226   *"grasp* below *"tyranny".*
227   This line, in its present form but partly canceled, appears near the middle of f. 29v; it is repeated, uncanceled, at the top of f. 30r. Following the first version were written several tercets, now canceled, on Rousseau and Voltaire (ff. 29v, 34, 31v). See Appendix C.
228   *MS:*

And all my thoughts were full of heaviness
And much I grieved to think *how all things are*

how far apart
how power & will

230   *"why"* above *"how"; "made"* after *"stamps".*
233   *"vision"* above *"shadows".*
234   *"dost thou behold"* below *"yet I behold".*
235   *MS:*

Said then my guide *Vo* those
   Chained in Life's triumph spoilers spoiled, Voltaire
   Like ?Voltaire   said   my guide
   The captive tors   captive led.—

Forman in a note conjectured the insertion of "then". The last *MS* line above (now canceled) was probably supposed to read: "The captors captive led.—"
236   "Kant" superimposed on *"Pitt".*
237–238   *MS:*

Chained   *an*   &
Each with his anarchs, *seers*
   And hoary *Kings*   *?sages* demagogues & sages
   ?With   *new*
   Whose names the   fresh world thinks already old—

Shelley first wrote: "Each with his"; canceling this, he began again "And hoary Kings" but canceled *"Kings"* and wrote above it "anarchs, seers"; he next canceled "seers", wrote "sages demagogues &"; about this time, deciding that "sages" was needed as a rhyme word, he canceled *"sages"*, adding an ampersand above and after "anarchs". After writing 238 (and perhaps 239), Shelley changed the plural nouns to singular (neglecting "demagogues"). "Chained" may represent either a false start or Shelley's latest intention. "Chained" may have been added when the removal of the "s" of "sages" shortened the line by one syllable. I do not follow *SN*'s reading (which has eleven syllables) because it is arbitrarily eclectic in using *"Each"*, rejected early and not, apparently, reconsidered.
238   *"new"* above *"fresh"; "fresh"* reinstated by underlining ("new world" may have carried geographical connotations foreign to Shelley's intention). The clause "Whose . . . old—" modifies only "sage."

"For in the battle Life & they did wage
     She remained conqueror—I was overcome   240
By my own heart alone, which neither age

f. 30v   "Nor tears nor infamy nor now the tomb
Could temper to its object."—"Let them pass"—
     I cried—"the world & its mysterious doom

"Is not so much more glorious than it was   245
     That I desire to worship those who drew
New figures on its false & fragile glass

     "As the old faded."—"Figures ever new
Rise on the bubble, paint them how you may;
f. 31r   We have but thrown, as those before us threw,   250

"Our shadows on it as it past away.
f. 32r   But mark, how chained to the triumphal chair
The mighty phantoms of an elder day—

239 For *in the* MS   battle, life *PP*   wage, *PP*
240 conqueror. *PP*
241 alone; *MS*   age, *PP*
242 Nor *MS*   tears, nor infamy, *PP*
243 object. let *MS*   pass— *MS*
                            pass," *PP, SN*
244 cried, *PP, SN*   the *MS*
245 Is *MS*   was, *PP*
248 As *MS*   faded.—Figures *MS*
249 bubble *MS*   how] as *PP*   may *MS*
250 we *MS*   us, threw— *MS*
251 Our *MS*   as] ere *SN*   passed *SN*   away *MS*
252 mark *PP*
253 day; *PP*

239–241 *MS:*

          Chill For   *strife* battle
              And in the war which Life & they did wage
          In the   was overcome
                        conqueror—I *have been subdued*
              She remained *?mistress of the ?field*
                        alone; which neither age
              By my own heart *which time could not assuage*

242–243 *MS:*

          Nor pain nor years pleasure
                  infamy, nor now the tomb
          Nor tears nor infamy nor now the tomb
          Could model to the its $\left\{\begin{array}{l} \textit{?plan.—} \\ \textit{spirit} \end{array}\right\}$
              Could temper to *the spirit.— the* Let them
                        its object—*let them pass*
          I said in scorn,—the world has not become
                  Frail ?ruin
                  I *said, and follow thou*   let them pass—

245 "much" is uncertain, though I can suggest no alternative reading.

247–249 *MS:*

          New *figures on its frail delusive glass—*
                        brittle sphere of
          Regard the other [*?*]
          Look onward then. . . . I looked & knew
              The *antique*   its   false & fragile glass
                        figures
              New *colours* on *that bubble like the*
              Fresh
                        Figures
              As the old faded.—*of among the crew*
                  Any delight [*?*] *Colours* ever new
                        them
              Rise on the bubble paint *it*   how you may

250 *MS:*

          And we like they of old   threw
                  but   those before us,
          And we have   thrown, as *elder*

251 Following this line are many false starts and canceled lines on f. 31r, the
      bottom of f. 31v, and the top of f. 32r before the text resumes (252) in the
      middle of f. 32r; see Appendix C.

252–253 *MS:*

          For *Mark the phantoms of* [*?*]
          ?For But mark how chained
                        to the triumphal chair
              But mark, *where*
                        the
              The mighty fantoms phantoms of an elder day—

"All that is mortal of great Plato there
Expiates the joy & woe his master knew not;   255
That star that ruled his doom was far too fair—

"And Life, where long that flower of Heaven grew not,
Conquered the heart by love which gold or pain

f. 32v   Or age or sloth or slavery could subdue not—

"And near   walk the   twain,   260
The tutor & his pupil, whom Dominion
Followed as tame as vulture in a chain.—

"The world was darkened beneath either pinion
Of him whom from the flock of conquerors
Fame singled as her thunderbearing minion;   265

"The other long outlived both woes & wars,
Throned in new thoughts of men, and still had kept
The jealous keys of truth's eternal doors

254   All *MS*
255   not *MS*
256   That] The *PP*   fair, *PP, SN*
257   And *MS*   life, *PP*   not *MS*
258   the] that *PP*   love, *PP*   gold, *PP*   pain, *PP*
                                Love *SN*
259   age, *PP*   sloth, *PP*   not. *PP*
                                                   not; *SN*
260   *And near MS*   walk, *MS*   twain *MS*
      "And near walk the [   ] twain, *PP*
      "And near walk the   twain, *SN*
262   chain. *PP, SN*
263   The *MS*
265   as] out for *PP*   thunder-bearing *PP*
                     for *SN*
266   The *MS*   wars *MS, SN*
267   new] the *PP, SN*
268   key *PP*   truths *MS*   doors, *PP*

254   *Orig.:* "All that *was* mortal of great Plato's *spirit*".
255–257 *MS:*

the

Walks, Expiates *the* joy & woe his master knew not

That star that ruled his *life*

The star of his Heaven   doom   far

And that his ∧ *ruling star which* was ∧ too fair—

flower of Heaven not

For And Life, where long that *?breathy blossom* grew

258   "the" superimposed on "*that*".
259–261 *MS:*

Or age or *sloth* sloth or slavery

And Slavery & age, or *sloth*   could subdue not—

Be

And near   walk, the   twain

Srumfredevi

The tutor & his pupil, & whom Dominion

The comma after "pupil" may indicate that "whom" refers to both "The tutor & his pupil"; "Srumfredevi" seems meaningless until one notices the same word written vertically along the left margin of the page, and under it "Sir Humphry Davy" above "Davi". This notation may tell us something about Shelley's attitude toward Davy as well as the nature of the adjective for which Shelley was searching: Davy, who received his baronetcy in 1818, spent 1818–20 in Italy working with the papyri of Herculaneum in the Neapolitan museum. In 1820 he became President of the Royal Society, where "he lent himself to the petty cabals of a coterie during his possession of the chair. His ill-concealed partiality for the aristocracy of birth . . . ; the presumptuous assumption in his own person, on some occasions, of a patrician haughtiness; and a neglect of the ordinary courtesies of society, procured him many enemies; and when he resigned the chair, he had become one of the most unpopular presidents that had for years ruled the society" (*Encyclopaedia Britannica*, 8th edition, 1854). Shelley may have heard of Davy's imperious ways at Naples or from England and with his inveterate hatred of authoritarianism may have set up Davy in his own mind as a symbol of the same kind of ruler-of-minds as is the Aristotle of the poem.

262   "vulture" below "*panther*".
263   "darkened beneath" above "*shadowed under*".
265   "singled" above "*nourished*"; "as" superimposed on "*for*"; *F* (and *MLR i*) suggested the omission of "out".
266–267 *MS:*

both

The other long outlived *both the wars* woes & wars

new   at the gate

Of Throned in the thoughts of men, and still had kept

"If Bacon's spirit   had not leapt
          Like lightning out of darkness; he compelled   270
The Proteus shape of Nature's as it slept

          "To wake & to unbar the caves that held
The treasure of the secrets of its reign—
f. 33r   See the great bards of old who inly quelled

"The passions which they sung, as by their strain   275
          May well be known: their living melody
Tempers its own contagion to the vein

          "Of those who are infected with it—I
Have suffered what I wrote, or viler pain!—

269 *If Bacon's spirit   had not leapt MS*
      "If Bacon's eagle spirit had not leapt *PP*
270 *Like lightning out of darkness; MS*
                              darkness— *PP*
271 *The Proteus MS*   Nature *PP*
      That Proteus *SN*
272 To *MS*
      "To wake, and lead him to the caves that held *PP*
      "To wake and follow to the caves that held *SN*
273 reign. *PP*
      reign.— *SN*
274 of old who inly quelled] of elder time, who quelled *PP*   old, *SN*
275 The *MS*
276 known, *MS, SN*   *their living melody MS*
                              for their soft melody *SN*
278 Of *MS*
279 pain! *PP, SN*

269–273   *MS* (to the bottom of f. 32v):

Had not that { *shadow* / *?spirit ?of* } *which*

If Bacon's spirit   had not leapt
                                he compelled
Like lightning out of darkness; and unveiled
If that
    The Proteus Nature   *Nature*
        Had   *?guard* shape of Nature's as it slept
        To wake & to { unbar / *?open* [*?*] [*?*] }
            yield a passage to the caves that held
    To resign a
    Unveil half
    The treasure of the secrets of its reign—
See Caesar   *who, when*
                                the slave who quelled
    ?Natures shapes to follow.—

"and unveiled" (270) is both canceled and underlined.

274   *MS* (beginning at top of f. 33r):
    Democritus was
    Diogenes was
        Diog   are
        And mighty bards were there
            See Homer & his brethren,—men who quelled inly
                            old
        See the great bards of *elder time* who   quelled

"inly" is partly superimposed on the end of *"quelled"*.

276–279   *MS:*
    May well be known, *by their infection flows*
                        for their *sweet sigh music* ever
                            their living melody
                    their *?soft the*
                its own
    With Tempers *the soft* contagion to the vein
                    [*?*]
            are infected with it— *but* I
    Of those who *hear . . . and so miserable they*
                I *sung* wrote
    Have suffered what *they paint, or* viler pain!—

As Matthews admits, his reading of 276 is eclectic; although "sigh" provides the closest rhyme, I fall back to *PP* and the canceled reading because:
(1) it contains no doubtful words ("soft" is very dubious); (2) it was written
as a unit and clearly conveys Shelley's intention at one point. I presume
that, in revising the poem, Shelley would have reconsidered this line and
the entire sequence of redundant rhymes in which it occurs (*PP*'s "chasm in
the manuscript").

"And so my words were seeds of misery—   280

f. 37v   Even as the deeds of others."—"Not as theirs,"
          I said—he pointed to a company

In which I recognized amid the heirs
Of Caesar's crime from him to Constantine,
The Anarchs old whose force & murderous snares   285

Had founded many a sceptre bearing line
And spread the plague of blood & gold abroad,
And Gregory & John and men divine

280   And *MS, PP*   were] have *PP*   misery"— *PP*
                                                  misery, *SN*
281   *omitted from PP*   others—not as theirs. *MS*
                                 others."—"Not as theirs?" *SN*
282   ——he pointed *PP*   company, *PP*
       I said, and pointed *SN*
283   Midst whom I quickly recognised the heirs *PP*
284   crime, *PP, SN*   Constantine; *PP*
285   Anarchs old] anarch chiefs, *PP*
286   sceptre-bearing *PP, SN*   line, *PP*
287   blood & gold] gold and blood *PP*   abroad *MS*
                                                abroad: *PP*
288   Gregory, *SN*   and John, *PP, SN*   divine, *PP, SN*

280   The remainder of f. 33r following this line is filled with cancellations that are continued on f. 37v, where the text resumes. Intervening in the MS are: (1) draft for lines 11–18 of "To Jane: 'The keen stars were twinkling' " (f. 33v); (2) continuation of the apocryphal passage that originally followed 227 (f. 34); (3) the only known draft of "Lines Written in the Bay of Lerici" (ff. 35, 36); (4) calculations, presumably of a monetary nature, and (5) fragments of lyrics as yet not collected in Shelley's works (f. 37r); see Appendix D.

281–284   *MS:*

not as

but

Even as the deeds of others—*even as* theirs.

And then   he pointed to a company

I said   { recognized amid }
         { *him of the* }

In which   *all who had been the* heirs

Midst whom I *knew Caesar whose withered hairs*

the Caesar whose withred hairs

Were circled by the priest

281–282   "I said" replaced *"And then"* at the same time "not as" replaced *"even as"*. To increase the dramatic interplay, Shelley has the Poet, who recognizes the nature of those captives now approaching, challenge Rousseau's classification of himself with such men as these whose deeds brought misery. The original period is thus rendered meaningless, though there is no reason why the Poet should ask (*SN*) rather than declare (*T*), inasmuch as "replied" (293) could appropriately introduce Rousseau's response in either case.

282–284   The original line alluded to Julius Caesar, while *"the Caesar whose withered hairs/ Were circled by the priest"* is Constantine: Shelley broadens his concept in the final text.

285   *MS:*

all   the *bloody chiefs whose* [?]

Amid   *Gregory*

Many   *fell chiefs*   *who by*   *or snares*

The Anarchs *&* old   whose force & murderous snares

286   "many a" above *"every"*.

288   "Gregory & John" above *"every hierarch"*; "men" after *"all"*; a comma after "divine" (*PP, SN*) would imply that all "men divine" are guilty of spiritual tyranny; Shelley's change in 286 of *"every"* to "many a" makes me hesitate to add a comma after "divine" and thereby suggest that this relative clause is nonrestrictive.

Who rose like shadows between Man & god
    Till that eclipse, still hanging under Heaven,   290
Was worshipped by the world o'er which they strode

    For the true Sun it quenched.—"Their power was
        given
f. 38r   But to destroy," replied the leader—"I
    Am one of those who have created, even

"If it be but a world of agony."—   295
    "Whence camest thou & whither goest thou?
How did thy course begin," I said, "& why?

    "Mine eyes are sick of this perpetual flow
Of people, & my heart of one sad thought.—
    Speak."—"Whence I came, partly I seem to
        know,   300

"And how & by what paths I have been brought
    To this dread pass, methinks even thou mayst guess;
Why this should be my mind can compass not;

    "Whither the conqueror hurries me still less.
But follow thou, & from spectator turn   305
    Actor or victim in this wretchedness,

289   man and God; *PP*
       Man and God, *SN*
290   eclipse *MS*   under Heaven,] under Heaven *MS*
                             over heaven, *PP*
291   oer *MS*   strode, *PP, SN*
292   sun *PP*   quenched—thier *MS*
                    quenched—"Their *PP*
293   destroy: *MS*   leader:— *PP*   I *MS*
                    leader, *SN*
295   If *MS*   agony *MS*
296   Whence *MS*   camest thou] comest thou? *PP*   thou?] thou *MS*
297   begin, I said, & *MS*   begin?" *PP*
298   Mine *MS*
299   heart of] heart sick of *PP*   thought— *PP, SN*
300   Speak.— *MS*   Whence *MS*   I came, partly I] I am, I partly *PP*
        Speak!"— *PP, SN*
        know *MS*
301   And *MS*
302   guess *MS*
        guess;— *PP*
303   be, *PP, SN*   not— *MS*
304   Whither *MS*   me, *PP, SN*   less *MS*
                             less;— *PP*
306   wretchedness *MS*

289   "Who rose" above *"Had stood"*; "Man" begins with a capital, "god" with a lowercase letter.

290   *MS:*

fated age
still hanging *twixt Heaven & earth*
Till that eclipse *which*   *not yet*
                    still   *over Heaven*
                                      under

291–292   *MS:*

Was worshipped by the world oer which they strode
                                          given
                      thier power was
For the true Sun it quenched—*these had their birth*
He answered from the death of such as I

A comma after "strode" (*PP, SN*) would convey the impression that "For" (292) is a conjunction (introducing a clause, "it quenched the true Sun") rather than a preposition (meaning "in place of" or "instead of"); the text returns to *MS* reading, leaving final interpretation a problem for the explicator; *"these had their birth"*, etc., canceled at the same time as *"Heaven & earth"* (290).

293–294   *MS:*

leader—
replied the *guide, but* I
But to destroy: *but I am* one of these
Who have created

Am { one   } of those who have created, even
    { *?him* }

293   *"guide"* was canceled to avoid an awkward internal rhyme with "replied".

296   *WR* corrected "comest" to "camest".

297   "How" after *"Where When"*; "did" above *"began"*.

299   "my heart" is not canceled, as it appears to be on microfilm: the line shows through from the other side of the folio; "one" above *"these"*; "thought" above *"thoughts.—"*

301–302   *MS:*

dread misery
And *how to this sad*   brought
    by how & by what paths I have been
To *what & where I am I not even* thou mayst
          dread   methinks even *you may*
    To this *sad* pass, *I fear*   I   guess

303   Below this line appears "devi" (Davy again? see 259–261[n]), below but to the left of "devi" are some letters that seem to be "ivəↄ" ("Devi" spelled backwards?).

f. 39r   "And what thou wouldst be taught I then may learn
                From thee.—Now listen . . . In the April prime
            When all the forest tops began to burn

                "With kindling green, touched by the azure
                    clime   310
                Of the young year, I found myself asleep
            Under a mountain which from unknown time

                "Had yawned into a cavern high & deep,
                And from it came a gentle rivulet
            Whose water like clear air in its calm sweep   315

                "Bent the soft grass & kept for ever wet
            The stems of the sweet flowers, and filled the grove
f. 39v   With sound which all who hear must needs forget

                "All pleasure & all pain, all hate & love,
                Which they had known before that hour of rest: 320
            A sleeping mother then would dream not of

307   And *MS*
308   thee—Now listen . . . In *MS*   prime, *PP*
      thee. Now listen:—In *PP*
      thee. Now listen . . . in *SN*
309   tops] tips *PP, SN*
310   With *MS*   green *MS*
311   Of the young year's dawn, I was laid asleep *PP*
      Of the young season, I was laid asleep *SN*
312   *Under a mountain MS*
                mountain, *PP, SN*
313   Had *MS*   cavern, *PP*   deep *MS*
                                              deep; *PP*
314   rivalet *MS*
      rivulet, *PP*
315   water, *PP*   air, *PP, SN*
316   Bent *MS*   grass, *PP, SN*   forever *PP*
317   And *MS*
318   *all who MS*
      With sounds, which whoso hears must needs forget *PP*
      With sound which whoso hears must needs forget *SN*
319   All *MS*   pain *MS*   love *MS*
320   they] he *SN*   rest *MS*
                            rest; *PP*
321   would] wd *MS*

307   At the top of f. 39r, above 307, appears: *"And I from thee may then the secret"*.

308   *MS:*

<blockquote>
In April
From thee—   *There is a cavern   years sweet*
                         prime
—Now listen . . . *In* In $\left\{ \begin{array}{l} \text{the} \\ \text{that} \end{array} \right\}$ season
</blockquote>

309   "forest tops" below *"willow buds"*; Shelley wrote "tops", not "tips" (cf. 415, f. 44r).

310   "azure" above *"starry"*, which is above *"azure"*.

311–312   *MS:*

<blockquote>
          year   found myself
Of the young season, I was laid asleep
  Of the *dawning* year dawn
Under a mountain which from *antient* time
             unknown
</blockquote>

     311   The text incorporates Shelley's latest thoughts: "found myself" was written later than "was laid asleep"; "year" was added to make the new reading metrically correct.

314   "came" above *"crept"*.

315   After three very confused (canceled) attempts to compose this line, Shelley wrote:

<blockquote>
                              sweep
                  clear   in its
Whose *lucid waves* water like *mild* air *in its* calm
</blockquote>

PP's punctuation arbitrarily prejudices the question of whether "its calm sweep" refers to "water" or "clear air"; *SN*'s punctuation separates the subject of the clause ("water") from its verbs ("Bent", "kept" [316], "filled" [317]).

316   "soft" above *"green"*.

317   *MS:*

<blockquote>
        the sweet flowers,   ?grove
The stems of *the* [*?*] *jonquils whose eyes for ever*
           And filled the *wood*
                 place
</blockquote>

318–320   *MS* (top of f. 39v):

<blockquote>
        such
  With murmur dull
                whoso   must needs forget
With sound*s* which *all who* hears *by force*
  Past pain & pleasure
    All pleasure & all pain   all hate & love
                   before that drowsy hour
     Which they had known *before they rested there*
             ere *sleep surprized them there*
             before that hour of rest
</blockquote>

     318   Both the "s" in "hears" and the final "s" in "sounds" are canceled; because Shelley first wrote "all who hear" and added the "s" to "hear" after "whoso" replaced *"all who"*, his cancellation of that "s" and his use of "they" in 320 clearly indicate that his latest intention was to return to the plural "all who" in 318. The hissing sound of the line, if all the sibilants were retained, may have played a part in this decision.

"The only child who died upon her breast
      At eventide, a king would mourn no more
          The crown of which his brow was dispossest

"When the sun lingered o'er the Ocean floor   325
      To gild his rival's new prosperity.—
Thou wouldst forget thus vainly to deplore

f. 40r   "Ills, which if ills, can find no cure from thee,
      The thought of which no other sleep will quell
          Nor other music blot from memory—   330

"So sweet & deep is the oblivious spell.—
      Whether my life had been before that sleep
The Heaven which I imagine, or a Hell

      "Like this harsh world in which I wake to weep,
I know not. I arose & for a space   335
      The scene of woods & waters seemed to keep,

"Though it was now broad day, a gentle trace
      Of light diviner than the common Sun
Sheds on the common Earth, but all the place

322   "The] The *MS*
              "Her *PP*
323   eventide— *PP*
324   brow, was dispossest *MS*
       brows were dispossest *PP*
       brow was dispossessed *SN*
325   When *MS*   oer *MS*   the] his *PP*   ocean floor, *PP*
                                                            ocean floor *SN*
326   rivals *MS*   prosperity. *PP*
                          prosperity— *SN*
328   Ills, *MS*   if ills *PP*   thee *MS*
329   *quell MS*
       quell, *PP, SN*
330   memory, *PP*
331   So *MS*   spell; *PP*
                      spell. *SN*
332   Whether my] whether my *MS*   *sleep MS*
                    And whether *PP*
333   heaven *PP*   hell *PP*
334   Like *MS*   weep *MS*
335   not *MS*   arose, *PP, SN*
       not . . . *SN*
336   keep *MS*
337   Though *MS*   day *MS*
338   sun *PP*
339   earth, *PP*   but] and *PP*

322 "breast" after "*heart*".
323 "eventide" above "*vesper bell,*".
324 "crown above "*throne*".
325 *MS:*

    An hour before   floor

    When { When } the sun lingered oer the Ocean
             { *Where* }

Although it is difficult to determine whether "When" is superimposed on "*Where*" or vice versa, the former reading seems to make better sense (as well as to have the authority of precedent); "Ocean" seems to begin with a capital letter.

327 "wouldst" above "*wilt*".
329 *MS:*

    The thought of which   will

    And which no others sleep *but*   *ever quell*

                     can quell [?]

I believe that the "s" in "other*s*" is canceled.

332 *MS:*

    And I hastened   my   had been

    And whether   *sleep been*

    And *as my*   *if my* ∧ life   before   that   *slumber*

                              hour had

333 "a" above "*the*".
334–339 *MS* (to bottom of f. 40r):

    Which I endure, I kno cannot know

                  my

    In which

       Th Like this harsh world in which I wake to weep

       know not   I arose &

       I *cannot know,*   and and for a moment thus

              awakening, for a space

    The *stream mountain & the*

       scene of woods & waters seemed to keep

             was now broad day   *heavenly* gentle

       Though it *was morning an ?unfading*

    A hue of *unremembered sunrise a*   trace

       Of light evening beams in day

       The sweet evening beams

    Of light

       Of evening beams,

       Of *evening sweetest evening beams*

         light

       Of *beams of more* diviner than the common Sun

    Rains on the   but

       Pours Sheds on the common Earth, & all the place

f. 40v   "Was filled with many sounds woven into one   340
                Oblivious melody, confusing sense
                  Amid the gliding waves & shadows dun;

                "And as I looked the bright omnipresence
                    Of morning through the orient cavern flowed,
                And the Sun's image radiantly intense   345

                    "Burned on the waters of the well that glowed
                Like gold, and threaded all the forest maze
                    With winding paths of emerald fire—there stood

                "Amid the sun, as he amid the blaze
                    Of his own glory, on the vibrating   350
                Floor of the fountain, paved with flashing rays,

---

340 Was *MS*   *filled with MS*   many] magic *PP*
                                                 mazy *SN*
342 Amid the gliding waves & amid the shadows dun *MS*
343 And *MS*   looked, *PP, SN*   *bright MS*
     "And, *PP*
344 flowed *MS*
345 sun's *PP, SN*
346 Burned *MS*
347 forest's *PP, SN*
348 emarald *MS*   fire; *PP*   *there stood MS*
349 Amid *MS*   sun *MS*
351 *fountain, MS*   rays *MS*

340   *"mazy"* seems to have been changed to "many" (after "maze" was used in 347?); the foot of the "z" is scored through and "n" is superimposed in heavy ink upon the top of the "z". The greatest difficulty is that the lower part of "y" is very faint; the word is not "magic", however, and is probably "many".

341   "sense" after *"thought;"*.

342   *MS:*

<blockquote>
                       waves
    Amid the gliding   *stream* &
Oer *the dark stream under* amid the shadows dun
    Floating
</blockquote>

The second "amid" (omitted from the text) was probably a replacement for *"under"* in the earlier version of the line (but cf. 349).

344   "morning" after *"sunlight"*; "flowed" above *"streamed"*, which is above *"burst"*.

345   Above this line appears: *"Veiling the Sun, & radiantly* intense".

347   "gold" after *"molten"*; *"forest"* has no "s": What appears to be one is the "t" from *"forest"* written immediately below it.

349   "blaze" above *"dawn"*.

350–351   *MS* (to bottom of f. 40v):

<blockquote>
                        ?yawning
                  on the restless floor
Of his own glory, *on the vibrating*
               a ?fair on the vibrating
               form
Crystal of that   *shape arrayed*
  Like the pure moon in clouds of soft
    Of that crystalline
       enkindled fountain,   moved
              paved with flashing rays
    Floor of the *fountain, waves*
             in the keenest rays
  A shape of whitest light
  A Woman
</blockquote>

f. 41r   "A shape all light, which with one hand did fling
            Dew on the earth, as if she were the Dawn
                Whose invisible rain forever seemed to sing

        "A silver music on the mossy lawn,   355
                And still before her on the dusky grass
            Iris her many coloured scarf had drawn.—

            "In her right hand she bore a crystal glass
            Mantling with bright Nepenthe;—the fierce splendour
                Fell from her as she moved under the mass   360

352   A *MS*   Shape *PP, SN*
353   *Dew on the MS*   Earth, *SN*   dawn, *PP, SN*
354   invisible] musical *SN*   And the invisible rain did ever sing *PP*
355   A *MS*   music] melody *SN*   lawn *MS*
                                                lawn; *PP*
356   her] me *PP*   grass, *PP*
357   *Iris her MS*   many-coloured *PP, SN*   drawn: *PP*
                                                              drawn. *SN*
358   In *MS*   chrystal *MS*   glass, *PP*
359   Mantling] Winking *SN*   Nepenthe; *PP*
                                       Nepenthe: *SN*

352   "shape" begins with a lower case "s", though it is higher on the page than the other letters of the word.

353   *MS:*

>earth, as if she were the Dawn
>*Dew on the grass path*
>   *world waters & the w*
>   *earth*
>   *grass & flowers*

Below 353 are six canceled attempts, the first of which is typical: *"Until the woods & waters seemed to ?ring"*.

354–357   *MS:*

>*In April rain*
>   *drops showers*
>Whose ?invisible rain forever seemed to
>And the *invisible rain did ever* sing
>   music *melody*
>A silver *melody upon*   mossy
>   *tune up*on the *flowery* lawn
>And *ever* still before her on the dusky *scene*
>*And underneath the darkness of   ?dell*
>*And still before her steps*   grass
>*Iris her* many coloured scarf had drawn.—
>   —— devi

Although "invisible" (354) is not a certain reading, the word begins exactly like *"invisible"* below; the use of "music" in 355 makes "musical" less likely here: "music may be canceled, though the line appears to be below it rather than through it. The word below 357 seems to be "devi" (Davy?) once again, though here it may be "deri" or "aeri".

358–359   *MS (to bottom of f. 41r):*

>*And in the other*
>*And in other hand she bore*   chrystal
> In her right hand she
>*And in the other hand she* bore a glass
>*Sparkling with purple liquor*   fierce splendour
>   ?every ?drink
>   ?strong ?spirits
>Mantling with *starry liquor;—* the *?fallen light*
>   bright Nepenthe
>   veil by
>Fell from her *like a veil as She did pass*
>   as she moved under the mass
>Out of the cavern
>*Out of the caverns*

The conventional spelling of "crystal" on f. 40v renders doubtful, I believe, any special significance for the archaic spelling in 358. The initial word in 359 is "Mantling" (*PP*) rather than "Winking" (*SN*); "Nepenthe" may begin with a lowercase "n".

f. 41v   "Of the deep cavern, & with palms so tender
                   Their tread broke not the mirror of its billow,
                Glided along the river, and did bend her

                "Head under the dark boughs, till like a willow
                Her fair hair swept the bosom of the stream   365
                   That whispered with delight to be their pillow.—

                "As one enamoured is upborne in dream
                   O'er lily-paven lakes mid silver mist
                To wondrous music, so this shape might seem

                "Partly to tread the waves with feet which kist   370
                The dancing foam, partly to glide along
                   The airs that roughened the moist amethyst,

f. 42v   "Or the slant morning beams that fell among
                   The trees, or the soft shadows of the trees;
                And her feet ever to the ceaseless song   375

                "Of leaves & winds & waves & birds & bees
                And falling drops moved in a measure new
                   Yet sweet, as on the summer evening breeze

361   "Of the] of the *MS*   *& MS*   & with] with *PP*   tender, *MS, PP*
          "Out of the *PP*
362   Thier *MS*   billow *MS*
                              billow; *PP*
363   Glided] She glided *PP*
364   Head *MS*   willow, *PP*
366   their] its *PP, SN*   pillow. *PP*
367   "As one enamoured] Swift As one enamoured, *MS*
368   Oer *MS*   mist, *PP*
369   *wondrous* music, so *this shape MS*
          music wondrous, so this Shape *SN*
370   Partly *MS*   kissed *PP, SN*
371   foam; *PP*
372   airs that] air which *PP*   *moist amethyst MS*
                              dewy amethyst, *SN*
373   Or *MS*   slant] faint *PP, SN*
374   trees;] trees *MS*
375   feet, *PP*
376   Of *MS*   "Of leaves, and winds, and waves, and birds, and bees, *PP*
377   drops, *PP, SN*   in] to *PP*
378   breeze, *PP*

361   *MS* (top of f. 41v):

        of the hollow mountain
      Out of the shadow of the crags
           deep
    Out of the cavern, *&* with palms so tender,

    "*Out*" is more firmly canceled (twice) than is "*&*". *WR* corrected this line.

362   "its billow stream" above "*the rill*", below which is "*river,*".
363   "Glided along" above "*She moved upon*"; "river" above "*waters,*".
364   "dark" above "*low*".
365   "fair hair" above "*long hair*".
366   I retain *MS* reading "their" (rather than "its": *PP, SN*). Matthews bases his emendation on the interpretive assumption that the antecedent of "their" must be "hair" or "head"; it is equally possible that "their" has as its antecedent a plural noun: "boughs" (364) or "palms" (361); cf. "Their" (362).
368   *Orig.:* "*Oer lakes & flowery meadows amid silver clouds*".
369   *MS:*

        planetary wondrous
      To *sweetest music, so this shape* might seem
        ?angel
        ?music
         music

    I retain Shelley's original order of adjective before noun; in this crowded and confused line there is no evidence that Shelley altered his intended word order.

370   "tread the waves with" below "*move upon the foam*"; "palms" above "feet".
371   "along" above "*upon*".
372   *MS:*

              [?]
      ?roughened   roughened the *moist*
    The airs that *which*   which [*?*]
                  amethyst

    The word above "*moist*" that Matthews reads as "dewy" may be "along" and go with 371.
373   The word that *PP* and *SN* read "faint" is actually "slant" superimposed on "*soft*"; "*soft*" is in the same ink as the rest of the line; the initial "s" of "slant" was written directly upon that of "*soft*", the "l" was written with very little ink, and Shelley dipped his quill before writing "ant".
374   "of the trees" after "*interposed*".
375   *MS:*

    And ever her slow slow feet
      to the ever unreposing song
      her [*?*] *feet to the*
        opiate song
    And her feet ever to the ceaseless song

    Shelley canceled "ceaseless" when he wrote "opiate" above it but later restored "ceaseless" by underlining.
376   "*trees*" changed to "bees".
377   "?dancing" above "falling"; "drops" above "*dew*"; "new" above "*strange*". When "new" became the rhyme-word, "*dew*" was replaced to avoid an internal rhyme.
378   "sweet" above "*beautiful,*"; "summer ?evening" above "*invisible*".

"Up from the lake a shape of golden dew
    Between two rocks, athwart the rising moon,   380
Moves up the east, where eagle never flew.—

    "And still her feet, no less than the sweet tune
To which they moved, seemed as they moved, to blot
    The thoughts of him who gazed on them, & soon

"All that was seemed as if it had been not,   385
f. 43r   As if the gazer's mind was strewn beneath
Her feet like embers, & she, thought by thought,

    "Trampled its fires into the dust of death,
As Day upon the threshold of the east
    Treads out the lamps of night, until the breath   390

379 Up *MS*
380 rocks *MS*   *the MS*   *moon MS*
381 *Moves MS*   Dances i' the wind, where never eagle flew; *PP*
                       Dances i' the wind where eagle never flew. *SN*
382 And *MS*   feet *MS*
384 them; *PP, SN*
385 All *MS*   was, *PP, SN*   not *MS*
                                   not; *PP*
386 *As if the gazer's mind was strewn beneath MS*
      And all the gazer's mind was strewn beneath *PP, SN*
387 embers; *PP*   thought,] thought *MS*
388 Trampled *MS*   fires] sparks *PP, SN*   death *MS*
                                         death; *PP*
389 day *PP*

380–382 *MS:*

a   planet

Moves twixt two rocks athwart *the* rising *moon*

Between

up the east,

Moves in wild

And tram

Tramples the wind where eagle never flew.—

Dances i' the

And still her *first in beauty*

feet no less than the sweet tune

"Between" may have replaced *"Moves twixt"* in 380 so that "Moves" could be used in 381; one must use some canceled word (either *"Moves"* or *"wind"*); "up the east," seems to have been written later than "Dances i' the". "And still her" (382) was first canceled and then reinstated by underlining.

383 "blot" above *"darken".*

386–388 *MS:*

all the

And *every form that peopling the busy mind*

Before,   were

Like stars at sunrise are forgot

As if the she trod

the gazer's mind was strewn beneath

Her path, and

The gazers mind $\left\{ \begin{array}{c} \text{was} \\ \textit{were} \end{array} \right\}$ strewn *beneath her feet*

She trampled out its   *thoughts*

waning

Like fading ashes, & she, thought by thought

embers

Her feet like *ashes*

fires

Trampled its *sparks* into the dust of death

stars

386 The reading found in *PP* and *SN* is unnecessarily eclectic: "And all the", though uncanceled, belongs to an entirely different version of the thought, whereas *"As if"* belongs to the only version of the line that fits the rhyme-scheme; *"As if"* remained uncanceled while *"the gazer's mind was strewn beneath"* was written; both were canceled when Shelley began again "The gazers mind was strewn *beneath her feet",* but the original line, metrically complete, must have been mentally reinstated when the *terza rima* again required *"beneath"* as the terminal word of the line,

389 "Day upon" above *"Morning".*

390 "lamps" above *"sparks".*

"Of darkness reillumines even the least
1824   Of heaven's living eyes—like day she came,
        Making the night a dream; and ere she ceased

        "To move, as one between desire and shame
    Suspended, I said—'If, as it doth seem,   395
        Thou comest from the realm without a name,

    " 'Into this valley of perpetual dream,
        Shew whence I came, and where I am, and why—
    Pass not away upon the passing stream.'

        " 'Arise and quench thy thirst,' was her reply.   400
    And as a shut lily, stricken by the wand
        Of dewy morning's vital alchemy,

    "I rose; and, bending at her sweet command,
        Touched with faint lips the cup she raised,
    And suddenly my brain became as sand   405

f. 44r   "Where the first wave had more than half erased
    The track of deer on desert Labrador,
        Whilst the fierce wolf from which they fled
            amazed

391 Of *MS*   re-illumine *PP*
392 *No MS available*   Day *SN*
393 *No MS available*
394 *No MS available*
395 *No MS available*   said: *SN*   If, *PP*
396 *No MS available*   name *SN*
397 *No MS available*   "Into *PP, SN*
398 *No MS available*   Show *SN*
399 *No MS available*   stream. *PP*
400 *No MS available*   "Arise *PP*   thirst, *PP*
401 *No MS available*
402 *No MS available*
403 *No MS available*   and *SN*   command *SN*
404 *No MS available*
405 *No MS available*
406 Where *MS*
407 desart *PP*   Labrader *MS*
                          Labrador; *PP*
408 fierce wolf] *fierce wolf MS*   amazed, *PP, SN*
                          wolf, *PP*
                          empty wolf, *SN*

391 The "s" at the end of "reillumines" may possibly be canceled; if so the subjunctive verb would express doubt (cf. Matthews' note: "the indicative ending is first canceled and then firmly replaced").

392–405 There is no draft of these lines in the Bodleian MS (see Appendix A). In the absence of such authority, the editor must rely on *PP*, based on the only authoritative transcript of the lines. I have differed from *PP* only in the use of quotation marks (which are all editorial additions anyway); *PP* omits single quotes to mark off dialogue within Rousseau's narration, but I have followed other editors in supplying these.

406 The first word ("Where") is not beyond question; it may instead be "When".

407–408 *MS:*

         track of   desert
   The *track of ?some* deer in *stormy* Labrader
     footsteps of some   timid animals
       empty   *ran*
   Whilst the *wolfs track* from which they *fled* amazed
       fierce wolf

407 "desert" was misspelled in *PP*, thus blurring Shelley's customary distinction between "desert" (adjective) and "desart" (noun): see Forman, III, 471–472.

408 This line is debatable, but since *"fierce"* (*SN* reads *"lean"*) and *"wolf"* were canceled in the same stroke, I reinstate them together on metrical grounds; *SN* says that the scansion of 408 is the same as that of 406, but 406 has ten syllables, 408 with "empty" instead of "fierce" contains eleven.

"Leaves his stamp visibly upon the shore
    Until the second bursts—so on my sight   410
Burst a new Vision never seen before.—

    "And the fair shape waned in the coming light
    As veil by veil the silent splendour drops
    From Lucifer, amid the chrysolite

"Of sunrise ere it strike the mountain tops—   415
    And as the presence of that fairest planet
Although unseen is felt by one who hopes

    "That his day's path may end as he began it
    In that star's smile, whose light is like the scent
    Of a jonquil when evening breezes fan it,   420

"Or the soft note in which his dear lament
    The Brescian shepherd breathes, or the caress
That turned his weary slumber to content.—

f. 44v (appears beside line 419)

409	Leaves *MS*	shore, *PP*		
410	bursts;— *PP*			
411	vision, *PP*	before, *PP*		
		before; *SN*		
412	And *MS*	shape, *MS*	light, *PP*	
		Shape *SN*		
415	Of *MS*	sun-rise, *PP*	strike] tinge *PP*	tops; *PP*
				tops, *SN*
416	planet, *PP, SN*			
417	unseen, *PP, SN*			
418	That *MS*	it, *PP*		
419	stars *MS*			
420	it *MS*			
421	Or *MS*	soft] true *SN*		
423	content; *PP*			
	content— *SN*			

409   Above 409 there appears: *"Was legible visible, until the second broke".*
410   "so" above "as".
411   "new" above *"strange".*
412–413 *MS:*

> The lovely shape grew pale *as beacon light*
>
> *?Mid sunrise, & soon faded* $\left\{ \begin{array}{c} in \\ like \end{array} \right\}$ *thin air*
>
> *And from the cavern came, rolled*   coming
>   waned in
> And *she* the fair shape, *the faded amid the* ∧ *light*
>   silent   drops
>   *Faded*   As veil by veil the *thrilling* splendour *falls*

415   "ere" above *"when";* "strike" actually "strikes" ("s" canceled); "strike"
       underlined: Above "strike" appear two uncanceled alternatives "tinge" and
       "touch".
416–417 Editorially added commas after "planet" and "unseen" are superfluous
       to comprehension of the passage.
418   Below this line (bottom of f. 44r) appear two line fragments: *"Under the*
       smile of the third sphere," and *"Amid that light* [?]".
419   *MS* (top of f. 44v):

> *Whilst With that calm sphere smiling with light,*
>   *Under that star*   the *air*
>   In that stars smile, whose light is like *sweet ?sound*
>   Of *some ?lut⟨e⟩* $\left\{ \begin{array}{c} scent \\ smell \end{array} \right\}$
>   *music, and*

421   *MS:*

> *sweet melody*   *stirs*
> Or *the soft music which*   *which*
>   soft *tune*   [?] *dear*
>   the *sweet notes* in which his *sweet* lament
>   ?those note

The sequence of composition of this line appears very complex; "those",
"note", "tune", and "his" were written with little ink, with the other words
written in heavier ink ("?those", which is very faint, is the word *SN* reads
"true"); apparently Shelley had not completely ruled out the possibility of
canceling "the" so that the phrase would be plural; as *MS* now stands,
"note" is the only appropriate uncanceled noun, "soft" the uncanceled
adjective.

"So knew I in that light's severe excess
   The presence of that shape which on the stream   425
     Moved, as I moved along the wilderness,

"More dimly than a day appearing dream,
   The ghost of a forgotten form of sleep,
f. 45r   A light from Heaven whose half extinguished beam

     "Through the sick day in which we wake to
       weep   430
   Glimmers, forever sought, forever lost.—
     So did that shape its obscure tenour keep

     "Beside my path, as silent as a ghost;
     But the new Vision, and its cold bright car,
   With savage music, stunning music, crost   435

     "The forest, and as if from some dread war
   Triumphantly returning, the loud million
f. 46r   Fiercely extolled the fortune of her star.—

"A moving arch of victory the vermilion
   And green & azure plumes of Iris had   440
   Built high over her wind-winged pavilion,

424 So *MS*
425 Shape *SN*
427 More *MS*   day-appearing *PP, SN*   dream *MS*
428 sleep *MS*
      sleep; *PP*
429 from Heaven] of heaven, *PP*   half-extinguished *PP, SN*
430 Through *MS*   weep, *PP*
431 for ever sought, for ever lost; *PP*
      for ever sought, for ever lost— *SN*
432 Shape *SN*
433 Beside *MS*
434 its] the *PP*   car *MS*
435 savage music, stunning music] savage music stunning music *MS*
                     solemn speed and stunning music, *PP*
                     solemn speed and stunning music *SN*
      crossed *SN*
436 The *MS*
437 returning *MS*
438 star. *PP, SN*
439 A *MS*   victory, *PP, SN*
441 pavilion *MS*

424–427 *MS:*

$$\text{So } \textit{did I} \left\{ \begin{array}{c} \text{knew} \\ \textit{know} \end{array} \right\} \text{ in that } \begin{array}{c} \text{I} \qquad \text{light's} \\ \text{severe excess} \end{array}$$

Of *light the presence of that form*   *still*

                              shape, which

                              ?forever

The presence of that shape which on the stream

Has been my guide across the wilderness

Fled like a herald oer the wilderness

Moved, as I moved along the wilderness,

           Obscurer than

    As aery

             dimly

           More *faint*   than a day appearing dream

429–431 *MS:*

    Amid the darkness of the

                 Heaven

      ?In beautiful, whose half

    Beckoning

      A light   from *Paradise*

    *Which glimmers like a smoke-*extinguished beam

    Amid the waking world

                 sick

    Upon Through the *pale* day in which we wake to weep

    ?Or And *paler glows more pale as the day grows more old.*

      Half seen, forever sought & ever lost—

$$\left\{ \begin{array}{c} So \\ As \end{array} \right\} \begin{array}{c} \text{Tormenting} \\ in \ the \end{array}$$

      Glimmers, forever sought, forever lost.—

432 Here as elsewhere in the description of the "shape all light" the "s" in "shape" is lowercase.

433 "Beside" above *"Before"*; "as silent" after *"as I"*.

434 "its cold bright car" above *"the car of beams"*.

435 *MS:*

       savage music   crost

   With *music new solemn speed &* stunning music *past*

       music

"savage music" is underlined in *MS;* the text requires only the insertion of two commas.

436 "dread" above *"new"*.

440 "plumes" above *"wings"*.

"And underneath aetherial glory clad
   The wilderness, and far before her flew
     The tempest of the splendour which forbade

"Shadow to fall from leaf or stone;—the crew   445
   Seemed in that light like atomies that dance
     Within a sunbeam.—Some upon the new

"Embroidery of flowers that did enhance
   The grassy vesture of the desart, played,
     Forgetful of the chariot's swift advance;   450

f. 47r   "Others stood gazing till within the shade
   Of the great mountain its light left them dim.—
     Others outspeeded it, and others made

"Circles around it like the clouds that swim
   Round the high moon in a bright sea of air,   455
     And more did follow, with exulting hymn,

"The chariot & the captives fettered there,
   But all like bubbles on an eddying flood
Fell into the same track at last & were

---

442   And *MS*   etherial *PP, SN*
444   splendour, *PP*
445   Shadow *MS*   or] and *PP*   stone; *PP*
                                         stone— *SN*
446   light, *PP*   that dance] to dance *PP*
447   sunbeam;— *PP*   some *MS, PP, SN*
      sunbeam: *SN*
448   Embroidery *MS*   flowers, *PP*
449   desert, *SN*
450   advance *MS*
451   Others *MS*   gazing, *PP*
452   dim; *PP, SN*
453   it; *PP*
454   Circles *MS*   it, *PP, SN*
455   air *MS*
      air; *PP, SN*
456   *exulting MS*   hymn *MS*
457   The *MS*   there *MS*
      there:— *PP*
      there; *SN*
459   last, *PP*   & *MS*

443   "wilderness," after *"forest"*.
444   "The tempest" below *"?A ?spirit"*.
446   "Seemed" after *"Who"*.
447   *MS:*

> *Within a ray that dimly struggles through*
>   Within a sunbeam.—some upon the new
>   *The cranny of a chamber*

The text line was inserted later between the two original lines.
448   "Embroidery" written above one or more canceled words that may be *"?Investitures"*.
449   "desart" above *"forest,"*.
450   *"fleet"* above "swift" (canceled and then underlined).
451   At the top of f. 47r appears a set of calculations and the beginning of a letter to Roberts (see Appendix A). Above 451 appears: *"Others before it"*.
452   "dim" above *"dark.—"*.
453   "and" after *"but"*.
454   "the clouds" above *"rapid"*.
455   "Round" after *"Around"*; "high" above *"white"*; "bright" above *"wild"*; "sea" may begin with a capital "S".
456   "And" above *"But"*; there is no alternative for *"exulting"*, which may be considered mentally reinstated.
458   *MS:*

> *And I who had made one of every band*
>   *Half phantoms & some*
>   *Phantoms & men & shadows in*
> But   flood
>   *And* all like bubbles on an eddying *river*

f. 47v   "Borne onward.—I among the multitude   460
      Was swept; me sweetest flowers delayed not long,
        Me not the shadow nor the solitude,

      "Me not the falling stream's Lethean song,
        Me, not the phantom of that early form
      Which moved upon its motion,—but among   465

        "The thickest billows of the living storm
      I plunged, and bared my bosom to the clime
        Of that cold light, whose airs too soon deform.—

      "Before the chariot had begun to climb
        The opposing steep of that mysterious dell,   470
f. 48r   Behold a wonder worthy of the rhyme

460 Borne *MS*   I, *MS*
461 swept— *PP*   me, *PP*   long *MS*
                                         long; *PP*
462 Me, *PP*   solitude; *PP*
463 Me *MS*   the] that *PP, SN*   song *MS*
    "Me, *PP*   song; *PP*
464 Not *MS*   form, *PP*
465 motion— *PP*   but] first *SN*
466 The *MS*   the] that *PP*
467 the clime] *the* cold clime *MS*
468 soon] *soon MS*   deform. *PP, SN*
          fierce *SN*
469 Before *MS*
470 dell *MS*

460 *"Hurried into the"* above "Borne onward.—".

461 *MS:*

> *After Was one whom neither fairest*
> *whom sweetest flowers delayed*
> Was swept; me sweetest flowers delayed not long

463 *MS:*

> *streams*
> Me not ⎰ the ⎱ *forests fair*
>   ⎱ *that* ⎰   falling stream's Lethean song

There is some question whether "that" or "the" was Shelley's final choice: A large "e" in lighter ink seems to be superimposed on "that" (had the words been written in the opposite order, there would be no reason for such a large "e"; cf. "the" in 466 below).

464–465 *MS:*

> *Me not that fairest shape*
> Me, *delayed not that*
>   Not the phantom of that early form
> Which
>
> *That* moved upon its motion,— ⎰ but ⎱ among
>   ⎱ for ⎰

466 *"that"* changed to "the"; the "l" of "living" goes too far below the line: Although I suspect the word may not be "living", I can suggest no alternative.

467–468 *MS* (an attempt to record the words in a chaotic mass of cancellation):

> I plunged, and *?saw was thus among the rest I*
>   *thus became*   *grew*
>   bared my bosom to
>   *?on the ?frail gulph of that*
>   *?Was made made naked to* the
>   *bare to the* cold clime
> *?Of that cold light, whose breath*
> *Whose blasts soon make ?airs*   too [?]
>   , *the limbs*
>   *brow*
>   *shape they*   *soon* deform—

In 467 I follow *PP* and *SN* in using "the" rather than "cold", because of the recurrence of "cold" in 468; in 468 I follow *PP* in retaining *"soon"* rather than trying to guess at the illegible word, which seems to end in "—ed" ("?formed").

469 "March" appears above "chariot": "March" may relate to the poem or may be the month (the numeral "12" appears across the page to the right).

471 *"thy"* changed to "the"; "rhyme" after *"rime"*.

"Of him whom from the lowest depths of Hell
Through every Paradise & through all glory
Love led serene, & who returned to tell

"In words of hate & awe the wondrous story   475
How all things are transfigured, except Love;
For deaf as is a sea which wrath makes hoary

"The world can hear not the sweet notes that move
f. 49r   The sphere whose light is melody to lovers—
A wonder worthy of his rhyme—the grove   480

"Grew dense with shadows to its inmost covers,
The earth was grey with phantoms, & the air
Was peopled with dim forms, as when there hovers

472 Of *MS*   *who MS*   hell, *PP*
                     who *PP*   Hell, *SN*
                     whom, *SN*
473 paradise *PP*   glory, *PP*
475 "In] In *MS*   awe] care; *PP*
        "The *PP*
476 transfigured *PP, SN*   Love *MS*
477 sea, *PP*   hoary, *PP*
478 "The] The *MS*
479 lovers.— *MS*
480 rhyme: *SN*
481 Grew *MS*   shadows, *MS*
483 *with MS*

472–476 *MS:*

        Of him *who sang the*
                 how
            how in the depths of Hell
            from the fabled depths of Hell
      The serpent &
        Sinner & the
            who [?]
    Ascended   from the lowest depths of Hell
     Through every Paradise & through all glory
       Love led
         Ascended on love thoughts
        Love   led   serene, & who returned to tell
               mate
     ?How L ?to
      How ?forever
      To ?ease that
        How Its power upon
        How from the highest Heaven unto the hoary
        Abyss, of whirling rain
           ?hoar doth Love alone eternal reign
                      awe

$\left\{\begin{matrix} \text{In} \\ \textit{And} \end{matrix}\right\}$ words of hate $\left\{\begin{matrix} \text{\&} \\ \textit{the} \end{matrix}\right\}$ *fear* the wondrous story
       Of strange tr
       How all ?things are transfigured, except Love

472 *MS* shows that Shelley's intention changed: *"who"* was to have been the subject of its clause, but when *"Love"* (474) became the subject, Shelley neglected to write in *"whom"* to replace *"who".*

477 "For deaf as is a sea" below line fragment: *"For the world, deaf even".*

480–482 *MS:*

     Behold I say a wonder, for the grove
      A wonder worthy of *that* his rhyme—*the grove*
   Was as   *above*
   Became   the grove
     Behind grew dark
      The Heaven grew dark
      Around, among, like tempest when it ?covers
               to its
     Grew dark with shadows, *as a*   inmost covers
     Grew dense
       The air
      From every was
       The earth was grey with phantoms, & the *?sky*
                     air   air
                         sky

480 This line is a parenthetical restatement of 471–472; *"?covers"* in the cancellation above 481 may be *"moves"* or *"roars".*

483 *MS:*

   Grew Became   *like In*
   Was peopled *with* dim forms, as when there hovers

"A flock of vampire-bats before the glare
Of the tropic sun, bringing ere evening   485
    Strange night upon some Indian isle,—thus were

"Phantoms diffused around, & some did fling
    Shadows of shadows, yet unlike themselves,
f. 49v   Behind them, some like eaglets on the wing

"Were lost in the white blaze, others like elves   490
Upon the sunny streams & grassy shelves;
    Danced in a thousand unimagined shapes

"And others sate chattering like restless apes
    On vulgar paws and voluble like fire.
Some made a cradle of the ermined capes   495

"Of kingly mantles, some upon the tiar
Of pontiffs sate like vultures, others played
    Within the crown which girt with empire

484   A *MS*
485   bringing, *PP*   evening, *PP*
486   isle,—] vale;— *PP*
            isle— *SN*
487   Phantoms *MS*   around; *PP*
488   themselves *MS*
489   them; *PP, SN*
490   Were *MS*   blaze,] blaze *MS*
                        day; *PP*
                        blaze; *SN*
493   And *MS*   sat *SN*
494   *and voluble like MS*
        On vulgar hands, * * * * * *PP*
        On vulgar hands, or over shoulders' fire; *SN*
496   Of *MS*   mantles; *PP, SN*   upon] across *PP*   tiar] tire *PP*
497   pontiffs, *MS*   sate like vultures,] sate like vultures *MS*
                        rode, like demons; *PP*
                        sat like vultures; *SN*
498   Within] Under *PP*

485   *MS:*
                          tropic
              evening   *strange*
          Of the *declining* sun, bringing *a night*
                      pale   *before* ere evening
486   *"islet"* changed to "isle".
487   "Phantoms" above *"Shadows"* and below *"Shadows & phantoms &"*.
489–490 *MS* (top of f. 49v):
              Across the ?forests
                                  like eaglets on the wing
              Before them them, some   *The cranes on*
                  Behind *them, others like wild birds on wing*
                          the   ?fury
              were lost in *the excess*
                          white   *beams,* others like elves
                                  blaze

       "?fury" (the word *PP* and *SN* read as "day") may be "day" or "fiery".
493   "restless" above *"filthy"*.
494   *MS* (the confused effect of *MS* here cannot be rendered in type):
              On vulgar ?paws   *or made*

       Upon the boughs, and on the shoulders $\left\{ \begin{array}{l} \text{leapt} \\ \textit{leaped} \end{array} \right\}$

          [*?*] [*?*] $\left\{ \begin{array}{l} \textit{?over shoulders} \\ \textit{voluble like} \end{array} \right\}$ fire

       The word "hands" does not appear (the supposed "a" in "hands" is really
       the top of the "h" from "boughs" below and the supposed "ds" is unlike
       any other "ds" Shelley wrote in *MS*); the questionable word is probably
       "paws"; "shoulders" (before "fire") is superimposed on two words, the last
       being *"like"* and the other, part of *"voluble"*, upon which is also super-
       imposed the word Matthews reads as "over". At one stage the line may
       have read: "On vulgar paws and voluble like fire"; Shelley then replaced
       this ending with "over shoulders leapt", but because the rhyme-scheme
       requires "fire"; the line does not make sense unless we return to the partially
       obliterated (and obviously discarded) reading.
495–498 *MS:*
              Some *With motions wild*
                  Or made a cradle of the ermined capes
                                      upon
              Of kingly mantles, or *sate & wept*
                                  across
              Within the some *within* the tiars
                              rode sate like vultures played
                  Of pontiffs, *hunched* like demons, others *sate*
                                              sate
                                      cowered
              Within *Upon* the crown which [*?*]
                  ?Under   girt with
                                              empire
497   "upon" and "sate like vultures" were added at the same time "played"
       replaced "sate" as the rhyme word (see 499).
498   "Within" canceled and then reinstated by underlining; "?Under" may
       be "Within" written again.

f. 50r   "A baby's or an idiot's brow, & made
             Their nests in it; the old anatomies   500
      Sate hatching their bare brood under the shade

f. 50v   "Of demon wings, and laughed from their dead eyes
      To reassume the delegated power
             Arrayed in which these worms did monarchize

      "Who make this earth their charnel.—Others more 505
             Humble, like falcons sate upon the fist
      Of common men, and round their heads did soar,

f. 51r   "Or like small gnats & flies, as thick as mist
      On evening marshes, thronged about the brow
             Of lawyer, statesman, priest & theorist,   510

      "And others like discoloured flakes of snow
             On fairest bosoms & the sunniest hair
      Fell, and were melted by the youthful glow

499 A *MS*   idiots *MS*
                  ideot's *PP*
500 nests, *MS*   it. The *PP*
                  it: the *SN*
501 Sat *SN*   broods *PP*
502 Of *MS*   demons' *SN*
503 power, *PP*
504 Array'd *PP*   these] those *PP*   monarchize, *PP*
505 Who *MS*   earth their] *earth* theier *MS*   charnel—others *MS*
                                          charnel. Others *PP*
506 falcons, *PP*   sat *SN*
507 soar *MS*
      soar; *PP, SN*
508 Or *MS*   flies *SN*
509 marshes *MS*
510 lawyers statesman priest & theorist, *MS*
      lawyers, statesmen, priest and theorist;— *PP*
      lawyer, statesman, priest, and theorist; *SN*
511 And *MS*   others, *PP*
512 *bosoms, & the sunniest hair MS*
                    hair, *PP*

499   *MS* (top of f. 50r):

whom   *whose state*

A baby's or an idiots brow, *and lowered & lowered*

whose

& or [*?*] *lowered*

ate   made

& ate

      "state" and *"ate"* were attempts to rhyme with *"sate"* in 497 (this shows clearly how Shelley pronounced "sate").

501   "bare"; the third letter in this word could be either an "r" or an "s'"; one familiar with Shelley's hand looking at *MS* without first consulting *PP* and *SN* could, I believe, read "base" just as readily as "bare"; the issue remains open.

502   The "n" of "demon" seems to have been written with a separate stroke, after the quill had been lifted from the paper, thus giving it an added flourish: It is reasonably certain that no "s" appears.

505   "Who make this *earth* theier charnel—" above an earlier version: "Of *which the shapes were shadows.*—others more".

506   "Humble," above *"Lowly,";* "*around* like falcons" above *"in shapes, of like shapes".*

508   "small" above *"the";* "as" after *"that".*

509   "thronged about the brow" above *"dazzled their weak sight";* a comma after "marshes" seems to be canceled.

510   The "s" in "lawyers" is clearly canceled; above this line is the fragment: *"Or like the   serpents twist".*

511–512   *MS:*

hoary living

And others *fell* like ⎰ *living* ⎱ flakes of snow
              ⎱ *rain* ⎰

discoloured

    Or   *Serpents & bats*

      Among our

      Fell at our feet, *and others with the*

                    And soon were trampled down

          Fell on

    Into a grey

          Were w   *Were tangled in the hair of those* [*?*]

          Caught

                 On fairest *bosoms, & the sunniest hair tresses*

"Which they extinguished; for like tears, they were
A veil to those from whose faint lids they rained   515
In drops of sorrow.—I became aware

"Of whence those forms proceeded which thus stained
f. 51v   The track in which we moved; after brief space
From every form the beauty slowly waned,

"From every firmest limb & fairest face   520
The strength & freshness fell like dust, & left
The action & the shape without the grace

"Of life; the marble brow of youth was cleft
f. 52r   With care, and in the eyes where once hope shone
Desire like a lioness bereft   525

514 Which *MS*   for] and, *PP*
516 sorrow. *PP*
517 Of *MS*
518 moved. After *PP*   space.— *MS*
     moved: after *SN*   space, *PP*
519 *beauty MS*   waned *MS*
                        waned; *PP, SN*
520 From *MS*
522 action] actions *SN*
523 Of life, *MS*
     "Of life. The *PP*
     "Of life: the *SN*
524 care; *PP*   the] those *PP*   shone, *PP*
525 Desire, *PP*

514–518 *MS* (to the bottom of f. 51r):

Which they extinguished; { *&* / *even* } *and their vapours*
                                      tears whi
                               and like tears, they were
                                        for
                                   on whom
A veil to those *whose, were*   rained
                         mourning lids they *fell*
                  from whose faint *eyes*
In drops of sorrow.—*Wonder* I became aware
                     Wonder
              forms   thus
Of whence those *phan* proceeded which *had* stained
        track   out of the
The *space with uncouth imagery*
           { in which } we moved; *from every one*
           { of the   }
                                   the shadows came
       images
   Came his own likeness, & the
   A mask &

518 The end of this line appears nearly two-thirds of the way down f. 51v;
the more significant intervening cancellations (in order of composition) are:
"*Fell shadowy masks*"; "*Came shadows, & the countenances waned/ From
which they fell*"; "*With form & countenance which ?ever ?craned*"; "*Sent
forth dense shadows of himself which*"; "*That weary as the moon when she
has waned*"; finally: "*That these strange shadows* after brief space.—*"
("*brief*" above "*short*"; "*space*" canceled and then reinstated by underlining).

519 "form the" below "*countenance*"; "*beauty*" probably canceled when
"*beauty*" was used in 521 and then mentally reinstated when "freshness'
replaced "*beauty*" (see 521[n]).
520 "*manliest* firmest limb" above "*fairest form*".
521 "freshness" above "*beauty*" (see 519[n]).
522 I believe that "action" is singular: The final upstroke of the "n" is not
unlike that of Shelley's usual "m" or "n" (cf. the final "m" of "form" and
of "From" above in 519, 520 on the same folio).
524 *MS* (top of f. 52r):

                                         shone
With *thought, and eyes*   ?shon
              desire burned where
     care, and in the eyes { where } once hope *lit*
                           { which }

"?shon" is the word Matthews reads as "Jane"; the word is very faint,
written with little ink; I believe that Shelley simply dipped his quill and
wrote "shone" clearly after his illegible attempt.
525 "like" after "*glared*"; "*sate*" below "*glared*".

"Of its last cub, glared ere it died; each one
Of that great crowd sent forth incessantly
   These shadows, numerous as the dead leaves blown

"In Autumn evening from a poplar tree—
   Each, like himself & like each other were,   530
At first, but soon distorted, seemed to be

   "Obscure clouds moulded by the casual air;
And of this stuff the car's creative ray
   Wrought all the busy phantoms that were there

526 Of *MS*   its] her *PP, SN*   *died; MS*
528 sha*dows, MS*
529 In *MS*   autumn evening *PP*   tree. *PP*
                    autumn evenings *SN*   tree.— *SN*
530 Each *PP, SN*   were *PP, SN*
531 first; *PP*   soon] some *PP*   distorted *PP*
532 Obscure *MS*   clouds, *PP*   air *MS*
533 cars *MS*
534 Wrought] Wrapt *PP*   phantoms, *MS*   were there] *were there MS*
                                                    were there, *PP*
                                                  flew there, *SN*

526–528 *MS:*

Of $\left\{\begin{matrix} \text{its} \\ \text{her} \end{matrix}\right\}$ last cub, glared ere it *died; turned to stone*
                                    each one
                              turned to stone

Its object & itself

Sent forth $\left\{\begin{matrix} a \\ in \end{matrix}\right\}$ *thousand shadows*
        Of that great crowd sent forth incessantly
        These   *as* numerous as the
A thousand shadows, *of himself &*
                    like the dead leaves blown

"its" (526) is partly superimposed on "*her*": "*her*" is in the same ink as "Of" and "last", while "its" is heavier; "sha*dows*" (528) is not heavily canceled and may have been accidentally touched by the quill.

529 "In" after "*Oer*"; "from" below "*out of*"; although more questionable than "action" (522), "evening" appears to be singular: Shelley often writes his "ing" hastily and carelessly, and although "s" could appear, it is by no means clear.

530 "were," may possibly be "wear," which would seem to make better rhyme than reason.

532–535 *MS* (to bottom of f. 52r):
        ?alike   vapour
          clouds
Like mounts   moulded by the casual air
        Obscure clouds
                    Chariots   ray
And left behind the ?car [*?*]   *car*
                cars cre ative *light*
        And of this stuff the *light of that* Vision
                                ?like
        ?busy   that   *were*
Wrought all the phantoms, *?fluttering there*
                        & on its far flight
        As the sun shapes the clouds—*& in derision*
                form   *mighty*
Wither Changes their shape ?at ?his ?whim ?at ?his ?will
                by his prevailing ray [*?*]
        So
        From

534 Matthews may have read the first part of "*?fluttering*" as "flew"; if "flew" does appear, it must be superimposed on part of a longer word; the line remains doubtful.

f. 52v   "As the sun shapes the clouds—thus, on the way   535
               Mask after mask fell from the countenance
           And form of all, and long before the day

           "Was old, the joy which waked like Heaven's glance
           The sleepers in the oblivious valley, died,
               And some grew weary of the ghastly dance   540

           "And fell, as I have fallen by the way side,
               Those soonest from whose forms most shadows past
           And least of strength & beauty did abide."—

               "Then, what is Life?" I said . . . the cripple cast
f. 53r   His eye upon the car which now had rolled   545
               Onward, as if that look must be the last,

           And answered . . . . "Happy those for whom the fold
               Of

535   As *MS*   clouds; thus *PP*
                        clouds—thus *SN*
537   all; *PP*
538   Was old *MS*   Heavens *MS*
                            heaven's *PP, SN*
539   valley *SN*   died *MS*
                            died; *PP*
540   dance, *PP*
541   And *MS*   fallen, *PP, SN*   way side *MS*
                                                 way side;— *PP*
                                                 wayside, *SN*
542   soonest, *MS*   past, *PP*
                            passed *SN*
543   abide.— *MS*
       abide. *PP*
544   Then, *MS*   Life I said . . . *MS*   *the cripple cast MS, omitted from PP*
                            life? I cried."— *PP*
545-548   *omitted from PP*
546   last *MS*
547   answered: *SN*   Happy *MS*

535   *MS* (top of f. 52v):

      As

        They

         Phantoms & men *&* &

         Compelling them

          With [*?*] *beams curdling the shapeless mass*

          So distinct

                             thus, on the way

537   *MS:*

      And form of every pilgrim

              ?long

    And form of all, *So when*

              and before the day

538   "waked" above *"was"*; "glance" above "Heavens".

539   "The" after *"Perished"*.

540   "some" above *"most"*.

541–542   *MS:*

      And *sank* fell, as I have fallen by the

               Alas I kiss you [*?*] way side

        Those soonest, *from whose limbs the*

               from whose forms most shadows

                         past

"Alas I kiss you [*?*]" was printed in an extremely fine hand after the quill had been sharpened (probably after *"limbs the"* below); the word *SN* reads as "Jane" I believe to be "Julie": At least there seem to me to be five rather than four letters, two of which rise above the level of the others.

543–544   *MS:*

               strength

    And least of *beauty*   & beauty did abide.—

    Then,   said

      And what is Life I *cried* . . . *the cripple cast*

Shelley probably replaced *"cried"* to avoid a misplaced rhyme with "abide" in 543.

545   *Orig.:* "*An* eye upon the *distant car* of *beams*".

548   "Of" is the last word on f. 53r; f. 53v is devoted to sketches of sailboats.

HISTORICAL COLLATIONS

3 splendor, *W*
4 Earth— *C, F, H, J*
   earth. *R*
   Earth; *W, L*
5 mountain-snows *R₂*
7 light *R, W*   ocean's *R*   arose, *C omnia*
9 forest, *W*
12 ray, *L*
14 air; *C omnia*
15 And, *C omnia*   continent, *C omnia*
16 ocean, *C omnia*
17 mould, *C omnia*
18 Rise, *W*   sun *C, J*
19 toil, *C, F, H, J*
20 own, *R, F, H*   them: *C, F, H, L, J*
                        them. *R, W*
23 night,— *L*   asleep *C, R, F, W, H, J*
25 chesnut *C, R, F, L, J*
26 Apennine. Before *R, W*
27 deep *C omnia*
28 heaven *R*   head, *C, F, J*
                     head;— *R, W, L*
                     head,— *H*
29 grew, *R, L*
31 transparent, *C₁, F, H, L*   through, *W*
32 As clear as, *C₂, R, L, J*
33 hills, *C₂, R, L, J*
34 dawn *C₂, R, W, H, J*
35 Bathe *C₂, R, W, H, J*   hair, *C omnia*
37 self-same *C, F, W, H, L, J*   bough,] tree, *J*   there] then *J*
   selfsame *R*
38 fountains, *C, R, J*   ocean *C, F, W, H, L*
                              ocean, *R*
   Ocean hold] sea still hold *J*
39 air, *C, F, H, J*
   air; *L*
40 vision *C, R, F, W, H, L*   rolled. *C omnia*
   And see those clouds o'er the horizon rolled. *J*
41 lay, *C omnia*
42 tenor *W*   dream:— *C, F, H, L, J*
                     dream.— *R*
43 way, *R₂*
44 Thick-strewn *R₂, L*   dust; *R, W, L*
45 fro, *C omnia*
46 gleam,— *R, W, L*
49 yet] and *C omnia*
50 crowd, *C, F, W, H, L, J*
51 Summer's *L*   bier; *C, F, H, L, J*
                        bier. *R, W*
52 infancy *F, L*
53 appear *C₁*
   appear: *C₂, R, J*
   appear; *W*

54 feared, *C omnia*
55 fear; *C, F, W, H, L, J*
    fear. *R*
56 others, *R, W, H, L*   tomb, *C omnia*
57 Poured *R₁*   beneath; *R, W*
59 walked *C, F, J*   death; *C omnia*
61 breath: *C, F, H, L, J*
    breath; *W*
62 more, *C₂, R, F, W, H, L, J*   motions, *C₁*   crost, *C, F, L, J*
                                                                crossed, *R, W, H*
63 shunned] spurned *C, R₁*   threw, *C, R, F, H, L, J*
64 noon-day *C, F, J*   aether *F, H, L, J*
65 grew, *C₁*
    grew,— *C₂, R, F, W, H, L, J*
66 And, *R, F, W, H*   thirst, *C omnia*
67 fountains, *C, F, H, J*
68 for ever *C, R, F, J*   burst; *C, F, H, L, J*
                                   burst, *R, W*
70 paths *C, R₂, F, W, H, L, J*   wood, lawn-interspersed, *C*
                                          wood lawn-interspersed, *R₁*
                                          wood-lawns interspersed *F, R₂, W, H, L*
                                          wood-lawn interspersed, *J*
71 over-arching *C, L, J*   elms, *R, W*
72 violet-banks *R*   brood;— *R*
                             brood; *W, L*
73 old. *C omnia*
74 And, *R, W*   gazed, *C omnia*
76 south *C omnia*   day, *C, F, H, J*
                            day; *R, W, L*
77 glare *C, J*   noon, *C, F, H, L, J*
78 icy-cold, *L*   with blinding light *C omnia*
79 sun, *C omnia*   moon— *R, W, H, L*
81 air, *C omnia*
82 might, *C, F, L, J*
    might— *R, W, H*
83 a] the *C omnia*
84 her] its *C, F, W, H, L, J*   mother, *C omnia*
85 aether *F, H, L, J*   chair,— *C, F, H, L, J*
                                 chair: *R*
                                 chair;— *W*
87 splendour; *R*
    splendor; *W*
88 within, *C omnia*   deform, *C omnia*
89 cape, *C omnia*
90 tomb; *C₂, F, W, H, L, J*
    tomb. *R*
91 head a cloud-like crape *C omnia*
92 bent, *C omnia*   ethereal *C, W*
                            aetherial *F, L*
                            aethereal *H, J*
93 light upon the chariot beam; *C₁*
    light: upon the chariot beam *C₂*
    light. Upon the chariot beam *R₁, F, J*
    light. Upon the chariot-beam *R₂, W, H, L*

94 shadow *C*, *J*
95 wonder-wingèd *R*, *F*, *W*, *H*, *L*, *J*   team; *C*, *F*, *W*, *H*, *L*, *J*
96 shapes *C omnia*   lightenings *R*, *H*, *L*
97 lost:— *C*, *R*, *F*, *H*, *L*, *J*
     lost— *W*
98 ever-moving *C omnia*
99 Charioteer *R*, *H*
100 banded; *C*, *F*, *W*, *H*, *L*, *J*   Little *R*
      banded. *R*
102 sun *C*, *F*, *L*, *J*
      sun: *R*
      sun,— *W*, *H*
103 that his] that with *C*, *F*, *W*, *H*, *L*, *J*
          that with *R*
104 been *F*, *W*, *H*, *L*   will be, *R*   done; *C*, *F*, *W*, *H*, *L*, *J*
                                                                    done. *R*
105 guided— *C omnia*   passed *R*, *W*, *H*
106 on. *C omnia*
107 way; *R*
109 saw, *C omnia*   thunder's blast, *C*, R_1
                                   thunder-blast, R_2, *H*, *L*, *J*
                                   thunder blast, *F*, *W*
111 around— *C*, *F*, *H*, *J*   Such *R*, *W*
      around. *R*, *W*
      around:— *L*
112 when, *C*, *R*, *J*   greet] meet *C*, R_1, *J*   advance, *C*, *R*, *J*
114 senate-house, and forum *C*, *F*, *W*, *H*, *L*, *J*   theatre, *C omnia*
      senate-house and forum *R*
115 When [   ] upon the free *C*
      When . . . upon the free *R*
      When   upon the free *F*, *W*, *H*, *L*, *J*
116 yoke, *C*, *F*, *W*, *H*, *L*, *J*
117 true] just *C omnia*
118 for, *R*, *W*
119 rolled, *C omnia*
120 driven;— *C*, *F*, *W*, *H*, *L*, *J*   althose] all those *C omnia*
      driven:— *R*
121 misery; *R*, *W*   have] had *C omnia*   subdued *C omnia*
124 flower;— *C*, *F*, *H*, *L*, *J*
126 Winter *L*
127 their own] this green *C omnia*   for ever *C*, *R*, *F*, *H*, *J*
      low;— *C*, *F*, *H*, *L*, *J*
      low; *R*, *W*
129 conquerors— *C*, *F*, *H*, *J*   but, *R*, *W*
      conquerors, *R*, *W*
      conqueror— *L*
130 flame, *C omnia*
131 noon,— *W*
      noon; *L*
133 gems, till the last one] gems [   ] *C*
                                   gems . . . *R*, *F*, *W*, *H*
                                   gems till the last *L*, *J*
134 Were there, of Athens or Jerusalem, C_1, *R*, *F*, *W*, *H*, *J*
      Were there of Athens or Jerusalem, C_2
      Were there, of Athens and Jerusalem, *L*

135 'mid *C, L, J*   seen, *C omnia*
136 'mid *C, R₁, L, J*   them, *C omnia*
137 Nor those who went before fierce and obscene. *C, R, F, W, H, J*
     Nor those who went before, fierce and obscene. *L*
138 van; *R, W*
139 it— *C, F, H, J*
140 chariot, *C omnia*
142 music, wilder *C, R, F, W, H, J*   grows. *R*
     music; wilder *L*
143 the] their *C omnia*
144 Convulsed, *R, L, J*
145 spirit *C₂, W*
     Spirit *R, L, J*
     Spirit, *H*
146 begun,— *C₂, J*
147 hair; *C omnia*
148 And, *R, W*   sun, *C omnia*
149 air; *C₂, J*
     air. *R₁*
150 twinkle *C₂*   recede,— *R₁*   now, *R, W*
     twinkle, *R₁*
     twinkle. They *R₂*
151 atmosphere, *R, F, W, H*
152 invisibly— *C, F, H, L, J*   and, *R, W*   glow, *C omnia*
     invisibly, *R, W*
154 new] their *C omnia*   go, *C, F, H, J*
                                   go; *R, L*
                                   go: *W*
155 Till (like *R*   impelled, *R, H, L*
     Till, like *W*
156 mingle, *R, L*
157 rain— *C, F, H, L, J*
     rain) *R*
     rain, *W*
158 snaps—the shock still may tingle; *C*
     snaps—the shock still may tingle. *R₁*
     snaps—while the shock still may tingle; *F, H, L, J*
     snaps, while the shock still may tingle. *R₂*
     snaps, while the shock still may tingle;— *W*
159 falls, *R*   another, *R*   path, *R*
160 Senseless— *C, R, F, H, L, J*   single. *R*
                                            single; *L*
161 Yet, *R*   *where— C, F, H*
                      where, R, W
                      'Ware, L
                      'Ware,— J
162 Passed *R, W, H*   them— *C omnia*
163 ocean's *C omnia*
164 shore;— *C, F, H, L, J*   behind, *C, F, H, L, J*
     shore. *R, W*
165 men *C omnia*   women, *R*   disarrayed, *C, R, F, H, L, J*
166 gray *F, W, H*   hairs *C omnia*   wind; *R*
                                                     wind *W*
167 And follow in the dance, with limbs decayed, *C, F, W, H, L, J*
     And follow in the dance with limbs decayed, *R*

168   To reach the car of] Seeking to reach the C, F, W, H, L, J
                        Limping to reach the R
171   wheel (though R
      wheel— L
172   other), R fulfil C omnia
      other— L
173   work] part, C to] in C omnia
          work, R, F, W, H, L, J
      whence they arose] from whence they rose C omnia
174   Sink, C omnia   lie, C omnia
175   frost] past C omnia   what [   ] in C those.— R_1
                                what . . in R
                                what   in F, W, H, L, J
177   said—And C, F
      said: "And R
      said—"And W, H, L, J
178   car?— R &] And C omnia   why— C, F
                                          why" R
                                          why—" H
179   (I R added—is C, F amiss?— C, F
              added) "is R amiss?"— R, W, L, J
              added—"Is L, J amiss?—" H
180   answered— C omnia   "Life!"— C, R_1, F, W, H, L, J
                                "Life."— R_2
      turned, C omnia
181   Heaven, C omnia
183   hill side, C, F, H, J
      hill-side R_2
      hillside W
      hill-side, L
184   that] those C, F, W, H, J crew; R, W
185   grass, C, F, W, H, L, J
186   white R discolored W hair; R, W
187   it] he F, W, H, J hide, C, F, H, L, J
188   eyes:— C, F, W, H, L, J canst, C, R, F, W, H, J
      eyes. R_2
189   dance,— L forborne!" C, F, W, H, L, J
190   Feature C_1 thought: C_1 "Aware, C_1
      Feature, (of C_2 aware); C_2
      Feature (of R, F, W, H, J aware). R, F, W, H
                                    aware;) J
191   now tell] unfold C omnia
193   morn. R, W
194   If R_2 doth not thus] shall not then C omnia
195   even] thou even C omnia   night; R, W, L
196   weary."—Then C, F, W, H, L, J
      weary."—Then, R
198   paused; C omnia   and, C, R cried: F, W, H, L
199   "First, C omnia   thou?"— C omnia   memory, C omnia
200   I R_2 did C, F, H, L, J died; R, L
201   And, R
202   Earth had] Had been C omnia   nutriment] sentiment C, R_1
      supplied, C omnia
203   Corruption R_2

204 Rousseau,— *C omnia*
205 Stain *R, F, W, H, L*
    that which ought to have disdained to wear *C omnia*
    it; *C, F, W, H, L, J*
    it. *R*
206 If *R₂*
207 bore"— *C, F, W, H, J*
    bore." *R*
208 car?"— *C, F, H, L, J*   wise, *C omnia*
209 The *R₂*   unforgotten,— *C omnia*
210 wreaths *C omnia*
211 thought;] thought— *C, F, H, J*   Their *R*
          thought. *R*
          thought: *L*
212 Taught *R₂*   this, *C omnia*
213 mutiny] mystery *C omnia*   within; *R*
214 And, *R, W, L, J*
215 Caught *R₂, W*   evening."— *C, F, H, L, J*
216 breast, *C omnia*   crossed *R, W, H*   chain?"— *C, F, H, L, J*
217 child *R, F, W, H*   hour. *R*   He *R*
218 The *R₂*   all it] all that it *C omnia*
220 virtue's *C omnia*
221 Without *R₂*
222 its] his *C₂*   eagle pinions *C omnia*
224 "Fallen, *C, R₁, F, W, H, L, J*   fell." *R*   cheek— *C₁*
    Fallen, *R₂*
225 Alter, *F, W, H*   great form] shadow *C, R, F, W, H, J*
                Shadow *L*
    away, *C, F, W, H, J*
226 weak, *C, F, L, J*
227 pygmy *R, L*   lay; *C, F, W, H, L, J*
           lay. *R*
229 day, *C omnia*
230 irreconcileable *R*
232 eyes' *C omnia*
233 were, *R*
234 be.— *C, R₁, F, H, L, J*   behold,' *C₁*
    be. *R₂, W*
235 Said then my] Said my *C, R, F, W, H*   spoiled,— *L*
        Said   my *L, J*
236 "Frederick, and Paul, *C, F, W, H, L, J*
    "Frederick and Paul, Catherine and Leopold, *R₁*
    Frederick and Paul, Catherine and Leopold, *R₂*
237 And hoary anarchs, demagogues, and sage— *C, R, F, W, H, J*
    And hoary anarchs, demagogues, and sage *L*
238 —names which the world thinks always old, *C*
    —names which the world thinks always old? *R₁*
       names which the world thinks always old, *F, W, H, J*
    . . . name the world thinks always old, *R₂*
       names which the world thinks always old? *L*
239 For, *R*   battle, *C₁*   life *C*   wage, *C omnia*
240 conqueror. *C omnia*
241 By] But *C₂*   age, *C, F, W, H, L, J*
242 Nor *R₂*   tears, *C, F, W, H, L, J*   infamy, *C omnia*   tomb, *R, W*

243 pass," *C, F, W, H, L, J*
     pass!" *R*
244 cried, *C, F, W, H, L, J*   "The *R*
     cried. *R*
245 Is *R₂*   was, *C, F, H, L, J*
248 As *R₂*
249 how] as *C omnia*
251 Our *R₂*   passed away.— *R*
                       passed away. *W, H*
252 mark *C omnia*
253 day; *C, F, W, H, L, J*
     day. *R*
254 All *R₂*
255 Master *R, W*   not: *C, J*
                            not. *R*
256 That] The *C omnia*   fair, *C, F, W, H, L, J*
                                  fair; *R*
257 And *R₂*   life, *C omnia*   heaven *R*
258 the] that *C omnia*   heart, *R*   love, *C omnia*
     gold, *C, F, W, H, L, J*   pain, *C, F, W, H, L, J*
259 age, *C, F, W, H, L, J*   sloth, *C, F, W, H, L, J*   slavery, *C, W, J*
     not. *C omnia*
260 "And near him walk the [   ] twain, *C*
     "And near him walk the . . . twain,— *R₁*
     "And near him walk the   twain, *F, W, H, L, J*
     And near him walk the . . . twain,— *R₂*
261 The Tutor, and his Pupil whom dominion *R₁*
     The Tutor and his Pupil whom dominion *R₂*
262 chain. *C omnia*
263 The *R₂*
265 as] out for *C omnia*   thunder-bearing *C omnia*   minion:— *R₂*
266 The *R₂*
267 new] the *C omnia*   men; *R*
268 key *C omnia*   Truth's *H, L, J*   doors, *C omnia*
269 If *R₂*   spirit] eagle spirit *C omnia*   lept *H*
270 darkness— *C, F, W, H, J*   He *R, L*
     darkness. *R, L*
271 Nature *C, F*   slept, *R, W, L*
     Nature, *R, W, H, L, J*
272 "To wake, and lead him to the caves that held *C, R₁, F, W, H, L, J*
     To wake, and lead him to the caves that held *R₂*
273 reign. *C, F, W, H, L, J*
     reign.— *R*
274 Bards *R*   old who inly] elder time, who *C omnia*
275 The *R₂*
278 Of *R₂*   it. I *R, W*
                     it: I *L*
279 pain, *C, J*
     pain; *R*
     pain! *F, W, H, L*
280 And *R₂, F, W, H, L, J*   were] have *C omnia*   misery!"— *C*
                                      misery."— *R₁*
281 *omitted from C, R₁*
     Even as the deeds of others, not as theirs." *R₂, L, J*
     "Even as the deeds of others, not as theirs." *F, W, H*

282 ——he pointed to a company, *C*
      He pointed to a company *R₁*
      And then he pointed to a company, *F, W, H, L, J*
      And then he pointed to a company *R₂*

283 'Midst whom I quickly recognised the heirs *C*
      'Midst whom I quickly recognized the heirs *R₁, F, W, H*
      Midst whom I quickly recognized the heirs *R₂*
      'Midst whom I [quickly] recognized the heirs *L*
      'Midst whom I [quickly] recognised the heirs *J*

284 crime, *C omnia*   Constantine; *C omnia*

285 Anarchs old] anarch chiefs, *C, R, F, W, H*
                    anarch [chiefs], *L, J*

286 sceptre-bearing *C omnia*   line, *C omnia*

287 blood & gold] gold and blood *C omnia*   abroad: *C, F, H, L, J*
                                      abroad; *R, W*

288 John, *C omnia*   divine, *C, F, W, H, L, J*

289 man and God; *C, F, H, L, J*
      man and God, *R, W*

290 under] over *C omnia*   heaven, *C, R, F, W, H, J*

291 worshiped, *R*   strode, *C omnia*
      worshipped, *W, L*

292 sun *C omnia*   quenched— *C, F, H, J*
                    quenched. *R, W, L*

293 leader:— *C omnia*

295 If *C₂, R₂, L, J*   agony." *R, W*

296 camest thou] comest thou? *C*
              comest thou, *R₁*
              camest thou? *F, W, H, L, J*
              camest thou, *R₂*

297 begin?" *C, F, W, H, L, J*

298 Mine *R₂*

299 heart of] heart sick of *C omnia*   thought— *C, F, W, H, J*
                              thought:— *R*
                              thought. *L*

300 Speak!"— *C, R₁, F, W, H, L, J*
      Speak!" *R₂*
      I came, partly I] I am, I partly *C omnia*   know; *R*

301 And *R₂*

302 may'st *C₂, J*   guess;— *C, F, H, L, J*
                 guess. *R, W*

303 be, *C omnia*

304 Whither *R₂*   me, *C omnia*   less;— *C, F, H, L, J*

306 wretchedness; *R, W*

307 And *R₂*

308 thee. Now listen:—In *C, R, F, W, H, J*   prime, *C omnia*
      thee. Now listen:—in *L*

309 forest tips *C, R₁, F, W, L, J*
      forest-tips *R₂, H*

310 With *R₂*

311 Of the young year's dawn, I was laid asleep *C, R₁*
      Of the young season, I was laid asleep *F, R₂, W, H, L, J*

312 mountain, *C, F, W, H, L, J*

313 Had *R₂*   cavern, *C, F, W, H, L, J*   deep; *C, F, W, H, L, J*
                                              deep. *R*

314 rivulet, *C omnia*
315 water, *C omnia*   air, *C omnia*
316 Bent R_2 grass, *C omnia*   forever *W, L*
318 sounds, *C, F, H, L, J*   all who hear] whoso hears *C omnia*
      sounds *R, W*
319 All R_2
320 they] he *R*   rest; *C, F, H, L, J*
                  rest. *R, W*
322 "The] "Her *C, R_1, F, W, H, L, J*   her] the *F, W, H, L, J*
         The R_2
323 eventide— *C, F, H, J*
      eventide; *R, W, L*
324 brow was] brows were *C omnia*   dispossessed *R, W, H*
325 When R_2 Sun R_2 the] his *C omnia*   ocean floor, *C, F, J*
                  ocean floor R_1, *W, H, L*
                  ocean-floor R_2
326 prosperity. *C, F, H, L, J*
      prosperity; *R, W*
328 "Ills which, R_1 if ills *C, F, H*   thee; *L*
      Ills which, R_2
      "Ills, which, *W, L, J*
329 quell, *C omnia*
330 memory, *C, F, H, J*
      memory;— R_1
      memory:— R_2
      memory,— *W, L*
331 So R_2 spell; *C, F, W, H, L, J*
                  spell. *R*
332 Whether my] And whether *C omnia*
333 heaven *C, R, F, W, J*   hell *C, R, F, W, L, J*
334 Like R_2
335 arose, *C, F, W, H, L, J*
      arose; *R*
336 seemed] seem C_2
337 Though *R*
338 sun *C omnia*
339 earth, *C omnia*   but] and *C omnia*
340 Was R_2 many] magic *C omnia*
341 sense, *L*
342 dun. *R*
343 "And, *C, R_1, F, W, H, L, J*   looked, *C omnia*
      And, R_2
345 sun's *C, R_1, F, W, H, L, J*
346 Burned R_2
347 forest's *C omnia*
348 fire; *C, F, H, L, J*   There *R, W*
      fire. *R, W*
349 Amid R_2 sun,— C_2, R_1, *J*
                  Sun— R_2
351 fountain C_2, *R, J*   rays,— C_2, *J*
                  rays— *R*
352 A R_2 Shape *C omnia*
353 dawn, *C, R, F, W, H, J*
      dawn; *L*

354 And the invisible rain did ever sing *C omnia*
355 A *R₂*   lawn; *C omnia*
356 her] me *C omnia*   grass, *C, F, W, H, L, J*
357 many-coloured *C, R, F, H, L, J*   drawn: *C, F, W, H, L, J*
     many-colored *W*   drawn. *R*
358 In *R₂*   glass, *C omnia*
359 Nepenthe; *C, F, H, L, J*   splendor *W*
     nepenthe; *R, W*
361 "Of the] "Out of the *C, R₁, J*   & with] with *C, R₁, J*
         Of the *R₂*   and, with *R₂, W*
     tender, *C, F, H, J*
362 billow; *C, J*
     billow. *R₁*
363 Glided] She glided *C, R₁, J*
364 Head *R₂*   boughs; *R*   till, *C, R, J*   willow, *C, R, F, W, L, J*
366 their pillow.—] its pillow. *C omnia*
367 As *R₂*
368 lakes, *H, J*   'mid *C, R₁, F, L, J*   mist, *C omnia*
369 music,— *R*   Shape *R₂, W, L*
370 Partly *R₂*   kissed *C omnia*
371 foam; *C, F, W, H, L, J*
372 airs that] air which *C omnia*
373 Or *R₂*   slant] faint *C omnia*
374 trees;] trees. *R*
375 feet, *C, R, F, W, H, J*   ever, *L*
376 "Of leaves, and winds, and waves, and birds, and bees, *C, F, H, L, J*
     Of *R₂*
377 drops, *R, F, W, H, L*   in] to *C, R₁, J*   new, *C, W, J*
                                              new,— *R*
378 summer-evening *R₂, L*   breeze, *C, R, F, H, L, J*
379 Up *R₂*   lake, *R*   dew, *R*
381 Moves up the east,] Dances i' the wind, *C omnia*
     eagle never] never eagle *C omnia*   flew; *C, F, W, H, L, J*
                                              flew. *R*
382 And *R₂*
383 moved to *C, R, F, W, H, J*
384 them; *C, F, W, H, L, J*   And *R*
     them. *R*
385 All *R₂*   was, *C, F, H, L, J*   not; *C omnia*
386 As if] And all *C omnia*
387 embers; *C omnia*
388 Trampled *R₂*   fires] sparks *C omnia*   death; *C₁, F, H, L*
                                              death,— *R*
389 day *C, F, H, J*   East *L*
391 Of *R₂*   re-illumine *C, R, F, H, L, J*
                 reillumine *W*
392 Heaven's *L*   eyes!— *C₂*   Like *R*
                     eyes. *R*
                     eyes; *W*
                     eyes! *J*
393 dream. And, *R₁*
     dream.
             "And, *R₂*
394 To *R₂*

395 said: *R*   If, *C, F, H, J*   seem *R₁*
396 name *R, H*
397 "Into *C, F, H, J*
   Into *R₂*
398 Show *C, R, F, W, H, J*   why: *L*
399 stream. *C, F, H, J*
400 "Arise *C, F, H, J*   thirst, *C, F, H, J*
   'Arise *R₂*
401 And, *R, W*   lily *R, F, W, H*
403 I *R₂*
404 lips the   cup *L*   raised. *R*
   lips   the cup *J*   raised; *L*
405 sand, *C*
406 Where *R₂*
407 Labrador; *C, F, H, L, J*
408 the fierce wolf] the wolf, *C, R, F, W, H*   amazed, *C omnia*
        the   wolf, *L, J*
409 Leaves *R₂*   shore, *C, F, H, L, J*
410 bursts;— *C omnia*
411 vision, *C, F, H, L, J*   before, *C, F, W, H, J*
   vision *R*   before. *R*
   Vision, *W*   before; *L*
412 And *R₂*   Shape *R₂, W, L, J*   light, *C omnia*
413 splendor *W*
414 Lucifer *R*
415 Of *R₂*   sun-rise, *C, F*   strike] tinge *C omnia*
        sunrise, *W, H, L, J*
   mountain tops; *C, F, W, J*
   mountain tops. *R₁*
   mountain-tops. *R₂*
   mountain-tops; *H, L*
416 And, *R*   planet, *C omnia*
417 unseen, *C omnia*
418 That *R₂*   end, *C₂, R, W, L, J*   it, *C omnia*
419 smile *R, W*
421 Or *R₂*
423 content; *C, F, H, L, J*
   content,— *R, W*
424 So *R₂*
425 Shape *R₂, W, H, L, J*
427 More *R₂*   day-appearing *C omnia*
428 sleep; *C, F, H, J*
429 from] of *C omnia*   heaven, *C, F, H, J*   half-extinguished *C omnia*
        heaven *R, W*
        Heaven, *L*
430 Through *R₂*   day, *W*   weep, *C, F, W, L, J*
431 for ever sought, for ever *C, R, F, H, J*   lost; *C, F, W, H, L, J*
                lost. *R*
432 Shape *R₂, W, L*   tenor *W*
433 Beside *R₂*   ghost. *R, W, L*
434 "But *R₂*   its] the *C omnia*
435 savage music, stunning] solemn speed and stunning *C omnia*
   crossed *R, W, H*
436 The *R₂*   forest; *R, W, L*   and, *R, W*

438   star. *C omnia*
439   A R_2 victory, *C, F, W, H, J*
441   wind-wingèd *R, F, W, H, L, J*   pavilion; *R, W*
442   And R_2 underneath, *L*   ethereal *C, W, J*
      "And, *L*   etherial *R*
                                                 aethereal *H*
443   wilderness; *R, W*
444   splendour, *C, F, H, L, J*
      splendor, *W*
445   Shadow R_2 or] and *C omnia*   stone; *C, F, H, L, J*   The *R, W*
                                                       stone. *R, W*
446   Seemed, *R*   light, *C omnia*   that dance] to dance *C omnia*
447   sunbeam;— *C, F, H, L, J*   some *C, F, H, L, J*
      sunbeam. *R, W*
448   Embroidery R_2 flowers, *C omnia*
449   desert, *C, R, W, H, L, J*
451   Others R_2 gazing, *C omnia*
452   dim; *C omnia*
453   it; *C omnia*
454   Circles R_2 it, *C omnia*
455   air; *C omnia*
457   The R_2 there:— *C, F, H, L, J*
                         there. *R*
                         there; *W*
458   all, *R*   flood, *R*
459   last, *C omnia*
460   Borne R_2 onward. *C, R, W, J*
461   swept— *C, F, H, J*   me, *C, F, H, L, J*   long; *C omnia*
      swept. *R, W*   Me *R, W*
      swept: *L*
462   Me, *C, R_1, F, H, L, J*   solitude; *C omnia*
463   "Me, *C, R_1, F, H, L, J*   the] that *C omnia*   lethean *R*
      Me R_2
      song; *C omnia*
464   Me R_2, *W*   form, *C, F, J*
                            Form R_2, *W, H*
                            Form, *L*
465   motion— *C, F, H, J*
      motion:— *R, L*
      motion; *W*
466   The R_2 the] that *C omnia*
468   light *R*   deform. *C omnia*
472   Of R_2 who *C, F, W, H*   hell, *C omnia*
473   paradise *C omnia*   glory, *C omnia*
474   tell, *L*
475   "In] "The *C, R_1, F, W, H*   words] world R_1 awe] care; *C*
              The R_2 care R_1
                                                                       awe; *F, H*
                                                                       awe,— R_2, *W*
                                                                       awe, *L, J*
476   transfigured *C omnia*
477   (For C_2 sea, *C, F, H, L, J*   hoary, *C omnia*
      For, *R*
478   "The] The R_2

479 lovers) C_2
     lovers. R
     lovers,— W
     lovers:— L
     lovers: J
480 rhyme! The R
     rhyme.—The F, H
     rhyme. The W, L, J
481 Grew R_2 covers; R, W
482 grey] gray W, H phantoms; R, W
484 A R_2
485 bringing, C omnia   evening, C omnia
486 isle,—] vale;— C Thus R, W
     vale. R_1
     isle;— F, H, L, J
     isle. R_2, W
487 Phantoms R_2 around; C, F, W, H, L, J And R
     around. R
488 themselves R_2
489 them; C omnia
490 Were R_2 blaze,] day; C omnia
493 And R_2
494 On vulgar hands, * * * C
     On vulgar hands. R
     On vulgar hands, ... F
     On vulgar hands, . . . W, H
     On vulgar hands, L
     In vulgar bands, J
496 Of R_2 mantles; C omnia   upon] across C omnia
     tiar] tire C
497 sate like vultures,] rode, like demons; C, R_1
                   sate like vultures; F, W, H, L, J
                   sate, like vultures; R_2
498 Within] Under C omnia
499 A R_2 ideot's F
500 it. The C omnia
501 broods C omnia
502 Of R_2 demon] daemon F, H wings; R
503 re-assume C, R, F, L, J power, C, F, W, H, J
504 these] those C omnia   monarchise, C, J
                   monarchize, F, H
505 Who R_2 make] made C omnia   charnel. C omnia   Others, R
506 falcons, C omnia   sat C, R, J
507 soar; C omnia
508 "Or, R_1 flies R
     Or, R_2
510 lawyers, statesmen, C, F, W, H, L, J priest, C, R, J
     theorist;— C, R, F, H, L, J
     theorist; W
511 And R_2 others, C omnia   discolored W snow, R, W, L
512 hair, C, F, W, H, J
514 Which R_2 for] and, C omnia
516 sorrow. C omnia
517 Of R_2

518 moved. After *C*, *R₁*, *F*, *W*, *H*, *L*, *J*　　　space, *C omnia*
　　　moved.
　　　　　"After *R₂*
519 waned; *C omnia*
520 From *R₂*
523 Of *R₂*　　　life. The *C omnia*
524 care; *C omnia*　　　and, *R*　　　the] those *C omnia*　　　shone, *C omnia*
525 Desire, *C omnia*
526 Of *R₂*　　　its] her *C omnia*　　　died. Each *R*
529 In *R₂*　　　autumn *C omnia*　　　tree, *C*, *J*
　　　　　　　　　　　　　　　　　tree. *R₁*, *F*, *W*, *H*
　　　　　　　　　　　　　　　　　poplar-tree. *R₂*, *L*
530 Each *C omnia*　　　himself, *R*　　　like each] each like *R*
　　　other, *R*　　　were *C omnia*
531 first; but *C*, *F*, *W*, *H*, *L*, *J*　　　soon] some *C*, *R*, *F*, *H*, *J*
　　　first. But *R₁*　　　　　　　　　　　some, *W*, *L*
　　　first: but *R₂*
　　　distorted *C*, *R*, *F*, *H*, *J*　　　be,— *R₁*
532 Obscure *R₂*　　　clouds, *C*, *F*, *W*, *H*, *L*, *J*
534 Wrought] Wrapt *C*　　　there, *C omnia*
　　　　　　Wrapped *R₁*
535 As *R₂*　　　clouds; thus *C*, *F*, *H*, *L*, *J*
　　　　　　clouds. Thus *R*, *W*
537 all; and *C*, *F*, *H*, *L*, *J*
　　　all. And, *R*
　　　all; and, *W*
538 Was *R₂*　　　joy, *W*　　　heaven's *C*, *R*, *F*, *W*, *H*, *J*
539 valley *R*, *J*　　　died; *C omnia*
540 dance, *C omnia*
541 And *R₂*　　　fallen, *C omnia*　　　way-side;— *C*, *R₁*, *F*, *L*, *J*
　　　　　　　　　　　　　　　　　wayside;— *R₂*, *W*, *H*
542 past, *C*, *F*, *L*, *J*
　　　passed, *R*, *W*, *H*
543 abide. *C*, *R₁*, *F*, *H*, *J*
　　　abide." *R₂*, *W*, *L*
544 " 'Then, *R₁*　　　life? *C*, *F*, *W*, *H*　　　said . . .] cried."— *C*, *R₁*, *F*, *W*, *H*
　　　"Then *R₂*　　　life?' *R₁*　　　　　　cried. *R₂*
　　　　　　　　　life?" *J*　　　　　　　　cried.— *L*, *J*
　　　the cripple cast *omitted C through H*
　　　The cripple cast *L*, *J*
545-548 *omitted C through H*
545 car, *L*, *J*
547 answered, *L*, *J*　　　fold] gold *L*, *J*
548 Of" *L*, *J*

THE BODLEIAN MANUSCRIPT

The Bodleian MS of "The Triumph of Life" (MS Shelley adds. c. 4, ff. 19–58) consists of forty leaves; some of these leaves are single and others are joined in conjugate pairs formed by folding larger sheets. Most leaves of the "Triumph" MS are of a greenish paper that before folding measured $10'' \times 15''$ and when folded (or torn in two) produced leaves $10'' \times 7\frac{1}{2}''$. This paper is watermarked BENEDETTO PARODI across the longest dimension ($15''$) of the full sheet, so that when the paper was properly folded and stacked, PARODI appeared on f. 1 recto (backwards on f. 1v) while BENE-DETTO appeared on f. 2 verso. Theoretically, then, when Shelley picked up a prefolded sheet from the stack of paper, he would begin to use the page upon which the PARODI watermark appeared "right side up." The order of the draft materials on the leaves of the conjugates indicates that this was indeed Shelley's practice.

When the Bodleian Library acquired this MS in 1946 as a part of the bequest of Sir John Shelley-Rolls, an assistant numbered the folios in c. 4 with pencil in the upper right-hand corner of each recto page. The leaves on which there is draft material for "The Triumph of Life" were numbered in the order of the appearance of lines included in the published poem, the discarded openings of the poem were relegated to the end (ff. 54–58), and certain leaves upon which appear no lines of "The Triumph" were numbered arbitrarily, presumably according to their place in the MS when it arrived at the Bodleian. The conjugate leaves ff. 29 and 34 are used as a folder to enclose ff. 30–31 and 32–33, which contain the continuing lines of "The Triumph." The following table provides an outline of the contents of *MS*. I have used the following abbreviations (arranged in alphabetical order):

C	Calculations: groups of numerals that seem to be calculations of a financial nature
LBL	"Lines Written in the Bay of Lerici"
S	Sketch: one or more sketches or drawings
TJKS	"To Jane: 'The keen stars . . .' "
TL	"The Triumph of Life"
TLA	The "Triumph of Life" Apocrypha
TLDO	The "Triumph of Life" Discarded Openings
UL	Uncollected lyrics (lyrical fragments not published in any collected edition of Shelley's poetry)

TABULATED INFORMATION ON BODLEIAN MS Shelley adds. c. 4, ff. 19–58

Folio No.	Conjugate Leaf	Watermark	Position of Watermark on Page (as numbered)	Contents	Remarks
19r	none	BENEDETTO	backwards and *reverso*	TL 1–13	fair copy "1" in upper left
19v			*reverso*	TL 14–31	fair copy "2" in upper left
20r	none	PARODI	correct	TL 32–48	fair copy "3" in upper center
20v			backwards	blank	
21r	22	BENEDETTO	*reverso*	*TLA*–"A" TL 48–54	lines follow *TLA*, f. 22v rough draft of 48 (fair copy on f. 20r)
21v			backwards and *reverso*	TL 55–68	
22r	21	PARODI	backwards and *reverso*	TL 69–83	
22v			*reverso*	*TLA*–"A"	draft *reverso* as leaves now ordered
23r	24	PARODI	correct	TL 84–97	
23v			backwards	TL 98–107	
24r	23	BENEDETTO	backwards	TL 108–118	
24v			correct	TL 119–130	
25r	26	BENEDETTO	*reverso*	TL 131–138	pencil corrections begin (one word)
25v			backwards and *reverso*	TL 139–147	one word in pencil
26r	25	PARODI	backwards and *reverso*	TL 148–157	several words in pencil

			reverso		
26v				*TL* 158–164 *UL:* "The earth quake" *S:* boats, plus word "Ricetti"	several words in pencil lyric (5 ll.) *reverso*
27r	28	PARODI	correct	*TL* 165–175	all but one word in pencil
27v			backwards	*TL* 176–185	"6" in upper right (pencil)
28r	27	BENEDETTO	backwards	*TL* 186–197	
28v			correct	*TL* 198–211	"8" in upper right (pencil)
29r	34	PARODI	correct	*TL* 211–221	last two words of 211 at top of page
29v			backwards	*TL* 222–227 *TLA*–"B"	227 partly canceled here
30r	31	PARODI	correct	*TL* 227–241	227 repeated at top
30v			backwards	*TL* 242–249	
31r	30	BENEDETTO	backwards	*TL* 250–251 *TLA*–"C"	
31v			correct	*TLA*–"B," "C"	
32r	33	PARODI	correct	*TLA*–"C" *TL* 252–258	
32v			backwards	*TL* 259–273	
33r	32	BENEDETTO	backwards	*TL* 274–280 *TLA*–"D"	
33v			correct	*TJKS* 11–18	
34r	29	BENEDETTO	backwards	*TLA*–"B" *S*	

Folio No.	Conjugate Leaf	Watermark	Position of Watermark on Page (as numbered)	Contents	Remarks
34v			correct	TLA–"B" S	
35r	36	BENEDETTO	reverso	LBL 1–18	
35v			backwards and reverso	LBL 19–28	
36r	35	PARODI	backwards and reverso	LBL 29–40	
36v			reverso	LBL 41–52	
37r	38	PARODI	correct	UL C	poetry in pencil calculations in ink
37v			backwards	TL 281–292	
38r	37	BENEDETTO	backwards	TL 293–306 C	
38v			correct	TLA–"D" TJKS 19–24	"To Jane" lines reverso
39r	40	PARODI	correct	TL 307–317	
39v			backwards	TL 318–327	
40r	39	PARODI	correct	TL 328–339	
40v			backwards	TL 340–351	
41r	none	PARODI	correct	TL 352–360	
41v			backwards	TL 361–372 C	
42r	43	PARODI	reverso	TL 378–385	according to the folding of the sheet, this page is 2v of the conjugate

Folio	No.	Watermark	Position	Contents	Notes
42v			backwards and *reverso*	blank	
43r	42	BENEDETTO	*reverso*	*TL* 386–391 *S*	according to the folding of the sheet, this is page 1r of the conjugate
43v			backwards and *reverso*	blank	
44r	45	GBA	backwards	*TL* 406–418	
44v			correct	*TL* 419–428	
45r	44	none		*TL* 429–437	
45v				*S*	large ink sketches of ornamental bows and sterns for a boat
46r	none	flower pot		*TL* 438–450	
46v				cover of letter addressed to Shelley at Villa Magni	postmarked at Pisa May 15
47r	48	BENEDETTO	*reverso*	*C* beginning of letter to Roberts *TL* 451–459	
47v			backwards and *reverso*	*TL* 460–470	
48r	47	PARODI	backwards and *reverso*	*TL* 471–478 *C*	
48v			*reverso*	"370" *S* beginning of letter to Roberts	*reverso*

Folio No.	Conjugate Leaf	Watermark	Position of Watermark on Page (as numbered)	Contents	Remarks
49r	50	PARODI	correct	TL 479–488 C	
49v			backwards	TL 489–498 S	
50r	49	none		TL 499–501	lower half of leaf torn away, apparently before TL written on upper half
50v				TL 502–507	
51r	none	eagle mounted in circle in which appear initials "JP"		TL 508–518	
51v				TL 518–523	last three words of 518 on f. 51v
52r	53 vertical	what seems to be elaborate capital "R" on its side in lower right corner		TL 524–535	
52v				TL 535–544	last four words of 535 on f. 52v
53r	attached to bottom of f. 52; that is, a long single sheet folded into two leaves; fold at top of f. 53r, bottom of f. 52v			TL 545–548	

54r	none	BENEDETTO	*reverso*	*TLDO*–"D" 1–13	
54v			backwards and *reverso*	*TLDO*–"D" 14–26	half of 26 missing
55r	56	BENEDETTO	*reverso*	*TLDO*–"B" 1–9	
55v			backwards and *reverso*	*TLDO*–"B" 10–25	
56r	55	PARODI	backwards and *reverso*	*TLDO*–"B" 26–30 *TJKS* 1–10	*TJKS* written with leaf "turned on its side" (left = top)
56v			*reverso*	*TLDO*–"A"	*reverso*
57r	58	BENEDETTO	*reverso*	*TLDO*–"C" 10–18	
57v			backwards and *reverso*	*TLDO*–"C" 19–26	
58r	57		backwards and *reverso*	*TLDO*–"C" 27–31	
58v			*reverso*	*TLDO*–"C" 1–9	*reverso*

DISCARDED OPENINGS

With the Bodleian MS of "The Triumph" are drafts of at least portions of four openings that Shelley discarded before writing the lines that now begin the poem. Mathilde Blind first published in *WR* the earliest and briefest of these attempts (*DO*-"A") on Garnett's authority; Matthews published the second and third (*DO*-"B" and *DO*-"C") in *TLS* and the final discarded opening (*DO*-"D"), which contains the title of the poem, in *SN*. At least one conjugate pair of leaves, an extension of *DO*-"D," became separated from *MS* and a rough transcription of its contents was published by Walter E. Peck as Appendix J of *Shelley: His Life and Work* (II, 402–404). The present location of this conjugate (called by Peck the Robert S. Garnett MS) is unknown.

The sequence of these openings, upon which I agree with Matthews, is evident both from their progressive development toward the eventual beginning of the poem and from their physical relationships to one another in *MS*. I have followed Matthews' designations of them as "A" to "D," preceding these with *DO* (for *Discarded Opening*) so that they will not be confused with the "apocryphal passages" discussed below. I have edited these discarded fragments upon the following principles: I have italicized words in the text that are canceled in *MS*, added punctuation where it is necessary to the sense of the passage, and recorded substantive variants between my text and *WR*, *TLS*, or *SN*.

DO-"A"

f. 56v   Out of the eastern shadow of the earth
reverso   Amid the clouds upon its margin grey—
           Scattered by Night to swathe in its bright birth

> In fleecy snow & gold the infant day,
> The glorious Sun arose . . . beneath his light   5
> The earth and all

DO-"B"

f. 55r   Swift as a spirit hastening to its task
> Of glory or of good, out of the gloom
> Of daily life; when through its mortal mask

> It burns, until the world it treads assume
> The beauty of the presence which makes bright   5
> Its desarts from the cradle to the tomb,

> So came the Sun out of the shade of night;
> And oer the clouds of crimson, gold & snow
> Which ?form the limits of the realm of ligh⟨t⟩

f. 55v   Moved through serenest air—the Ear⟨th⟩ below   10
> Lay *like the* fairest of the wandering Seven
> *Beneath* her father's wings in the *clear* glow

> Of his bright smile, and all the stars of Heaven
> Were hidden by the luminous expanse
> Of those wide wings which *to the utmost even*   15

> Beare him mid the indefatigable dance
> Of all the fires of the abyss.—The tops
> Of the white mountains, kindling at his glance,

> Like smokeless altars flame, with clouds whose drops
> Make sacrifize of sanguine fire, and breath   20
> Of incense of sweet morning airs—the copse

> And the deep forest, & the woods beneath
> The wetting Ocean, and the flowers which pave
> The vallies *of the earth* or interwreath

> With mimic stars the caverns of the wave.   25
f. 56r   Their painted censers swing on high to gre⟨et⟩
> The presence of the God whose smile first ⟨gave⟩

> The light which kindled them . . their odours swe⟨et⟩
> And orient incense touched by that mild ray
> Burn slow & inconsumably & meet

DO-"A"
  4   In gold and fleecy snow *WR*

DO-"B"
  4   treads] heats *TLS*
  9   Which form *TLS* [The second word may be "frame".]
 10   Moved] Burned *TLS*
 12   Her brooding wings in the *parental* glow *TLS*
 14   luminous] immense *TLS*
 16   Beare him] Wave clear *TLS*
 18   white] high *TLS*
 23   wetting] weltring *TLS*
 28   odours] colours *TLS*

DO-"C"

f. 58v   Swift as a Spirit hastening to its task
reverso   Of glory & of good, the Sun came forth
            Rejoicing in his splendour and the mask

            Of darkness fell from the awakened earth.—
            Whilst she, the fairest of the wandering Seven,   5
            Laughed to behold how in their fiery mirth

            The clearest Stars were blotted out of Heaven
            While every palest flower on her own brow
            Shone, diamonded with dewy splendour, and even

f. 57r   The buds which hang their waned lamps below   10
            The emerald twilight of the sea, half spent
            Glimmered and in the sapphire morning glow

            Their censers swinging to the element
            With orient incense touched by the mild ray
            Burned slow & inconsumably, & sent   15

            Their odourous sighs up to the smiling day.—
            The smokeless altars of the mountain snows
            Flamed amid crimson clouds, and far away

f. 57v   Every successive region slowly rose
            Out of the death of daily life, and bore   20
            Its portion in the ruin of repose . . . .

            It was the year, the season & the hour
            When *the* high tide of life has ceased to flow,
            Its stormy reflux pauses, and *the* shore

            Looks gay with anchored hopes, whose pennons glow   25
            In the false wind & oer the flattering *wave*
f. 58r   When I went forth *with silent steps & slow;*

            She rose in glory from her billowy grave:
            Before me was the day, behind the night,
            The Heaven above me, and its cloudless cave   30

            Was *mirrored in the ocean at my feet*

DO-"D"

DO-"D" is incomplete in *MS* and probably continued on at least
two conjugate pairs of leaves, one of these being the "Garnett MS."
Besides printing a text that parallels *SN*'s version of "D" (1–26), I

DO-"C"
   10   buds] stars *TLS*
   12   Glimmered *with* light, and in the morning glow *TLS*
   26   oer] on *TLS*
   27   &] how *TLS*
   29   *was*] rose *TLS*

have attempted to wrest a few additional lines (26–38) from Peck's transcription of the Garnett leaf. To do so has necessitated conjectural emendation of Peck's work, based on my own problems in deciphering Shelley's writing. Though I have collated that portion of my text with Peck, neither his readings nor my conjectures can be considered authoritative.

f. 54r   The Triumph of Life

    Swift as a Spirit hastening to its task
      Of glory & of good, the Sun sprang forth
    Rejoicing in his splendour; & the mask

    Of darkness fell from the awakened earth;
    The smokeless altars of the mountain snows   5
      Flamed above crimson clouds, and at the birth

    Of light the Ocean's orison arose
      Amid the music of *the* birds of day.
    All flowers in field or forest which unclose

    Their veiled lids to the tēpid kiss of day   10
    Swinging their censers in the element
      With orient incense touched by *the new ray*

    Burned slow & inconsumably & sent
f. 54v   Their odourous sighs up to the smiling air.—
    And in succession slow, did Continent,   15

    And Ocean, isle & cave that in them wear
    The form and character of mortal mould
      Rise as the Sun their father rose, to bear

    Their portion in the toil which he of old,
      Took as his own, & then imposed on them.   20
    But I, whom thoughts which must remain untold

    Had kept as wakeful as *the* stars which gem
    The cone of night, now they were laid asleep
      Stretched my faint limbs beneath the *hoary* stem

    Which an old chesnut flings athwart the steep   25
      Of the green Apennine—
Garnett   before me fled
  MS   The night, behind me rose the day, the deep

    Was at my feet, & Heaven above my head.
    Gazing awhile, my charmed senses grew
      Part of the scene which I contemplated   30

DO-"D"
  16   And isle, and *all things* that within them wear *SN*

And *suddenly as Heaven changed I* knew
    That as the birds & waves made melody
And as the clouds *over* the horizon flew

                .   .   .   .

Under the self same tree, & heard as there
    The birds the fountains & the Ocean hold   35
Sweet talk in music through the enamoured air;

And see these clouds oer the horizon rolled—

                .   .   .   .

Balanced on wings of crimson snow & gold,   38

33   *over*] *ever Peck*
34   there] then *Peck*
36   sweet talke *Peck*

APOCRYPHAL PASSAGES

Following Matthews' terminology in *TLS,* I use the term "apocryphal passages" to designate those passages of three or more complete lines in "The Triumph" MS that were at one time part of the text but were later canceled or superseded; the passages reproduced here (abbreviated *TLA*-"A," "B," "C," and "D") contain images or ideas that were radically revised or eliminated from the final text.

The apocryphal passages I designate "A" and "B" were first transcribed and published by Matthews—with a few different readings —in *TLS,* and many of the lines of "C" and "D" were recorded in *SN* amid notes to the appropriate folios. I have followed *MS* as closely as the imperfect and fragmented nature of the draft would permit: (1) words canceled separately—that is, before the entire passage was discarded—are printed in italics; (2) doubtful words are preceded by question marks; (3) I have retained Shelley's punctuation except when he seems obviously to have changed his intention; (4) I have added minimal punctuation and capitals necessary to the sense, including all quotation marks; (5) in "B" 5 I have omitted the final "s" of "tends" (*MS*), which Shelley obviously intended to be canceled when he replaced *"it"* with "they"; (6) I have numbered the lines of each apocryphal passage. (Line numbers in brackets are those of "The Triumph of Life.")

TLA-"A"

After "The Triumph of Life," lines 44–46, that read,

f.20r   . . . & a great stream
      Of people there was hurrying to & fro
        Numerous as gnats upon the evening gleam,

Shelley began the following passage on a new conjugate:

f.22v   And all the flowers which the vain wind could sow   1
reverso   Beside this way *were bruised* & trampled down
           Not one among the many seemed to know   3

              His way, but as grey moths when grass is mown
              Go blindly fluttring from the moving heap,   5

At this time Shelley introduced a new rhyme-word in the middle of
the initial tercet, canceling *"were bruised"* while adding "& spoiled"
(the sense would seem to imply that he meant to cancel "bruised &").
First canceling the last three lines above ("A" 3–5), he then composed several more lines, completely turning over the conjugate so
that the last three lines of "A" ("A" 9–11, below), which appear on
f. 21r are *reverso* from "A" 1–8. This may indicate that Shelley was
already thinking that he would probably have to cancel the lines
and begin again. Just before most of "A" was finally canceled, the
passage read:

f. 22v   And all the flowers which the vain wind could sow
reverso   Beside this way *were* trampled down & spoiled;   7
           The heartease, which where nothing else will grow

              Lives in old walls,
f.21r   for want of dew was soiled   9
           And died within the hand that gathered it.—
              But few sought flowers there; they rather toiled   11

Matthews suggests that Shelley probably canceled "A" because "the
aloof, alienated description of the crowd on the public way, in terms
of dust and gnats, becomes compromised by inappropriately homely
imagery" (*TLS*). Beyond this lapse in tone—including the introduction of overt allegory in the lines on the "heartease"—there is a
more fundamental fault in the juxtaposition of images that would
have gnat-like people trampling down flowers.

TLA-"B"

On f. 29v Shelley (who had just finished his description of
Napoleon—which, in turn, follows his general picture of all physical, intellectual, and spiritual tyrants) began a new passage designed
to focus on the new age that had dawned with the French
Revolution.

f. 29v   "Fall'n as Napoleon fell."—I felt my cheek
           Alter to see the great form pass away   [225]
              Whose grasp had left the giant world so weak

That every pigmy kicked it as it lay . . .   1 [227]
    Nor mid the many shapes around him chained
    Pale with the toil of lifting their proud clay

f. 34r   Or those gross dregs of it which yet remained
    Out of the grave to which they tend, should I   5
    Have sought to *mark* any who may *have* stained

    Or have adorned the doubtful progeny
    Of the new birth of this new tide of time
    In which our fathers lived & we shall die

    Whilst others tell our sons in prose or rhyme   10
    The manhood of the child; unless my guide
    Had said, "Behold Voltaire—We two would climb

f. 34v   "Where Plato & his pupil, side by side,
    Reigned from the *centre to the circumference*
    Of thought; till Bacon, great as either, spied   15

    "The spot on which they met and said, 'From hence
    I soar into a loftier throne.'—But I—
    O World, who from full urns dost still dispense,

    "Blind as thy fortune, fame & infamy—
    I who sought both, prize neither *now;* I find   20
    What names have died within thy memory,

    "Which ones still live;
f. 31v   I know the place assigned
    To such as sweep the threshold of the fane
    Where truth & its inventors sit enshrined.—

    "And if I sought those joy*s* which now are pain,   25
    If he is captive to the car of life,
    'Twas that we feared our labour wd be vain

This passage focuses on the problem of history and its meaning for the individual life. The Poet, considering history as a black record of past horrors, is not interested in identifying the figures of the pageant who "may have stained/ Or have adorned the doubtful progeny" (6, 7) of "this new tide of time" that began sometime in the mid-eighteenth century ("In which our fathers lived & we shall die," [9]). Rousseau, however, tries to impress on the Poet that it was exactly this attitude toward the past struggles of great men that led him and Voltaire to abandon their reforming zeal and succumb to life. Thus the Poet's contemptuous allusion to Wordsworth (10, 11) turns against him as Rousseau endeavors to show the Poet how the mistakes of those who have preceded him, especially idealists like himself, can serve as a warning to him: Rousseau and Voltaire fell because they adopted the same contemptuous attitude toward

history (25–27) that the Poet now displays; the child *is* the father
of the man, and Shelley's generation, representing the full maturity
of the new age that dawned in the French Revolution, can learn
from the mistakes of that age's earlier generations (those of Rousseau and Voltaire and of Wordsworth).

TLA-"C"

After canceling *TLA-*"B," Shelley turned the conjugate leaves
numbered ff. 30–31 and began again by recopying line 227 at the
top of f. 30r; the text continues on ff. 30r, 30v, and 31r, incorporating many of the implications of *TLA-*"B"; on f. 31r, however,
Shelley once again began a series of lines that he finally rejected.
In these later lines, as in those canceled earlier, Shelley attempts to
illustrate the paradoxical lesson of history:

f. 31r   We have but thrown, as those before us threw,   [250]

          "Our shadows on it as it past away.   1
          See Zoroaster, Solomon and those
          Great forms to whom Egypt & India

          "Owed what they were & are, *but no repose*
          Found these in the creation or the wreck   5
          On which they spent their ?fate in joys & woes

Shelley seems to have been stopped at the bottom of f. 31r; he canceled the lines and attempted to begin again in the blank space at
the bottom of f. 31v (below the end of *TLA-*"B"):

f. 31r   We have but thrown, as those before us threw,   [250]

          "Our shadows on it as it past away."   7
f. 31v   I answered not, but contemplated long
          The mighty phantoms which old India   9

Finally, at the top of f. 32r Shelley made still another attempt, one
that in its central figure parallels a speech attributed to Woodville,
Shelley's surrogate in Mary Shelley's novelette *Mathilda* (ed. Elizabeth Nitchie [Chapel Hill, N.C., 1959], pp. 55–56; cf. note, p. 86):

f. 31r   "Our shadows on it as it past away."
f.32r   "Or as you passed," I interrupted; "thus   11
          One who awakes within a ship would say

          That the stars move; as it appears to us   13
          So is it not, however it may be."—
          "The last of beings multitudinous   15

          "*Phantoms of those who*

The attempt here breaks off, and Shelley, mentally returning to his "base" on f. 31r, proceeded to write what are now lines 252ff. of the text.

TLA-"D"

Shelley attempted at least three times to bridge the so-called "chasm" in the poem (*TL*, 273–282): at the bottom of f. 33r, at the top of f. 38v, and at the top of f. 37v; although he was not able to go beyond the text we now have, it is illuminating to follow his efforts:

f. 33r   "The passions which they sung, as by their strain   [275]
              May well be known: their living melody
          Tempers its own contagion to the vein

              "Of those who are infected with it—I
          Have suffered what I wrote, or viler pain!—

              "And so my words were seeds of misery—   [280]

Unable to continue with the "pain" rhyme (used immediately above), Shelley wrote only two other complete lines at the bottom of f. 33r:

f. 33r   *These the creators, the destroyers those*   1
              Who stalk before, slaves of one victory

These lines were soon canceled because they failed to solve the problem of continuing the "pain" rhyme and created a new difficulty by introducing as the medial rhyme of the tercet the "I" rhyme that should have been ended, not reinitiated, in this tercet. Turning then to f. 38v (f. 33v apparently having already been filled with *TJKS*), Shelley tried a rhyme for "pain":

f.38v   *See Caesar, Aurunzebe & Tamerlane*   3
                Of the destroyers, in one victory

but once again he failed to find a line to close the tercet. Finally, turning back to f. 37v (f. 37r must have been already filled, partly with poetry written in pencil), Shelley wrote:

f. 37v   These *the creators, the destroyers those*—   7
              By words & deeds,—& *thou & such as thee*
           Are both *or* neither

He then rejected these lines and, still anchored to 278–279, wrote lines 280ff., permitting the redundancy that now exists.

APPENDIX D

ORDER AND DATING OF MATERIALS
IN THE BODLEIAN MANUSCRIPT

As one can see from the "Tabulated Information" in Appendix A, the Bodleian manuscript contains, besides the text of "The Triumph" and the various discarded or canceled fragments relating directly to it, the drafts of other poems, some ink sketches or drawings (chiefly just doodling), and calculations that seem to be of a financial nature. The most important poetry other than "The Triumph" itself is the work in tetrameter couplets occupying the conjugate folios 35 and 36 that Richard Garnett first published in *Macmillan's Magazine* and *Relics of Shelley* under the title "Lines Written in the Bay of Lerici," as well as the lines also printed in *Relics of Shelley* as "Miscellaneous Fragment" XL and titled in Hutchinson's Oxford text as "Fragment: To the Moon" (p. 675), which is really the opening of the "Lines." G. M. Matthews has put the two parts together, deciphered the interlined intervening words (which apparently baffled Garnett), and in "Shelley and Jane Williams" given a corrected text of the expanded "Lines Written in the Bay of Lerici." Though I take issue with Mr. Matthews' interpretation and use of the poem as biographical evidence, I accept his text in all but a few points. Here, for the record, are all my variants from Matthews' text *(RES)*.

Line 3   ever . . . *RES*] ever . . . . . *MS*
13   Ocean *RES*] ocean *MS*
29   alone *RES*] alone, *MS*
41   For ministrations *RES*] To ministrations *MS*
56   & *RES*] and *MS*

58 Seeking *RES*] *Destroying MS*
    peace. *RES*] peace: *MS*

(I discuss the variants in line 58 in my essay on the "Biographical Problem," p. 538.)

On three widely separated folios of *MS* appears a complete holograph draft of the lyric "To Jane: 'The keen stars were twinkling' " (untitled, of course, here). Below I have transcribed the text as it appears in the draft and collated it with the accepted text in Hutchinson's Oxford edition (*H*). Italicized words are canceled in *MS*.

f. 56r   The keen stars were twinkling
      And the fair moon was rising among them,
        Dear Jane
      The guitar was tinkling
      But the notes were not sweet till you sang them   5
        Again

      As the moon's soft splendour,
      O'er the faint cold starlight of Heaven
        Is thrown
      So one voice sweet & tender   10
f. 33v   To the strings without soul had then given
        Its own.

      The stars will awaken,
      Though the moon, sleep a full hour later,
        To night.   15
      Not a leaf will *be* shaken
      Whilst the dews of your melody scatter
        Delight.—

f. 38v   Though the sound overpowers
reverso

"To Jane: 'The keen stars . . .' "
1 twinkling, *H*
3 Jane! *H*
4 tinkling, *H*
5 sang] sung *H*
6 Again. *H*
7 splendour *H*
9 thrown, *H*
10 So your voice most tender *H*
14 moon *H*
15 To-night; *H*
16 No leaf will be shaken *H*
18 Delight. *H*
19 overpowers, *H*

> Sing again—for thy voice is revealing   20
>   A tone
> Of some world far from *ours*
> Where moonlight & music & feeling
>   Are won.

Of the substantive variants between *MS* and *H*, the *MS* readings at 5 ("sang" for "sung"), 10, and 20 seem to me to be definite improvements in the poem, as does the order of "moonlight & music & feeling" in 23. I tend to favor the reading of *MS* in 16, though Shelley's cancellation of *"be"* may indicate that Shelley wished to eliminate one syllable from the line (as is done in *H*). Of greatest interest, however, is the change in 24 of "Are one." (*H*) to "Are won." (*MS*); the variant version of 23–24 (written on f. 33v) provides the basic reading in *H*, and although a later *holograph* MS of the poem containing this reading would claim precedence, there is nothing in *MS* itself to suggest greater authority for the version on f. 33v.

On f. 26v *reverso* Shelley began a lyric that he seems to have abandoned before writing *TL*, 131–164. The text is collated with a version of the lines in a footnote to *SN* (p. 285):

f. 26v	*The* earth quake is rocking	1
reverso	The corpse in its cradle within the grave	
	The thunder is mocking	
	The spasm of the earth from its cloudy cave	
	The clear air awakes	5

Below I have transcribed in their order of composition some lines that appear in pencil on f. 37r. Lines 1–3 are, quite obviously, a rough draft of 4–6. Neville Rogers published lines 4–11 in *Shelley at Work* (p. 288); earlier Sir John Shelley-Rolls and Roger Ingpen had printed a version in *Verse and Prose* (p. 71) that was arranged in a different stanzaic pattern to give the impression that the fragment was a continuation of "Autumn: A Dirge" (printed by Mary Shelley with the poems of 1820).

f. 37r	The hours are flying	1
	And joys are dying	
	And hope is sighing	

20   again, with your dear voice revealing *H*
22   ours, *H*
23–24   Where music and moonlight and feeling
       Are one.   *H*
   Where moonlight & music & feeling are one *MS* [f. 33v]

f. 26v
reverso
 5   The clouds are mockin *SN*

Time is flying   4
Joy is dying
Hope is sighing
    For there is

Far more to fear   8
In the coming year
Than desire can bear
    In this

Can I say that sorrow   12
?No mask cd borrow
?If to day like tomorrow
    ?Wd ?remain

And between short is bliss   16
And a state such as this
Would

To conclude the examination of the contents of *MS,* I shall set down physical evidence for the order of composition of the poetry in *MS* and then relate this order to the meager evidence for dating these compositions. It is impossible to determine exactly when during the composition of *TL* Shelley wrote "Lines Written in the Bay of Lerici," though in all likelihood before he ran out of his main supply of BENEDETTO PARODI paper and used odd papers (ff. 44–45, 46), a conjugate of BENEDETTO PARODI paper on which he had already begun a letter (ff. 47–48), and one which was torn (ff. 49–50); *LBL* seems to have been composed before *TL,* 406–437 (ff. 44–45) and, I would guess, also before *TL* 373–391 (ff. 42–43), so strangely written on the outside pages of a conjugate pair of leaves. But ff. 35–36, the conjugate leaves on which *LBL* is composed, seem now not to be properly placed relative to the other leaves of *MS;* f. 34 (conjugate of f. 29) also intervenes between leaves that were probably written consecutively.

The lyric on f. 37r, written in pencil, may have been composed about the same time as the other penciled portions of *MS* (ff. 25–27r). The watermarks indicate that f. 37r was written before Shelley reversed the conjugate to complete *TJKS* (f. 38v *reverso*); later, Shelley again reversed the page before writing *TLA*-"D" at the top of f. 38v and *TL,* 281–306, on the two inner pages of the conjugate (ff. 37v–38r). *TJKS,* 19–24, was thus probably composed sometime between the writing of *TL,* 175 (in pencil on f. 27r), and *TL,* 281 (f. 37v, following the lyric in pencil on f. 37r); moreover, *TJKS,* 11–18 (f. 33v), must also have preceded Shelley's attempts to fill the chasm after 280, or f. 33v would have been used to continue *TLA*-

"D." "To Jane: 'The keen stars . . .' " was written, I should guess, during the time that Shelley found himself struggling to continue with "The Triumph," for had more space been available on the conjugate of which f. 33v is a part (i.e., if ff. 32–33r had not already been filled with *TL*, 252–280), he would not have needed to write *TJKS*, 19–24, on a fresh page.

As I have said, *TJKS* is written on three widely separated folios: lines 1–10 are written "sideways" on f. 56r (the conjugate ff. 55–56 also contains *TLDO*-"A" and "B"); lines 11–18 on f. 33v; and lines 19–24 on f. 38v. Because Shelley had long since rejected *TLDO*-"B" (and hence, ff. 55–56), we must assume that he had the entire sheaf of loose papers before him as he wrote, including both blank sheets and rejected passages. This would seem almost to preclude his having written the bulk of "The Triumph" while sailing, as Mary ("Note on Poems of 1822") and Lady Jane Shelley (*Shelley Memorials*) suggested. (There is no evidence that Shelley discussed the poem with the others at Casa Magni, and if he had written while sailing, he probably would have mentioned "The Triumph," just as he discussed with Trelawny the draft of "With a Guitar, To Jane.") Because all conjugates of BENEDETTO PARODI paper were first begun on the same page, I think that he must have written at a table or desk, where the unused papers could be stacked and where he could spread out at least two pages at once, as he must have in order to continue from one page to the next of *TL* or *TJKS*. Although Shelley is known to have composed in a pocket notebook while wandering or sailing, the size (and presently good condition) of *MS* makes it highly unlikely that he carried this loose sheaf of large sheets around with him. Where could Shelley have found a quiet retreat away from the overcrowded bustle of Casa Magni? Apparently near the end of May he set up a study in one of the outbuildings in which the servants lived, for he wrote to Claire Clairmont on the thirtieth: "My health is much better this summer than it has been for many years; but the occupation of a few mornings in composition has somewhat shaken my nerves.—I have turned Maria's room into a study, and am in this respect very comfortable" (Julian, X, 397). Inasmuch as Claire had left Casa Magni just nine days before (21 May), Shelley must have "turned Maria's room into a study" sometime between then and 30 May.

Shelley has written dates on three folios of *MS;* on two folios these dates accompany financial calculations and seem to relate to future budgeting—perhaps dates when his quarterly income would arrive

or when large obligations would fall due. On f. 37r Shelley wrote
three different dates: "June 4" (twice), "July 4," and "July 15"; on
f. 48r he wrote "1st July" (twice); on f. 58r he wrote "15 June" three
times and "12th June" once. (This last folio has no calculations
accompanying the dates.) The dates are cryptic and the accompanying calculations shed no light (for me, at least). Edward Williams'
journal hints at no significant event on 4, 15, or 30 June. In writing
"1st July," the date that Shelley and Williams sailed to Leghorn,
Shelley could have been anticipating this journey, for ff. 47–48 form
that conjugate on which Shelley began a letter to Roberts, asking
him to accompany Shelley and Williams on a sail to Genoa in
response to Hunt's appeal. After canceling plans for this hurried
trip, Shelley may have calculated 1 July as the proper time to sail
to Leghorn and meet Hunt there. Finally, 15 July was a week after
Shelley's death and thus must represent Shelley's anticipation of
some event; it does not, at any rate, help us to date "The Triumph."

Only two dates in the sequence of the composition of *TL* can be
definitely established from *MS;* 15 May [1822] is the postmark date of
the letter-cover on the back of which Shelley wrote *TL,* 438–450; 24
June 1822 is the date upon which Shelley wrote the unfinished beginnings of a letter to Roberts that appear on ff. 47r and 48v, and which
preceded the composition of *TL,* 451–478. Because Shelley seems
to have employed these odds and ends of partly used paper only
after his supply of BENEDETTO PARODI paper was exhausted,
we cannot assume that there was any great time lapse between the
writing of *TL,* 438–450 and 451–478. The letter-cover that was post-
marked at Sarzana on 15 May was probably that of the letter from
Lega (with another from Collini enclosed) concerning the Masi
incident. Shelley received this letter (he tells Byron) on the morning
of 16 May. Shelley's letter to Byron, asking advice on whether to
proceed with the prosecution of Masi, contains this clause: "as to
Lega's compositions, and that enclosed as they seem written under
the supposition of my having a secretary at my elbow as learned in
the law as himself, they are and probably will continue to be totally
unintelligible to me" (Julian, X, 391; corrected from Jones, II, 420).
Because the letters from Lega and Collini contained detailed discussion of the legal aspects of the Masi case, the value of which Shelley
felt himself incompetent to judge, I think it reasonable to suppose
that he retained the letters. Thus the arrival of the 15 May letter
may have preceded and, I believe, probably did precede the composition of the early lines of *TL.*

In his letter to Claire of 30 May, Shelley says that "the occupation of a few mornings in composition has somewhat shaken my nerves." Though I am not sure that this was always the case, I suspect that a failure to record his conceptions was more likely to disturb Shelley than a successful session of composition, which, as he records elsewhere, tended to calm him. Thus, if the composing he alludes to did involve "The Triumph of Life," I suspect that he was either just beginning it (and hence four times rewriting the opening lines of the poem) or else was reaching one of the places where he found it difficult to continue his composition. Although internal evidence demonstrates that 24 June is the earliest possible date for writing of *TL*, 451ff., Shelley's composition can hardly have continued uninterrupted from late May through the end of June. Both the evidence of *MS* and our knowledge of Shelley's method of composing indicate that he probably wrote rapidly—several pages, rather than a few lines, on each day of successful composition. Though there is no incontrovertible evidence, it seems probable either that Shelley began "The Triumph of Life" late in May 1822 and returned to it late in June, after having put it aside while he sailed, traveled to Massa (6 June), cared for Mary (her first serious attack occurred 9 June and her miscarriage, 16 June), and entertained Trelawny and Roberts during the visit of the "Bolivar" (13–18 June), or else that Shelley wrote the entire fragment after 18 June, the composing he refers to in his 30 May letter to Claire involving some other work. It is perhaps significant that Shelley's letter to Horace Smith of 29 June 1822 (the last surviving letter that Shelley wrote from Casa Magni) is written on BENEDETTO PARODI paper. In any event, Shelley was still working on "The Triumph of Life" when Hunt's arrival at Leghorn took him away from the MS on 1 July 1822.

CHECKLIST

This checklist enumerates books, articles, and reviews cited in the monograph, as well as others that contain extended or historically significant mention of "The Triumph of Life." In addition, it includes works that have been important to me when assembling an initial checklist of Shelley studies and while forming my ideas on Shelley's life, thought, and art, and it lists the editions (and translations) that are the sources of my quotations from writers who influenced Shelley's later poetry. A few recent titles appear here that, though published too late to leave a substantive mark on this monograph, treat some of the same problems here discussed.

Abinger MSS. Microfilms of the Shelley-Godwin collection of James Richard Scarlett, 8th Baron Abinger. Duke University Library. Durham, North Carolina, 1952.

Allott, Kenneth. "Bloom on 'The Triumph of Life,' " *EC*, X (April 1960), 222–228.

American Quarterly Review. "The Shelley Papers," XIX (June 1836), 257–287.

[Anster, Henry]. "Life and Writings of Percy Bysshe Shelley," *North British Review*, VIII (November 1847), 218–257.

Arnold, Matthew. *Essays in Criticism: Second Series.* London: Macmillan, 1888.

[Ascham, John, ed.]. *The Beauties of Percy Bysshe Shelley.* London: John Ascham, 1836.

———. *The Works of Percy Bysshe Shelley with His Life.* 2 vols. London: John Ascham, 1834.

The Athenaeum. Review of *The Poetical Works of Percy Bysshe Shelley,* ed. Mrs. Shelley, 27 April 1839, p. 313.

Aveling, Edward B., and Eleanor Marx Aveling. "Shelley and Socialism," *The Shelley Society's Papers,* 1st ser., I, pt. 2 (1891), 180–203.

Axson, Stockton. "Shelley's 'The Triumph of Life,' " *The Citizen*, I (November 1895), 209–212.

Babbitt, Irving. *Rousseau and Romanticism.* Boston: Houghton Mifflin, 1919.

Baker, Carlos H. "The Bottom of the Night," *The Major English Romantic Poets: A Symposium in Reappraisal,* pp. 185–199. See Clarence D. Thorpe.

————. *Shelley's Major Poetry: The Fabric of a Vision*. Princeton: Princeton University Press, 1948.

————, ed. *The Selected Poetry and Prose of Percy Bysshe Shelley*. New York: Random House, 1951 (Modern Library Edition).

Bald, Marjory A. "The Psychology of Shelley," *Contemporary Review*, CXXXI (March 1927), 359–366.

————. "Shelley's Mental Progress," *Essays and Studies by Members of the English Association*, XIII (Oxford: Clarendon Press, 1928), 112–137.

Barnard, Ellsworth. *Shelley's Religion*. Minneapolis: University of Minnesota Press, 1937.

————, ed. *Shelley: Selected Poems, Essays, and Letters*. New York: Odyssey Press, 1944.

Barrell, Joseph. *Shelley and the Thought of His Time: A Study in the History of Ideas*. New Haven: Yale University Press, 1947.

[Barrett, Joseph Hartwell]. "Characteristics of Shelley," *American Review: A Whig Journal*, V (May 1847), 534–537.

Beers, Henry A. *A History of English Romanticism in the Nineteenth Century*. New York: Henry Holt, 1901.

[Benbow, William, ed.]. *Miscellaneous and Posthumous Poems of Percy Bysshe Shelley*. London: William Benbow, 1826.

Bernbaum, Ernest, ed. *Anthology of Romanticism*. 3rd ed. New York: Ronald Press, 1948.

————. *Guide Through the Romantic Movement*. 2nd ed. New York: Ronald Press, 1949.

Biagi, Guido. *The Last Days of Percy Bysshe Shelley: New Details from Unpublished Documents*. London: Unwin, 1898.

Blackstone, Bernard. *The Lost Travellers: A Romantic Theme with Variations*. London: Longmans, 1962.

Blessington, The Countess of. "Journal of Conversations with Lord Byron," *New Monthly Magazine*, XXXV, pt. 2 (1832), 5–23 129–146, 228–241, 305–319, 521–544.

[Blind, Mathilde]. "Shelley," *Westminster Review*, N.S., XXXVIII (July 1870), 75–97.

Bloom, Harold. *Shelley's Mythmaking*. New Haven: Yale University Press, 1959.

————. *The Visionary Company: A Reading of English Romantic Poetry*. Garden City, N.Y.: Doubleday, 1961.

Blunden, Edmund. *Shelley: A Life Story*. London: Collins, 1946.

Bostetter, Edward E. *The Romantic Ventriloquists: Wordsworth, Coleridge, Keats, Shelley, Byron*. Seattle: University of Washington Press, 1963.

Boston Quarterly Review. "Poetical Works of Percy Bysshe Shelley," IV (October 1841), 393–436.

Bower, George Spencer. "The Philosophical Element in Shelley," *Journal of Speculative Philosophy*, XIV (October 1880), 421–454.

Bradley, A. C. *A Miscellany*. London: Macmillan, 1929.

————. "Notes on Passages in Shelley," *MLR*, I (October 1905), 25–42.

————. "Notes on Shelley's 'Triumph of Life,'" *MLR*, IX (October 1914), 441–456.

————. *Oxford Lectures on Poetry*. London: Macmillan, 1909.

Brand, C[harles] P. *Italy and the English Romantics: The Italianate Fashion in Early Nineteenth-Century England.* Cambridge: Cambridge University Press, 1957.

Brooke, Stopford A. *Naturalism in English Poetry.* New York: Dutton, 1920.

———. "Some Thoughts on Shelley," *Macmillan's Magazine,* XLII (June 1880), 124–135.

———. *Studies in Poetry.* London: Duckworth, 1907.

———, ed. *Poems from Shelley.* London: Macmillan, 1880.

Bruca', Renzo. "L'ultima dimora di Shelley: Villa Magni," *Emporium,* XXVIII (August 1908), 113–122.

Butter, Peter. *Shelley's Idols of the Cave.* Edinburgh: University Press, 1954.

———. "Sun and Shape in Shelley's *The Triumph of Life,*" *RES,* N.S., XIII (1962), 40–51.

Byron, Lord. *The Works of Lord Byron: A New, Revised and Enlarged Edition,* eds. Ernest Hartley Coleridge and Rowland E. Prothero. 13 vols. London: John Murray, 1898–1904.

Cambridge University Magazine. "The Poets of England Who Have Died Young: Percy Bysshe Shelley," I (May 1839), 81–101.

———. Review of *The Poetical Works of Percy Bysshe Shelley,* ed. Mrs. Shelley, I (March 1839), 78–79.

Cameron, Kenneth Neill. *The Young Shelley: Genesis of a Radical.* New York: Macmillan, 1950.

———. Review of Bice Chiappelli, *Il Pensiero religioso di Shelley, MP,* LV (August 1957), 62–63.

———, ed. *Percy Bysshe Shelley: Selected Poetry and Prose.* New York: Rinehart, 1951.

———, ed. *Shelley and His Circle: 1773–1822.* Vols. I and II. Cambridge, Mass.: Harvard University Press, 1961.

Campbell, Olwen Ward. *Shelley and the Unromantics.* London: Methuen, 1924.

Cherubini, William. "Shelley's 'Own Symposium': *The Triumph of Life,*" *SP,* XXXIX (July 1942), 559–570.

Chiappelli, Bice. *Il Pensiero religioso di Shelley: con particolare riferimento alla "Necessity of Atheism" e al "Triumph of Life."* Rome: Edizioni di Storia e Letteratura, 1956.

Clark, David Lee. *Shelley's Prose; or, the Trumpet of a Prophecy.* Albuquerque: University of New Mexico Press, 1954.

Clutton-Brock, A[rthur]. *Shelley: The Man and the Poet.* London: Methuen, 1910.

Coleridge, Samuel Taylor. *The Complete Poetical Works of Samuel Taylor Coleridge,* ed. E. H. Coleridge. 2 vols. Oxford: Clarendon Press, 1912.

———. *The Complete Works of Samuel Taylor Coleridge,* ed. W. G. T. Shedd. 7 vols. New York: Harper, 1884.

Colvin, Sidney. *John Keats.* 2nd ed. London: Macmillan, 1918.

Courthope, William John. *A History of English Poetry.* 6 vols. London: Macmillan, 1895–1910.

Cowling, George Herbert. *Shelley and Other Essays.* Melbourne: Melbourne University Press, 1936.

Dante Alighieri. *La Divina Commedia,* ed. C. H. Grandgent. Rev. ed. Boston: D. C. Heath, 1933.

———. *The Inferno of Dante Alighieri,* trans. by J. A. Carlyle; ed. H. Oelsner. London: Dent, 1900 (Temple Classics Edition).

———. *The Purgatorio of Dante Alighieri,* trans. by Thomas Okey; ed. H. Oelsner. London: Dent, 1901 (Temple Classics Edition).

———. *The Paradiso cf Dante Alighieri,* trans. by P. H. Wicksteed; ed. H. Oelsner. London: Dent, 1899 (Temple Classics Edition).

Davie, Donald A. *Purity of Diction in English Verse.* London: Chatto & Windus, 1952.

De Gruyter, J. "Shelley and Dostoievsky," *English Studies,* IV (1922), 129–151.

Dixon, James Henry. "Emendations of Shelley," *N & Q,* 4th ser., I (25 January 1868), 79–81.

Dowden, Edward. *The Life of Percy Bysshe Shelley.* 2 vols. London: Kegan Paul, Trench & Co., 1886.

———. *Transcripts and Studies.* London: Kegan Paul, Trench, Trübner & Co., 1888.

———, ed. *The Poetical Works of Percy Bysshe Shelley.* London: Macmillan, 1890.

———. See Robert S. Garnett.

Drummond, William. *Academical Questions.* London: W. Bulmer, 1805.

Edinburgh Review. Review of *The Poetical Works of Percy Bysshe Shelley,* ed. Mrs. Shelley, LXIX (July 1839), 503–527.

———. Review of *The Poetical Works of Percy Bysshe Shelley,* ed. Mrs. Shelley, XC (October 1849), 419–425.

———. Review of *The Prose Works of Percy Bysshe Shelley,* ed. H[arry] Buxton Forman, CLXIV (July 1886), 42–72.

———. Review of *Shelley and Mary,* CLVI (October 1882), 472–507.

Eiloart, A. "Shelley's 'Skylark': The 'Silver Sphere,' " *N & Q,* CLXI (4 July 1931), 4–8.

Eliot, T[homas] S[tearns]. "The Metaphysical Poets," *Selected Essays.* 2nd ed. London: Faber and Faber, 1934.

———. "Talk on Dante," *The Adelphi,* XXVII (1st quarter, 1951), 106–114.

———. *The Use of Poetry and the Use of Criticism.* London: Faber and Faber, 1933.

Elliott, G. R. *The Cycle of Modern Poetry.* Princeton: Princeton University Press, 1929.

Ellis, F. S. *A Lexical Concordance to the Poetical Works of Percy Bysshe Shelley.* London: Quaritch, 1892.

Elton, Oliver. *A Survey of English Literature: 1780–1830.* 2 vols. London: Edward Arnold, 1912.

Erdman, David V. See Ralph Houston.

Ervine, St. John. "Shelley as a Dramatist," *Essays by Divers Hands. Transactions of the Royal Society of Literature of the United Kingdom.* N.S., XV, ed. Hugh Walpole. London: Oxford University Press, 1936.

The Examiner. "Byron-Shelley," 3 October 1824, p. 635.

————. Review of *Posthumous Poems of Percy Bysshe Shelley*, 14 June 1824, p. 370.

Fairchild, Hoxie Neale. *Religious Trends in English Poetry: Romantic Faith*, III, *1780–1830*. New York: Columbia University Press, 1949.

————. *The Romantic Quest*. Philadelphia: Albert Saifer, 1931.

Firkins, O. W. *Power and Elusiveness in Shelley*. Minneapolis: University of Minnesota Press, 1937.

Foakes, R. A. *The Romantic Assertion: A Study in the Language of Nineteenth Century Poetry*. New Haven: Yale University Press, 1958.

Fogle, Richard Harter. *The Imagery of Keats and Shelley: A Comparative Study*. Chapel Hill: University of North Carolina Press, 1949.

Forman, Harry Buxton, ed. *The Poetical Works of Percy Bysshe Shelley*. 4 vols. London: Reeves and Turner, 1876.

————, ed. See Thomas Medwin.

Freeman, Martin J. See Carl H. Grabo.

Friederich, Werner Paul. *Dante's Fame Abroad: 1350–1850*. Rome: Edizioni di Storia e Letteratura, 1950.

[Galignani, A. and W., eds.]. *The Poetical Works of Coleridge, Shelley, and Keats*. Paris: A. and W. Galignani, 1829.

Gardner, Edmund G. "The Mysticism of Shelley," *Catholic World*, LXXXVIII (November 1908), 145–155.

Garnett, Richard. "Percy Bysshe Shelley," *Dictionary of National Biography*. 63 vols. London: Smith, Elder, 1897.

————, ed. *Relics of Shelley*. London: Edward Moxon, 1862.

[————, ed.] " 'Lines Written in the Bay of Lerici' by Percy Bysshe Shelley," *Macmillan's Magazine*, VI (June 1862), 122–123.

———— and Edmund Gosse. *English Literature: An Illustrated Record*. 4 vols. London: William Heinemann, 1903.

Garnett, R[obert] S., ed. *Letters About Shelley Interchanged by Three Friends—Edward Dowden, Richard Garnett and William Michael Rossetti*. London: Hodder and Stoughton, 1917.

Gates, Eunice Joiner. "Shelley and Calderón," *PQ*, XVI (January 1937), 49–58.

Gérard, Albert. *L'idée romantique de la poésie en Angleterre*. Paris: Société d'Edition "Les Belles Lettres," 1955.

Gilfillan, George. *A Gallery of Literary Portraits*. Edinburgh: William Tait, 1845.

Gingerich, Solomon F. *Essays in the Romantic Poets*. New York: Macmillan, 1924.

————. "Shelley's Doctrine of Necessity *versus* Christianity," *PMLA*, XXXIII (September 1918), 444–473.

Giovannini, G. Review of Bice Chiappelli, *Il Pensiero religioso di Shelley*, *MLQ*, XVIII (June 1957), 158–160.

Gisborne, Maria, and Edward E. Williams. *Maria Gisborne & Edward E. Williams, Shelley's Friends: Their Journals and Letters*, ed. Frederick L. Jones. Norman: University of Oklahoma Press, 1951.

Godwin, William. *Caleb Williams*, ed. George Sherburn. New York: Rinehart, 1960.

——. *Enquiry Concerning Political Justice and Its Influence on Morals and Happiness. Photographic Facsimile of the 3rd Edition Corrected*, ed. F. E. L. Priestley. 3 vols. Toronto: University of Toronto Press, 1946.

Goethe, Johann Wolfgang von. *Faust*, ed. Georg Witkowski. Leipzig: Hesse & Becker, 1929.

——. *Faust*, trans. by Bayard Taylor. 2 vols. Boston: Houghton Mifflin, 1879.

Gosse, Edmund. *Aspects and Impressions*. London: Cassell, 1922.

——. See Richard Garnett.

Grabo, Carl H. *The Magic Plant: The Growth of Shelley's Thought*. Chapel Hill: University of North Carolina Press, 1936.

—— and Martin J. Freeman, eds. *The Reader's Shelley: Selections with Introduction, Bibliography, and Notes*. New York: American Book Company, 1942.

Grierson, Herbert J. C., and J. C. Smith. *A Critical History of English Poetry*. 2nd ed. (rev.) London: Chatto & Windus, 1947.

Groom, Bernard. *The Diction of Poetry from Spenser to Bridges*. Toronto: University of Toronto Press, 1955.

Gulliver, Julia Henrietta. "Shelley—The Poet," *New Englander and Yale Review*, N.S., XVI (February 1890), 138–146.

Hancock, Albert E. *The French Revolution and the English Poets: A Study in Historical Criticism*. New York: Henry Holt, 1899.

Havens, Raymond D. "*Hellas* and *Charles the First*," *SP*, XLIII (July 1946), 545–550.

——. "Shelley the Artist," *The Major English Romantic Poets: A Symposium in Reappraisal*, pp. 169–184. See Clarence D. Thorpe.

[Hazlitt, William]. "*Posthumous Poems* of Percy Bysshe Shelley," *Edinburgh Review*, XL (July 1824), 494–514.

Herford, C. H. *The Age of Wordsworth*. 8th ed. London: G. Bell, 1911.

——. "Shelley," *Cambridge History of English Literature*. 15 vols. Cambridge: Cambridge University Press, 1915.

——, ed. *The Narrative Poems of Percy Bysshe Shelley*. 2 vols. London: Chatto & Windus, 1927.

Hewlett, Maurice H. "Shelley's Swan-Song," *Extemporary Essays*. London: Oxford University Press, 1922.

Hogg, Thomas Jefferson. *The Life of Percy Bysshe Shelley*. 2 vols. London: Moxon, 1858.

Hopkins, Gerard Manley. *Poems of Gerard Manley Hopkins*, ed. W. H. Gardner. 3rd ed. London: Oxford University Press, 1948.

Hough, Graham. *The Romantic Poets*. London: Hutchinson House, 1953.

Houston, Ralph. "Shelley and the Principle of Association," *EC*, III (January 1953), 45–59.

——, W. Milgate, David V. Erdman, and Valerie Pitt. "Reading Shelley," *EC*, IV (January 1954), 87–103.

Hughes, A. M. D. *The Nascent Mind of Shelley*. Oxford: Clarendon Press, 1947.

——. "Shelley and Nature," *North American Review*, CCVIII (August 1918), 287–295.

————. "The Theology of Shelley," *Proceedings of the British Academy, 1938,* XXIV (London: Oxford University Press, 1938), 191–203.

————, ed. *Shelley: Poetry and Prose, with Essays by Browning, Bagehot, Swinburne, and Reminiscences by Others.* Oxford: Clarendon Press, 1931.

Hunt, Leigh. *Lord Byron and Some of His Contemporaries with Recollections of the Author's Life and of His Visit to Italy.* London: Henry Colburn, 1828.

Hutchinson, Thomas, ed. *The Complete Poetical Works of Percy Bysshe Shelley.* London: Oxford University Press, 1905, 1934.

————, ed. *The Complete Poetical Works of Shelley.* Oxford: Clarendon Press, 1904.

Hutton, Richard H. *Essays: Theological and Literary.* 2 vols. London: Strahan, 1871.

Ingpen, Roger. *Shelley in England.* 2 vols. London: Kegan Paul, Trench, Trübner & Co., 1917.

———— and Walter E. Peck, eds. *The Complete Works of Percy Bysshe Shelley.* 10 vols. London: Ernest Benn, 1926–30 (Julian Edition).

James, D[avid] G. *Byron and Shelley.* Nottingham: Byron Foundation Lecture, University College, 1951.

Jeffrey, Lloyd N. "Shelley's Life-Images," *N & Q,* CCII (November 1957), 480–481.

————. "Shelley's 'Triumph of Life' and the 'Dhammapada,'" *N & Q,* CCI (March 1956), 116–117.

Jones, Frederick L. "Shelley and Milton," *SP,* XLIX (July 1952), 488–519.

————. "Shelley's *On Life,*" *PMLA,* LXII (September 1947), 774–783.

————. "The Vision Theme in Shelley's *Alastor* and Related Works," *SP,* XLIV (January 1947), 108–125.

————, ed. See Maria Gisborne, Mary Wollstonecraft Shelley, and Percy Bysshe Shelley.

Keats, John. *The Letters of John Keats: 1814–1821,* ed. Hyder Rollins. 2 vols. Cambridge: Harvard University Press, 1958.

————. *The Poetical Works of John Keats,* ed. H. W. Garrod. 2nd ed. Oxford: Clarendon Press, 1958.

Kermode, Frank. *Romantic Image.* London: Routledge & Kegan Paul, 1957.

King, R. W. Review of C. P. Brand, *Italy and the English Romantics, RES,* N.S., X (May 1959), 205–207.

————. Review of Bice Chiappelli, *Il Pensiero religioso di Shelley, MLR,* LII (April 1957), 261–263.

King-Hele, Desmond. *Shelley: His Thought and Work.* London: Macmillan, 1960.

Knight, G. Wilson. *The Starlit Dome: Studies in the Poetry of Vision.* London: Oxford University Press, 1941.

Knight's Quarterly Magazine. Review of Shelley's *Posthumous Poems,* III (August 1824), 182–192.

Kuhns, Oscar. *Dante and the English Poets from Chaucer to Tennyson.* New York: Henry Holt, 1904.

Kurtz, Benjamin P. *The Pursuit of Death: A Study of Shelley's Poetry.* New York: Oxford University Press, 1933.

Laird, John. *Philosophical Incursions into English Literature.* Cambridge: Cambridge University Press, 1946.

Lea, F. A. *Shelley and the Romantic Revolution.* London: Routledge, 1945.

Leavis, F. R. *Revaluation: Tradition and Development in English Poetry.* London: Chatto & Windus, 1936.

Lehmann, John, ed. *Shelley in Italy: An Anthology.* London: John Lehmann, 1947.

Lemaitre, Hélène. *Shelley: poète des éléments.* Paris: Didier, 1962.

Lewis, C. S. *Rehabilitations and Other Essays.* London: Oxford University Press, 1939.

The Liberal: Verse and Prose from the South, vols. I and II (1822, 1823). London: Printed by and for John Hunt.

Lind, L. Robert. "Shelley Reappraised," *Sewanee Review,* XLIII (October-December 1935), 413–435.

Literary Journal and Weekly Register of Science and Arts [Providence, R.I.]. "Character and Writings of Shelley," I (11 January 1834), 252–253.

Lockard, Thaddeus C., Jr. Review of Bice Chiappelli, *Il Pensiero religioso di Shelley, K-SJ,* VI (Winter 1957), 122–125.

Locock, C. D. *An Examination of the Shelley Manuscripts in the Bodleian Library.* Oxford: Clarendon Press, 1903.

———, ed. *The Poems of Percy Bysshe Shelley, with an Introduction by A. Clutton-Brock.* 2 vols. London: Methuen, 1911.

London Quarterly Review. Review of *The Poetical Works of Percy Bysshe Shelley,* ed. William Michael Rossetti, XXXVIII (1872), 124–149.

Lucretius. *De Rerum Natura,* with an English translation by W. H. D. Rouse. London: William Heinemann, 1947 (Loeb Classical Library Edition).

Madariaga, Salvador de. *Shelley and Calderon and Other Essays on English and Spanish Poetry.* London: Constable, 1920.

Male, Roy R., Jr. "Shelley and the Doctrine of Sympathy," *University of Texas Studies in English,* XXIX (1950), 183–203.

——— and James A. Notopoulos. "Shelley's Copy of Diogenes Laertius," *MLR,* LIV (January 1959), 10–21.

Marchand, Leslie A. *The Athenaeum: A Mirror of Victorian Culture.* Chapel Hill: University of North Carolina Press, 1941.

———. *Byron: A Biography.* 3 vols. New York: Knopf, 1957.

Marsh, George L. "The Early Reviews of Shelley," *MP,* XXVII (August 1929), 73–95.

Mason, Francis Claiborne. *A Study in Shelley Criticism . . . in England from 1818–1860.* Mercersburg, Pennsylvania: Privately printed, 1937.

Massey, Irving. "Shelley's 'Music when Soft Voices Die': Text and Meaning," *JEGP,* LIX (1960), 430–438.

Matthews, G. M. "On Shelley's 'The Triumph of Life,'" *Studia Neophilologica,* XXXIV (1962), 104–134.

———. "Shelley and Jane Williams," *RES,* N.S., XII (February 1961), 40–48.

————. "The 'Triumph of Life' Apocrypha," *TLS*, 5 August 1960, p. 503.

————. " 'The Triumph of Life': A New Text," *Studia Neophilologica*, XXXII (1960), 271–309.

Mayor, J[oseph] B. "Shelley's Metre," *The Shelley Society's Papers*, 1st ser., I, pt. 2 (1891), 220–261.

Medwin, Thomas. *The Life of Percy Bysshe Shelley: A New Edition . . .*, ed. Harry Buxton Forman. London: Oxford University Press, 1913.

Meldrum, Elizabeth. "The Classical Background of Shelley," *Contemporary Review*, CLXXIII (1948), 160–165.

Meyer, Hans. *Rousseau und Shelley: Ein Typologischer Vergleich.* Würzburg: K. Triltsch, 1934.

Milgate, W. See Ralph Houston.

Milton, John. *The Student's Milton*, ed. Frank Allen Patterson. Rev. ed. New York: Appleton-Century-Crofts, 1933.

Monroe, Harriet. *Poets and Their Art.* New York: Macmillan, 1926.

Mousel, Sister M. Eunice. "Falsetto in Shelley," *SP*, XXXIII (October 1936), 587–609.

Nathan, Norman. "Shelley's 'Eagle Home,' " *N & Q*, CXCIX (January 1954), 30.

New Monthly Magazine and Literary Journal. "Byron and Shelley on the Character of Hamlet," XXIX, pt. 2 (1830), 327–336.

————. Review of *Posthumous Poems of Percy Bysshe Shelley*, XII (July 1824), 316–317.

————. Review of Thomas Medwin, *The Life of Percy Bysshe Shelley*, LXXXI (November 1847), 295–296.

Norman, Sylva. *Flight of the Skylark: The Development of Shelley's Reputation.* Norman: University of Oklahoma Press, 1954.

Notes and Queries. "Emendations of Shelley," 4th ser., I (15 February 1868), 151–152.

Notopoulos, James A. "The Dating of Shelley's Prose," *PMLA*, LVIII (June 1943), 477–498.

————. *The Platonism of Shelley: A Study of Platonism and the Poetic Mind.* Durham: Duke University Press, 1949.

————. See Roy R. Male, Jr.

O'Malley, Glenn. "Shelley's 'Air-Prism': The Synesthetic Scheme of *Alastor*," *MP*, LV (February 1958), 178–187.

Oras, Ants. *On Some Aspects of Shelley's Poetic Imagery (Acta et Commentationes Universitatis Tartuensis*, B, XLIII, no. 4). Tartu, Estonia, 1939.

O'Sullivan-Kohling, Ilsa. *Shelley und die Bildende Kunst.* Halle, Salle: Max Niemeyer, 1928.

Peacock, Thomas Love. See Humbert Wolfe.

Peck, Walter E. *Shelley: His Life and Work.* 2 vols. Boston: Houghton Mifflin, 1927.

————, ed. See Roger Ingpen.

Perkins, David. *The Quest for Permanence: The Symbolism of Wordsworth, Shelley, and Keats.* Cambridge: Harvard University Press, 1959.

Petrarca, Francesco. *Rime di Francesco Petrarca*, ed. Giacomo Leopardi. Firenze: Successori Le Monnier, 1896.

————. *The Triumphs of Petrarch,* trans. by Ernest Hatch Wilkins. Chicago: University of Chicago Press, 1962.

Pitt, Valerie. See Ralph Houston.

Pliny. *Natural History, with an English Translation.* 10 vols. London: William Heinemann, 1938 (Loeb Classical Library Edition).

Pottle, Frederick A. "The Case of Shelley," *PMLA,* LXVII (September 1952), 589–608.

Power, Julia A. *Shelley in America in the Nineteenth Century (University of Nebraska Studies,* XL, no. 2). Lincoln: University of Nebraska Press, 1940.

Pratt, Willis Winslow. "Shelley Criticism in England: 1810–1890." Unpublished Ph.D. thesis, Cornell University, 1935.

Prescott, Frederick Clarke. *The Poetic Mind.* New York: Macmillan, 1922.

Prideaux, W. F. "Shelley: A Poliad," *N & Q,* 6th ser., VIII (15 September 1883), 205.

Pulos, C. E. *The Deep Truth: A Study of Shelley's Scepticism.* Lincoln: University of Nebraska Press, 1954; reprinted, Bison Books, 1962.

————. "Shelley and Malthus," *PMLA,* LXVII (1952), 113–124.

Purser, J. W. R. Review of Bice Chiappelli, *Il Pensiero religioso di Shelley, RES,* N.S., IX (February 1958), 121.

Quiller-Couch, Arthur T. *Studies in Literature, Second Series.* Cambridge: Cambridge University Press, 1922.

Rabbe, Felix. *Shelley: The Man and the Poet: From the French . . . .* 2 vols. London: Ward and Downey, 1888.

Raben, Joseph A. "Milton's Influence on Shelley's Translation of Dante's 'Matilda Gathering Flowers,'" *RES,* N.S., XIV (May 1963), 142–156.

Raleigh, Walter, ed. *Poems by Percy Bysshe Shelley.* London: George Bell, 1902 (Endymion Series Edition).

Raysor, Thomas M., ed. *The English Romantic Poets; a Review of Research.* Rev. ed. New York: Modern Language Association, 1956.

Read, Herbert. *In Defense of Shelley and Other Essays.* London: William Heinemann, 1936.

Reiman, Donald H. "Shelley's 'The Triumph of Life': The Biographical Problem," *PMLA,* LXXVIII (December 1963), 536–550.

————. "Structure, Symbol, and Theme in 'Lines Written Among the Euganean Hills,'" *PMLA,* LXXVII (September 1962), 404–413.

Reul, Paul de. "The Centenary of Shelley," *Essays by Divers Hands. Being the Transactions of the Royal Society of Literature,* ed. F. S. Boas. London: Oxford University Press, 1923.

Richards, I. A. *Principles of Literary Criticism.* 14th impression. London: Routledge & Kegan Paul, 1955.

Richter, Helene. *Percy Bysshe Shelley.* Weimar: Emil Felber, 1898.

Rideout, John Granville. "Rhetoric, Symbolism, and Imagery in the Poetry of Percy Bysshe Shelley." Unpublished Ph.D. thesis, Brown University, 1945.

Roe, Ivan. *Shelley: The Last Phase.* London: Hutchinson, 1953.

Rogers, Neville. *Shelley at Work: A Critical Inquiry.* Oxford: Clarendon Press, 1956.

————, ed. *Keats, Shelley & Rome: An Illustrated Miscellany.* London: Johnson, 1949.

Rollins, Hyder. *Keats' Reputation in America to 1848.* Cambridge: Harvard University Press, 1946.

———, ed. See John Keats.

Rossetti, William Michael. "Notes and Emendations on Shelley," *N & Q,* 4th ser., I (18 April and 25 April 1868), 357–360, 384–387.

———. "Shelley's Life and Writings," *Dublin University Magazine,* N.S., I (February and March 1878), 138–155, 262–277.

———, ed. *The Complete Poetical Works of Percy Bysshe Shelley.* 3 vols. London: Moxon, 1878.

———, ed. *The Complete Poetical Works of Percy Bysshe Shelley.* 3 vols. London: Gibbings, 1894.

———, ed. *The Poetical Works of Percy Bysshe Shelley.* 2 vols. London: Moxon, 1870.

———, ed. *The Poetical Works of Percy Bysshe Shelley.* London: Ward, Lock & Co., n.d. [1879] (Moxon's Popular Poets Edition).

———. See Robert S. Garnett.

Rousseau, Jean Jacques. *Eloisa: Or, a Series of Original Letters.* . . . Translated from the French. 3rd ed. 4 vols. London: T. Becket and P. A. De Hondt, 1764.

———. *Œuvres complètes de J. J. Rousseau.* 2nd ed. 25 vols. Paris: Baudouin Frères, 1826.

Royce, Josiah. *Fugitive Essays.* Cambridge: Harvard University Press, 1920.

Sackville-West, Edward. "Books in General," *New Statesman and Nation,* N.S., XXVII (1 April 1944), 227.

Saintsbury, George. *History of Nineteenth Century English Literature (1780–1895).* London: Macmillan, 1896.

Salt, Henry S. *Percy Bysshe Shelley: A Monograph.* London: Swan Sonnenschein, Lowrey, & Co., 1888.

———. *Percy Bysshe Shelley, Poet and Pioneer: A Biographical Study.* London: William Reeves, 1896.

———. *A Shelley Primer. The Shelley Society's Publications,* Ser. 4, No. 4. London: Reeves and Turner, 1887.

Santayana, George. *Winds of Doctrine.* London: Dent, 1913.

Scots Magazine. Review of *Posthumous Poems of Percy Bysshe Shelley,* XCIV (N.S., XV) (July 1824), 11–17.

Scott, Walter S., ed. *New Shelley Letters.* London: Bodley Head, 1948.

Scott, William O. "Shelley's Admiration for Bacon," *PMLA,* LXXIII (June 1958), 228–236.

Sen, Amiyakumar K. *Studies in Shelley.* Calcutta: University of Calcutta, 1936.

Sharp, William. *Life of Percy Bysshe Shelley.* London: Walter Scott, 1887.

Shaw, George Bernard. *Pen Portraits and Reviews.* London: Constable, 1932.

Shelley, Lady [Jane Gibson], ed. *Shelley Memorials: From Authentic Sources.* London: Smith Elder, 1859.

Shelley, Mary Wollstonecraft. *The Letters of Mary W. Shelley,* ed. Frederick L. Jones. 2 vols. Norman: University of Oklahoma Press, 1944.

———. *Mary Shelley's Journal,* ed. Frederick L. Jones. Norman: University of Oklahoma Press, 1947.

————. *Mathilda*, ed. Elizabeth Nitchie. Chapel Hill: University of North Carolina Press [1960].

————, ed. *Essays, Letters from Abroad, Translations and Fragments by Percy Bysshe Shelley*. 2 vols. London: Edward Moxon, 1840.

————, ed. *The Poetical Works of Percy Bysshe Shelley*. 4 vols. London: Edward Moxon, 1839.

————, ed. *The Poetical Works of Percy Bysshe Shelley*. London: Edward Moxon, 1839 [1840].

————, ed. *The Poetical Works of Percy Bysshe Shelley*. 3 vols. London: Edward Moxon, 1847.

————, ed. *Posthumous Poems of Percy Bysshe Shelley*. London: John and Henry L. Hunt, 1824.

Shelley, Percy Bysshe. Bodleian MSS, especially MS Shelley adds. c. 4. Bodleian Library, Oxford, England.

————. *The Letters of Percy Bysshe Shelley*, ed. Frederick L. Jones. 2 vols. Oxford: Clarendon Press, 1964.

————. Pierpont Morgan Library MS of "On Life." Pierpont Morgan Library, New York, New York.

————. Prose and poetical works. See various editors.

Shelley-Rolls, Sir John, and Roger Ingpen, eds. *Verse and Prose from the Manuscripts of Percy Bysshe Shelley*. London: privately printed, 1934.

Sismondi, J. C. L. Simonde de. *A History of the Italian Republics, Being a View of the Origin, Progress, and Fall of Italian Freedom*. London: Dent, n.d. (Everyman Edition).

Slaughter, Gertrude. "Percy Bysshe Shelley: 1822–1922," *North American Review*, CCXVI (July 1922), 67–82.

Smith, J. C. See Herbert Grierson.

Solve, Melvin. *Shelley: His Theory of Poetry*. Chicago: University of Chicago Press, 1927.

Spender, Stephen. *Shelley*. London: Longmans, 1952.

La Spezia a P. B. Shelley. Spezia: "La Sociale," 27 October 1907.

Stawell, F. Melian. "Shelley's 'Triumph of Life,'" *Essays and Studies by Members of the English Association*, V (Oxford: Clarendon Press, 1914), 104–131.

Stephen, Leslie. "Godwin and Shelley," *Cornhill Magazine*, XXXIX (March 1879), 281–302.

Stovall, Floyd. *Desire and Restraint in Shelley*. Durham: Duke University Press, 1931.

————. "Shelley's Doctrine of Love," *PMLA*, XLV (March 1930), 283–303.

Strong, Archibald T. *Three Studies in Shelley and an Essay on Nature in Wordsworth and Meredith*. London: Oxford University Press, 1921.

Suddard, S[ara] J[ulie] Mary. *Keats, Shelley and Shakespeare: Studies and Essays in English Literature*. Cambridge: Cambridge University Press, 1912.

Swinburne, A. C. "Percy Bysshe Shelley," *Chambers's Cyclopaedia of English Literature*. New ed. by David Patrick (Philadelphia: Lippincott, 1904), III, 107–118.

————. "Notes on the Text of Shelley," *Fortnightly Review*, N.S., V (1 May 1869), 539–561.

Symonds, John Addington. *Shelley*. London: Macmillan, 1878 (English Men of Letters Series).

Tait's Edinburgh Magazine. "Chapters on English Poetry: Shelley," N.S., VIII (November 1841), 681–685.

———. "Percy Bysshe Shelley," II (October and December 1832), 92–103, 331–342.

Taylor, Charles H., Jr. *The Early Collected Editions of Shelley's Poems: A Study in the History and Transmission of the Printed Text*. New Haven: Yale University Press, 1958.

Thayer, Mary Rebecca. *The Influence of Horace on the Chief English Poets of the Nineteenth Century*. New Haven: Yale University Press, 1916.

Thomson, James. *Shelley, a Poem: With Other Writings Related to Shelley*. Privately Printed: Chiswick Press, 1884.

Thorpe, Clarence D., Carlos Baker, Bennett Weaver, eds. *The Major English Romantic Poets: A Symposium in Reappraisal*. Carbondale: Southern Illinois University Press, 1957.

Todhunter, John. "Notes on 'The Triumph of Life,' " *The Shelley Society's Papers*, 1st ser., I, pt. 1 (1888), 73–80.

———. *A Study of Shelley*. London: C. Kegan Paul, 1880.

Toynbee, Paget. *Dante in English Literature: From Chaucer to Cary*. 2 vols. London: Methuen, 1909.

Trelawny, Edward John. *Recollections of the Last Days of Shelley and Byron*. London: Edward Moxon, 1858.

———. *Records of Shelley, Byron, and the Author*. 2 vols. London: Basil Montagu Pickering, 1878.

Turner, Paul. "Shelley and Lucretius," *RES*, N.S., X (August 1959), 269–282.

Ullman, James Ramsey. *Mad Shelley*. Princeton: Princeton University Press, 1930.

Vance, Thomas H. "Dante and Shelley." Unpublished Ph.D. thesis, Yale University, 1935.

Wain, John. "Terza rima: A Footnote on English Prosody," *Rivista di letterature moderne*, N.S., I (1950–51), 44–48.

Wasserman, Earl R. *"Adonais:* Progressive Revelation as a Poetic Mode," *ELH*, XXI (December 1954), 274–326.

———. *The Subtler Language: Critical Readings of Neoclassic and Romantic Poems*. Baltimore: Johns Hopkins University Press, 1959.

Weaver, Bennett. *Toward the Understanding of Shelley*. *University of Michigan Publications: Language and Literature*, IX. Ann Arbor: University of Michigan Press, 1932.

Westminster Review. "The Poets of Our Age, Considered as to Their Philosophic Tendencies," XXV (April 1836), 60–71.

White, Newman Ivey. *Shelley*. 2 vols. New York: Knopf, 1940.

———. "Shelley's Charles I.," *JEGP*, XXI (1922), 431–441.

———. *The Unextinguished Hearth: Shelley and His Contemporary Critics*. Durham: Duke University Press, 1938.

Williams, Edward E. See Maria Gisborne.

Wilson, Milton. *Shelley's Later Poetry: A Study of His Prophetic Imagination.* New York: Columbia University Press, 1959.

Winstanley, Lilian. "Platonism in Shelley," *Essays and Studies by Members of the English Association,* IV (Oxford: Clarendon Press, 1913), 72–100.

Wolfe, Humbert, ed. *The Life of Percy Bysshe Shelley, as Comprised in The Life of Shelley by Thomas Jefferson Hogg,* The Recollections of Shelley & Byron *by Edward John Trelawny,* Memoirs of Shelley *by Thomas Love Peacock.* 2 vols. London: Dent, 1933.

Woodberry, George E. *Studies of a Litterateur.* New York: Harcourt Brace, 1921.

————, ed. *The Complete Poetical Works of Percy Bysshe Shelley.* 4 vols. Boston: Houghton Mifflin, 1892 (Centenary Edition).

————, ed. *The Complete Poetical Works of Percy Bysshe Shelley.* Boston: Houghton Mifflin, 1901 (Cambridge Edition).

Woodman, Ross Greig. "The Apocalyptic Vision in the Poetry of Percy Bysshe Shelley." Unpublished Ph.D. thesis, University of Toronto, 1956.

Wordsworth, William. *The Poetical Works of William Wordsworth,* eds. E. de Selincourt and Helen Darbishire. 5 vols. Oxford: Clarendon Press, 1940–49.

Yeats, William Butler. *Essays: 1931–1936.* Dublin: Cuala Press, 1937.

————. *Ideas of Good and Evil.* New York: Macmillan, 1903.

Young, George. *An English Prosody on Inductive Lines.* Cambridge: Cambridge University Press, 1928.

Zacchetti, Corrado. *Shelley e Dante.* Milano: Remo Sandron, 1922.

Zillman, Lawrence John, ed. *Shelley's Prometheus Unbound: A Variorum Edition.* Seattle: University of Washington Press, 1959.

INDEX

"Accent," 89–90
Adam and Eve, 67
Æschylus, 12, 17
Alexander, 30n, 50, 53, 103–104, 108n; Godwin on, 53n
Alfieri, Vittorio, Count, 6
Aristotle, 6, 50, 53–54, 103, 108n, 171, 241
Arnold, Matthew, viii–ix, x
Arve, River, 32
Aster (youth beloved by Plato), 51, 52
Athens, 36, 43, 115, 153
Augustine, 6
Aurunzebe: in draft of *TL*, 243

Bacon, Francis, Lord, 11, 19, 53–54, 173, 241; his scepticism, 5n; S on, 49n, 52, 115
Baker, Carlos, xi, 8, 31n–32n, 60n
Barnard, Ellsworth, 26n
Beatrice. *See* Dante Aligheri
Berdyaev, Nikolai, 111, 113
Berkeley, George, Bishop, 4, 5n
Bible, 6, 10, 12, 49n, 115; Ecclesiastes, 72; Genesis, 73n; Psalms, 22
Blessington, Marguerite, Lady, 72
Blind, Mathilde, 118, 143, 151, 177, 187, 234, 235; contributions to text of *TL*, 122–123
Bloom, Harold, xi, 2, 8, 23n; on parallels to chariot in *TL*, 30; on Rousseau and Virgil, 40n; on Rousseau's vision, 39; on S's religious orthodoxy, 23
Blunden, Edmund, xi
Boccaccio, Giovanni, 49n, 115
Booth, Wayne C., 51
Boscombe Manor, viii

Bowles, William Lisle, Rev., 88
Bradley, A. C., x, 2, 23, 24n–25n, 27n, 37n, 44n, 49n, 51n, 60, 61n, 78n, 118, 171; contributions to text of *TL*, 125–126
Brooke, Stopford, 78n
Browning, Robert, 65n
Buffon, Georges Louis Leclerc, Comte de, 34n, 72n
Bunyan, John, 46n
Burns, Robert, 61n, 110
Butter, Peter, xi, 8
Byron, George Gordon, Lord: conception of Rousseau in *Childe Harold*, Canto III, 60n; defends Pope, 88; S distinguishes between man and poet, 52; and S on Shakespeare, 99–100; on S's *beau idéal*, 72; S's letters to, 70n, 88–89, 101n, 249
—*Don Juan*, 38n; *Manfred*, 109; *The Vision of Judgment*, 22n

Caesar, 50, 175, 243
Cain, 102
Calderón de la Barca, Pedro, 6, 12; S on, 49n, 115
—*Cypriano*, 59n
Cameron, Kenneth Neill, xi
Casa Magni, 82, 85, 100, 248–250
Cenci, Beatrice, 42
Chatterton, Thomas: in *Adonais*, 36
Chaucer, Geoffrey, 49n, 115
Chiappelli, Bice, 65
Christ. *See* Jesus Christ
Cicero, 5n
Circe, 64
Clairmont, Claire: S's letters to, 49n, 85, 248, 250

265

Hunt, Leigh, vii, 249, 250; S's letters to, 85, 86
Hutchinson, Thomas, 2, 118, 126, 143, 145, 212–225, 244, 245, 246; his text of *TL*, 124–125; on S's punctuation, 131

India: in draft of *TL*, 242
Ingpen, Roger, 246; and Walter E. Peck (editors of Julian Edition), 2, 118, 126, 139, 143, 212–225

"Jane," 207, 211
Jerusalem, 36, 153
Jesus Christ, 34, 36, 47, 107, 116; in *Adonais*, 102; in *Hellas*, 83; in *Prometheus Unbound*, 46; S on, 52n
John, 50, 104, 175
Jones, Frederick L., xi, xi n
Julian Edition. *See* Ingpen, Roger
Julie. *See* Rousseau: *Julie, ou la Nouvelle Héloïse*
"Julie," 211

Kant, Immanuel, 4; in *TL*, 48, 167
Keats, John: in *Adonais*, 36; alliteration and assonance in poems, 97n–98n; Eliot on, vii; letter to Benjamin Bailey, 43; letter to J. H. Reynolds, 61n; on Newton, 116n; on Pope, 88
—*Endymion*, 21n, 78n; "The Fall of Hyperion," 21n; "Lamia," 116n; "Ode to a Nightingale," 69, 97n–98n
Kermode, Frank, 107n
Kierkegaard, Sören, 111, 113
Kuhns, Oscar, 67n
Kurtz, Benjamin P., 32n

Lamb, Charles, 116n
Lega (Antonio Lega Zambelli, Byron's secretary), 249
Locke, John, 4
Locock, C. D., 24n–25n, 31n–32n, 65n, 78n, 82n, 118, 126, 143, 147, 212–225; his text of *TL*, 125
Lovell, Ernest J., 100n
Lucan: in *Adonais*, 36

Lucretius, 6, 11, 19; *simulacra*, 79, 101
—*De Rerum Natura*, 24n–25n, 75n–76n

Male, Roy R., Jr., 4n
Malthus, Thomas: Malthusians, 80n; S on, 35, 48n
Marvell, Andrew, 76
Masi incident, 249
Massey, Irving, xi
Matthews, G. M., xi, xii, 2, 34, 60n, 83, 118, 120, 122, 129, 136–211 *passim*, 240, 244–245; and apocryphal passages of *TL*, 239; and discarded openings of *TL*, 234; his text of *TL*, 127–128; repunctuates *TL* lines 281–282, 55; on Rousseau as botanist, 77n; on Mary Shelley's editions of *TL*, 119; on *TL* and Rousseau's *Confessions*, 26
Medwin, Thomas, 100n
Metaphor. *See* Shelley: poetic techniques, simile and metaphor
Michelangelo: S on, 49n, 115
Milton, John, ix, 2, 12, 18, 19, 89–90; in *Adonais*, 36; S on, 49n, 115
—*Comus*, 21–22, 35, 64–65, 78, 83n, 84, 101; *Lycidas*, 64, 68n; "Ode on the Morning of Christ's Nativity," 83; *Paradise Lost*, 22n, 24n–25n, 27n, 33n, 38n, 60n, 61n, 63n, 65n, 73n, 77n, 78, 82n, 101; "Chariot of Paternal Deitie" in, 30–31, 31n–32n; Death in, 29, 40–41, 105; Nimrod in, 76n; S on, 101n; spelling of "wreathes" in, 165; use of "anarch" in, 48n, 50n; use of "crew" in, 40n, 76n; "Il Penseroso," 75n–76n; *Samson Agonistes*, 90n
Mind. *See* Shelley: ideas and opinions on
Montaigne, Michel de, 5n
Mont Blanc, 32, 34n
Moxon, Edward, 121

Napoleon Bonaparte, 45n; in *TL*,